Lecture Notes in Computer Science   13912

Founding Editors

Gerhard Goos
Juris Hartmanis

Editorial Board Members

The series Lecture Notes in Computer Science (LNCS), including its subseries Lecture Notes in Artificial Intelligence (LNAI) and Lecture Notes in Bioinformatics (LNBI), has established itself as a medium for the publication of new developments in computer science and information technology research, teaching, and education.

LNCS enjoys close cooperation with the computer science R & D community, the series counts many renowned academics among its volume editors and paper authors, and collaborates with prestigious societies. Its mission is to serve this international community by providing an invaluable service, mainly focused on the publication of conference and workshop proceedings and postproceedings. LNCS commenced publication in 1973.

Mir Abolfazl Mostafavi · Géraldine Del Mondo
Editors

Web and Wireless Geographical Information Systems

20th International Symposium, W2GIS 2023
Quebec City, QC, Canada, June 12–13, 2023
Proceedings

Editors
Mir Abolfazl Mostafavi (iD)
Université Laval
Québec, QC, Canada

Géraldine Del Mondo (iD)
INSA
Saint Etienne du Rouvray Cedex, France

ISSN 0302-9743   ISSN 1611-3349 (electronic)
Lecture Notes in Computer Science
ISBN 978-3-031-34611-8   ISBN 978-3-031-34612-5 (eBook)
https://doi.org/10.1007/978-3-031-34612-5

This Springer imprint is published by the registered company Springer Nature Switzerland AG
The registered company address is: Gewerbestrasse 11, 6330 Cham, Switzerland

Preface

This volume contains the papers selected for presentation at the 20th International Symposium on Web and Wireless Geographical Information Systems (W2GIS 2023), hosted by Université Laval in Quebec City, Canada, on June 12–13, 2023.

W2GIS 2023 aimed to provide a forum for discussing advances in theoretical, technical, and practical issues in the field of wireless and Internet technologies suited for the dissemination, usage, and processing of georeferenced data. W2GIS is a unique forum to address new research challenges in the development of location-based and GIS. It now represents a recognized and regular event within the research community that continues to develop and expand.

For this 2023 edition, we received 14 submissions from more than 8 countries on 4 continents. Each paper received at least three reviews, and based on these reviews, 9 full papers and 2 short papers were selected for presentation at the symposium and inclusion in the Springer LNCS proceedings. We also had the privilege of having two invited papers authored by Alexis Comber and his collaborator from the University of Leeds, UK, and Marlène Villanova-Oliver and her collaborator from Université Grenoble Alpes, France.

The accepted papers are all of excellent quality and cover topics that range from sensor webs to location-based services and Geospatial Artificial Intelligence. The program covered a wide range of topics including sensor network deployment for smart environments, smart and inclusive mobility and navigation, deep-learning algorithms applied to urban mobility assessment, and network analysis and geovisualization.

We wish to thank all authors that contributed to this symposium for the high quality of their papers and presentations. Our sincere thanks go to Springer's LNCS team. We would also like to acknowledge and thank the Program Committee members for the quality and timeliness of their reviews. We also wish to thank all the members of the local organizing committee, especially Maryssa Moffatt St-Pierre and Sonia Rivest for their valuable help with the organization of the conference. Finally, we would like to thank the Steering Committee members for providing continuous support and advice.

June 2023

Mir Abolfazl Mostafavi
Géraldine Del Mondo

Organization

General Chair

Mir Abolfazl Mostafavi   Université Laval, Canada

Program Committee Chairs

Mir Abolfazl Mostafavi   Université Laval, Canada
Géraldine Del Mondo   INSA, France

Steering Committee

Michela Bertolotto   University College Dublin, Ireland
Christophe Claramunt   Naval Academy Research Institute, France
Sergio di Martino   University of Naples Federico II, Italy
Jerome Gensel   Université Grenoble Alpes, France
Farid Karimipour   Institute of Science and Technology Austria (ISTA), Austria
Miguel R. Luaces   Universidade da Coruña, Spain
Sabine Storandt   University of Konstanz, Germany
Kazutoshi Sumiya   Kwansei Gakuin University, Japan
Martin Tomko   University of Melbourne, Australia

Local Organizing Committee

Ali Afghantoloee   Laval University, Canada
Sanaz Azimi   Laval University, Canada
Saeid Doodman   Laval University, Canada
Elizabeth Dionne   Laval University, Canada
Ali Ahmadi   Laval University, Canada
Maryam Naghdizadegan   Laval University, Canada
Reihaneh S. Razavi   Laval University, Canada
Maryssa Moffatt   Laval University, Canada
Sonia Rivest   Laval University, Canada
Mir Abolfazl Mostafavi   Laval University, Canada

Program Committee

Michela Bertolotto	University College Dublin, Ireland
Alain Bouju	La Rochelle University, France
Christophe Claramunt	Naval Academy Research Institute, France
Claude Duvallet	LITIS, Le Havre University, France
Zhixiang Fang	Wuhan University, China
Rob Feick	Waterloo University, Canada
Jerome Gensel	Université Grenoble Alpes, France
Eric Guilbert	Laval University, Canada
Kyoung-Sook Kim	AIST, Japan
Daisuke Kitayama	Kogakuin University, Japan
Thierry Le Pors	ISEN, France
Songnian Li	Ryerson University, Canada
Xiang Li	East China Normal University, China
Feng Lu	IREIS, China
Nicolas Malandain	LITIS, INSA, France
Miguel Mata	UPIITA-IPN, Mexico
Gavin McArdle	University College Dublin, Ireland
Kamaldeep S. Oberoi	IRIT, Paul Sabatier University, France
Kostas Patroumpas	Athena Research Center, Greece
Peng Peng	State Key Lab. of Resources & Env. Info. System, China
Stéphane Roche	Laval University, Canada
Miguel R. Luaces	University of A Coruña, Spain
Sara Saeedi	University of Calgary, Canada
Raja Sengupta	McGill University, Canada
Sabine Storandt	University of Konstanz, Germany
Pierrick Tranouez	LITIS, University of Rouen Normandie, France
Yuanyuan Wang	Yamaguchi University, Japan
Yousuke Watanabe	Nagoya University, Japan
Francisco J. Zarazaga Soria	University of Zaragoza, Spain

Contents

Keynote

Geosensor Network Optimisation to Support Decisions at Multiple Scales

Alexis Comber[1]([envelope]) [iD] and Paul Harris[2] [iD]

[1] School of Geography, University of Leeds, Leeds, UK
a.comber@leeds.ac.uk
[2] Sustainable Agriculture Sciences, Rothamsted Research,
North Wyke, Harpenden, UK
paul.harris@rothamsted.ac.uk

Abstract. Geosensor networks are often used to monitor processes at different spatial scales. Existing approaches for configuring geosensor locations (i.e. sample design) do not address two key challenges: 1) they are limited to a single scale of analysis and do not support multiple scales of evaluation, and 2) they assume that the geosensor network, once established at whatever scale, does not change either in terms of location or number of geosensors. While approaches exist in part for 1) and 2) they do not for both combined. This paper describes a novel approach for optimising geosensor locations in support of multi-scale decisions. It uses the local variation in environmental gradient as a cost surface to approximate the process of interest a proxy for measurements of the process of interest. Cross-scale evaluations of geosensor spatial configurations are supported by measurements of the information loss within spatially nested decision scales. The methods described in this paper fill an important gap as they are i) suggest appropriate sample and geosensor network designs to support cross-scale monitoring, ii) inform on how current network or geosensor coverage could be enhanced by filling gaps, and iii) quantify the information trade-offs (information loss) associated with designs when they are evaluated from the perspective of different decision scales.

Keywords: Sensor · Network Design · Optimisation

1 Introduction

The use of *in situ* geosensors is increasing. In an agricultural context, geosensors are being used to inform on a farm's current and long-term sustainability. They can provide valuable and timely information on soil nutrient and moisture status, nutrient loss to water and air, biodiversity change, crop performance, etc, thus provide valuable information for farm management and decisions. Organisations and individuals that use geosensors are frequently members of formal and informal communities of practice and geographic communities. Many farms,

M. A. Mostafavi and G. Del Mondo (Eds.): W2GIS 2023, LNCS 13912, pp. 3–16, 2023.
https://doi.org/10.1007/978-3-031-34612-5_1

for example, are members of local catchment networks with the broad aim of improving catchment water quality and sustainability. Pooling data and information from members' geosensors can enable the network or catchment status to be monitored. Thus, geosensors are increasingly being used to support monitoring across different scales of decision-making. Using the agriculture example, farmers may wish to monitor at a field and farm scale, whilst also supporting evaluations at other scales. However, there are currently no methods or tools for determining geosensor locations in such a way that they data they provide can support different scales of decision making.

Consider the following scenarios:

1. **Farmer A** wants to instrument her farm with *in situ* geosensors (e.g. soil moisture probes) to inform the real-time performance of her new farm strategy which emphasises sustainable, resilient, regenerative, organic practice. Where should she put them to optimise the coverage for each field as well as the whole farm?. What if she has some sensors in place already, and / or a limited budget?

2. **Farmer B** is in the same situation, but is in an informal network with her neighbouring farm(s) in the local catchment. Some of of the neighbouring farms already have some *in situ* geosensors. She has the same questions as Farmer A, as well as wanting to know whether her land is already effectively covered by her neighbours' sensors as they are nearby, under the same land use and similar management.

3. **Farmer C** is the local chair of the Catchment Soil Network. They have received some funding to distribute geosensors amongst their members, some of whom already have them. They want to optimise sensor coverage across the catchment, and for each member. How should the distribute them? Where should the sensors be located? Do they need to recruit new farms to the network to monitor the run-off in the catchment effectively?

4. The **Department of Agriculture and Environment** wants to link information from different environmental networks to inform national policy and strategies. They also want effective information at multiple scales, for example to evaluate performance at catchment, regional and national levels. Some networks overlap geographically, some are dense covering small areas, some are sparse covering large areas, some are both (i.e. geographically unbalanced), some areas have no sensor coverage. So there are different gaps at different scales and the gaps change according to what process is being measured. How do they evaluate these networks and fill gaps in orderto be able to generate synoptic and robust overviews of performance?

5. **AgriConsult** is developing a framer focussed tool which uses crop models to monitor the growth of crops nationwide to improve the use of integrated pest management. They want to understand where they should locate ground-based geosensors to provide training data for use with Earth observation data to train models that give nationwide coverage. Where should these be located to support these activities?

There is a well-established literature on sample designs for agri-environment monitoring, especially for soil (e.g. [3]), and designs exist for single, multiple and scale-nested processes, together with those for multiple objectives (e.g. [8]). Typically, they follow a design- or model-based philosophy [3,14,16]. The nature of the design is driven by the goals of the farmer, the particular models chosen, and the scale and context of the analysis. These designs generally support only analysis of a pre-determined, spatially bounded system (e.g. a field, farm holding or catchment), with known environmental gradients (e.g. slope, soil type) and management (land use and treatment) and for a specific process.

However, existing approaches to sample design do not address two key challenges :

1. They are limited to a single scale of analysis. They do not support multiple scales and the needs of individual users who may want a geosensor distribution on their land that is able to simultaneously support both field- and farm-scale information (and thus decisions), as well as ones pertaining to their local network, or who may want to link across different networks and identify where current gaps in coverage need to be filled.
2. They assume that the network, once established at whatever scale, does not change. These days it is rare that the spatial configuration of any geosensor network is static and has a limited spatial extent. Members may join or leave at any time; individuals may add sensors at different times; new sensors may be added that do not augment current coverage; networks may be linked to other networks.

1.1   Case Study

A spatially nested case study was selected to demonstrate the approach. The North Wyke Farm Platform (NWFP) is a heavily instrumented experimental farm that contains 3 non-contiguous farmlets, named Red, Green and Blue, each with 7 fields, which in this study are hypothesised to comprise an informal farm network (Fig. 1a). The paper uses these to illustrate the process, to quantify the information trade-offs and to identify further considerations associated with supporting cross-scale decisions. To demonstrate the approach, an empirical case study of soil water geosensor sampling over the 3 farms is explored, with slope and soil physical properties combined to form a cost surface or single environmental gradient (Fig. 1b).

While sample designs exist in part for 1) and 2) above [e.g. [15,17], they are not for both combined/

This paper describes a novel approach for optimising geosensor locations such that they support evaluations of the process across different spatial scales. It is predicated on an assumption that data are available to construct a *cost* surface that approximates the process being monitored by the geosensor.

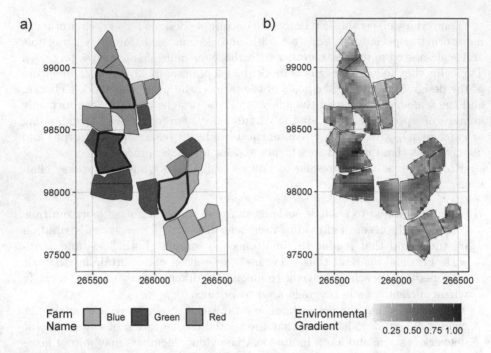

Fig. 1. a) The NWFP farms and single fields (highlighted), b) the distribution of a composite environmental gradient, both with OSGB projection coordinates (ESPSG 27700).

Cross scale evaluations are supported by evaluations of the information loss, when locations that were determined for one scale, are subsequently used to monitor the same process at another scale. It uses an empirical case study where the objective is to support the monitoring of environmental processes at different scales of decision making, in this case these are a field, a farm and a group of neighbouring farms (for example within an informal geographic farm network). It informs user decisions about the siting of new geosensors within spatially nested decision scales. In so doing, the methods described in this paper fill an important gap concerning tools able to i) suggest appropriate sample and geosensor network designs to support cross-scale monitoring, ii) inform on how current network or geosensor coverage could be enhanced by filling gaps, and iii) quantify the information trade-offs (information loss) associated with designs when they are evaluated from the perspective of different decision scales.

2   Methods

2.1   Overview

In overview, a case study is used for three adjacent experimental farms and a model-based methodology and a cost surface to approximate the soil-water process. An environmental gradient was constructed from interpolated local measures of soil bulk density combined with slope data, under the conceit that the increased availability of such data supports a different type of approach for determining optimal geosensor locations (e.g. CEH's COSMOS soil moisture and temperature data - https://cosmos.ceh.ac.uk/). This overcomes the more usual approach of fitting models to a large sample (e.g. $n >= 100$) of the process of interest and the typical situation of process measurement data being unavailable. The approach used a moving window variance of the cost surface to weight the spatial coverage evaluated for potential designs and to evaluate the relative value of the design over different scales. In this way, it supports potential decisions for geosensor location decisions.The proposed approach is parsimonious, generic, and takes advantages of the increased availability of spatial data about all kinds.

Consider a hypothetical case of a local sustainability network offering 4 soil moisture geosensors to each farm in the local catchment area. The Green farmer already has 7 geosensors, the Red farmer has 4 and the Blue farm does not have any. The Green farm has one sensor in each field and the Red farm in has them in the 4 largest fields and in both cases, they are located in the centre of each field for maximal (field scale) coverage.

One approach for locating the additional geosensors is locate them on the basis of maximising the areal coverage of their farm holding. The coverage optimisation problem conceptualised in this way is one that seeks to minimise:

$$\sum_{i=locs} d_{ij} \tag{1}$$

where i indexes the candidate geosensor locations, and d_{ij} is the distance between each location i and candidate location j. In this instance, a p-median search heuristic locates sensors that maximise spatial coverage. However, any allocation undertaken in this way take no account of the spatial variation in the process being measured. This is addressed in the next section.

2.2 Parsimony With Variance

An important component of the geosensor optimisation approach described in this paper is that of parsimony. Spatial sample design is usually undertaken sequentially, with new sample locations selected as those that minimise the variance of the as yet unmeasured process being considered. Here, that concept is flipped by incorporating a gradient that approximates the process of interest into geosensor location selection (as in Fig. 1b)).

The basic idea is that it is now relatively straightforward to construct gradients that approximate to the process of interest, given the huge amounts of environmental data that are routinely collected and available. The local variance in these gradients can be used to inform the evaluation of potential geosample locations, shown in Fig. 2a).

The approach taken to do this was to calculate a moving window variance of the cost surface or environmental gradients. The bandwidth for the moving window was determined using a cross validation of the cost surface mean under the commonly used assumption of a proportional effect between the mean and variance. The variance for the study area calculated in this way is shown in Fig. 2b).

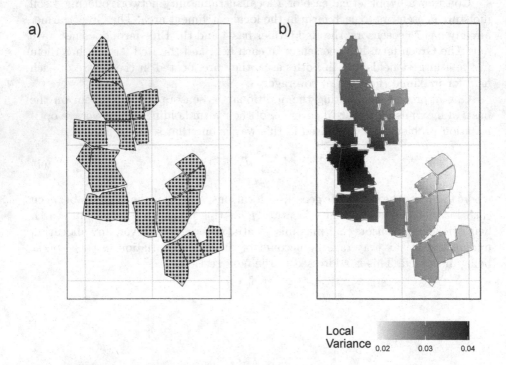

Fig. 2. a) The potential geosensor locations, spaced on a 25 m grid, and b) the estimates the moving window variance in the study area at those locations.

2.3   Modified P-Median and Search heuristic

Here a p-median model was adapted to include local variance of potential geosample locations within the evaluation function and sets of geosensor locations were identified using a Teitz and Bart search heuristic. The p-median model [6,12] seeks to identify sets of locations that minimise some kind of weighted distance. It is frequently used in accessibility analyses and is formulated as follows:

$$\sum_i^m \sum_j^n a_i d_{ij} x_{ij} \tag{2}$$

where i is again the index of potential locations (1 to m) and j is the index of supply (1 to n), a_i represents the demand at demand location i, d_{ij} is the distance between i and j and x_{ij} is an allocation decision variable with a value of 1 if demand at location i, is served by a supply j and 0 otherwise.

In this case the supply and demand locations are the same (as shown in Fig. 2b)) and the p-median model accepts new potential sample locations if they reduce the sum of the (variance) weighted distance between them. Thus optimal sets of sampling locations are conceptualised as those that minimise the variance weighted distance produced by the design, while maximizing coverage:

$$\frac{\sum_{i=locs} v_i d_{ij}}{\sum_{i=locs} v_i} \tag{3}$$

where i indexes the candidate geosensor locations, d_{ij} is the distance between each location i and candidate location j as before, and v_i is the cost surface derived local variance at location i. In this extended case, the distance matrices used by the search heuristic are weighted by v and the optimisation procedure identifies locations in areas of high variability, balanced by spatial coverage. The implementation of the algorithm in the Teitz and Bart (1968) heuristic starts with an initial set of n locations and then proceeds to swap these with other locations (exchange operation), testing for improvement in the evaluation function (the sum of the weighted distance) and accepting the new location in the set if improvement is found.

2.4   Cross-Scale Evaluations

The preceding sections have described a parsimonious approach to sample design using the local variance of the cost surface. Potential geosensor locations are determined for a single scale of interest. An optimal geosensor design at one scale of decision making (for example a field) is likely to result in sub-optimal designs when evaluated at another scale (for example a farm). However, users may want to understand how well the design captures the process, such as soil water run-off, at a different scale. Specifically in relation to the case study, farms may only have the resources for a limited number of geosensors, increasingly would like to filed level and whole-farm understanding of environmental process, and would like to the activities of the informal networks, of which they are members. Thus, users may wish to locate their new geosensors in locations that provide effective coverage (i.e. capture the variation in the process being monitored) at different scales:

– at an individual field scale;
– to provide whole-farm monitoring as well;
– to support network monitoring.

The question is then, how to support user evaluations of the coverage provided by any given spatial arrangement of sensors determined over one scale, when evaluated over other scales.

Recall that in this approach, an approximation of the process spatial variation is captured in the environmental gradient. The selected geosample locations can be used to model (predict) the value of the environmental gradient for a set of target locations. The predictions can be compared with observed environmental gradient observations in order to quantify the relative value of geosensors located in support of one scale of decision, when used to measure process over a different decision scale.

To do this, the approach in outline was to model (krige) the environmental gradient values at the selected sample, over the potential sample locations at other decision scales. The predicted and observed values were then compared using standard measures of fit: R^2, RMSE and MAE, giving relative measures of, for example, how well the farm scale spatial arrangement predicts the environmental gradients over the field, the farm and the network.

2.5 Summary

Geosensor locations that maximise coverage or some other constraint can be identified. However, users may wish to monitor particular fields, as well as undertake whole-farm monitoring. Many farms are also part of local networks and users may wish to monitor at field, farm and network scales. The design methodology to support this is as follows (see also [4]):

1. Create a set of candidate geosensor locations including any existing sensor sites (see Fig. 2a));
2. Determine the local variance of the cost surface at all locations (see Fig. 1b));
3. Weight the distance matrix for all candidate locations by the local variances;
4. Search for the set of n locations that minimise the sum of the variance weighted distances;
5. Repeat for each specified decision scale;
6. Evaluate each model when applied to across all decision scales.

3   Results

Analyses were undertaken to determine and evaluate the locations for 4 new sensors for each farm under 3 decision scales: over a single field, over each whole farm holding and then when the farms combined forces ad shared the 12 sensors over the whole network. The subsections below consider each of these scenarios for each farm, with any existing sensors remained fixed in place to illustrate the approach here. However the existing geosensors could be relocated and the re-configuration of existing geosensor plus new ones is demonstrated in the final subsection.

3.1   The Green Farm

The Green farm has 7 sensors located in the centre of each of its fields. The results of allocating the 4 new sensors to the field, the farm and the network, without relocating any of the existing sensors are shown in Fig. 3. Here we can see that at the field level (Fig. 3a)) the sensors are evenly located around the existing sensor, reflecting the even pull of the local variance (Fig. 2b)) on the allocation. The high levels of variance around this field are also reflected in the sample locations identified at the farm level (Fig. 3b)). Because each field has an existing sensor, the 4 new geosensor locations are located to the west in order to capture this variance. At the network level, with 11 sensors existing

a)   b)   c)

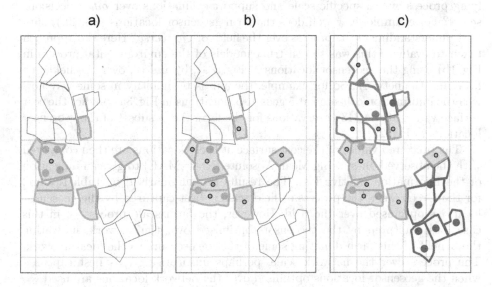

Fig. 3. The Green farm, with the locations of 4 new geosensors indicated under a) field, b) farm and c) network objectives, with existing geosensor locations indicated in black. (Color figure online)

Table 1. The evaluations of the Green farm geosensor locations when used to infer over different scales.

	n_model	n_target	MAE
Field locations to capture field process	5	104	0.123
Field locations to capture farm process	5	343	0.133
Field locations to capture network process	5	1013	0.183
Farm locations to capture field process	11	104	0.149
Farm locations to capture farm process	11	343	0.113
Farm locations to capture network process	11	1013	0.145
Network locations to capture field process	23	104	0.132
Network locations to capture farm process	23	343	0.103
Network locations to capture network process	23	1013	0.098

sensors across the 3 farms, the locations (coverage) for 12 new sensors over the Green farm area are remarkably similar for this farm. Interestingly the geosensor locations optimised over the network would suggest that the Green farm donates 1 of its geosensors and the Red farm donates 2 in order to support the activities of the network.

The question is then how well do these spatial configurations of geosensors, whose locations have been optimised to provide information about the underlying process over a specific scale and support evaluations over *other* decisions scales? For example, how well does the farm geosensor locations (Fig. 3b)) support understanding of the process over the field, or *vice versa*? Here the approach taken to evaluate this was to construct models of the environmental process in Fig. 1b) using the geosensor locations in Fig. 3 a), b) and c), over the field, the farm and the network. So for example, the aim is to quantify in some way how well the information collected at 5 geosensor locations in Fig. 3a) predict the cost surface values at the 343 observations for the farm (i.e. a subset of the geosensor locations in Fig. 2a)).

The predicted values of the cost surface at these locations are then compared with the observed ones, using Mean Absolute Error (MAE) to give an indication of the information relative loss. The results are summarised in Table 1. Here, for the Green farm, the process at field scale is best captured by the geosensor locations optimised over the field. However, the farm scale process is, in this case, best captured by the geosensors optimised over the network, indicating the benefit of this farm donating some of their geosensors to the local network. The process over the network scale, perhaps unsurprisingly, is best captured when the geosensor locations optimised over the network locations are used.

By comparing the MAE values across individual decision scales (field, farm and network), it is possible to quantify the information losses and gains. For example using network locations to capture the field process, increases the MAE by 0.009, an information loss of around 7.3%, and if the farm scale is used this loss is around 21.1% (MAE increase of 0.026, relative to the baseline MAE of 0.123). By contrast, the information gain of donating sensors to the network from the farm is around 9.7%.

3.2   Re-configuring Geosensor Design

It is also possible to suggest alternative locations for any existing geosensors, as well as the new ones in order to improve monitoring at different scales. This was done for the Green farm and the results are shown in Table 2 and in Fig. 4. Whilst, the changes in geosensor location may seem subtle, the effect of the local variance is to pull the geosensor towards locations that balance coverage in a classic p-median sense with capturing areas of high variance in the underlying environmental gradient. In the case of the Farm the benefit is small, but at the field level the improvement is considerable, reducing the MAE score by 0.012, and information gain of around 10.8%.

Table 2. The changes in MAE for the Green farm when existing geosensor locations are allowed to be relocated.

	n_model	n_target	MAE	MAE_new
Field locations to capture field process	5	104	0.123	0.111
Field locations to capture farm process	5	343	0.133	0.147
Field locations to capture network process	5	1013	0.183	0.216
Farm locations to capture field process	11	104	0.149	0.149
Farm locations to capture farm process	11	343	0.113	0.108
Farm locations to capture network process	11	1013	0.145	0.144
Network locations to capture field process	23	104	0.132	0.148
Network locations to capture farm process	23	343	0.103	0.113
Network locations to capture network process	23	1013	0.098	0.100

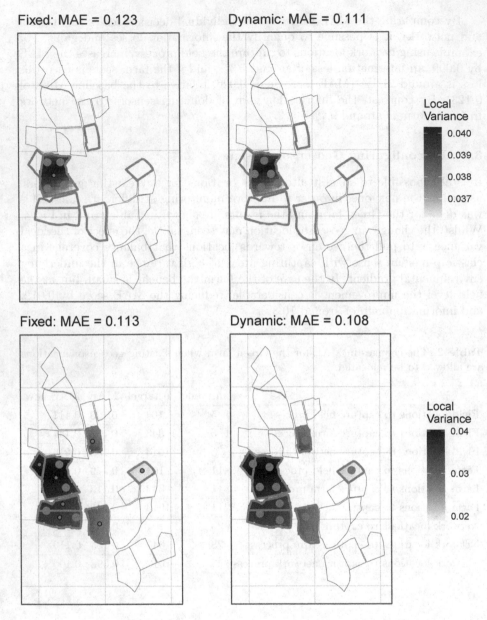

Fig. 4. Comparisons of the optimised geosensor locations when existing geosensors are fixed (as by the smaller dots) and relocated, for the field (top) and the farm (bottom).

4   Discussion and Conclusions

In situ sensors are increasing being used in a variety of domains including those used to monitor pollutants in water [18], air [7], soils [5], noise [9], traffic [1], where data streams combined with appropriate analysis supports timely and robust decision making and mitigation strategies. In an agricultural context, sensors are typically used to inform on a farm's current and future sustainability. Sensor data streams can provide valuable and timely information on soil nutrient [5] and moisture status [13], emissions to water and to air [2], biodiversity change [11] and crop performance [10]. In doing so, they provide valuable information for farm management decisions, both in the short- and long-term.

Farmers may wish to monitor at a within-field, field and farm scale, whilst also supporting evaluations at the catchment and broader scales. However, typically, individuals and organisations that deploy sensors are members of formal and informal communities of practice, most of which are geographically clustered in nature, but not always. Such communities may wish to deploy sensors in order to capture the status of each farm sought (for example for soil nutrient loss) and also to pool information form community sensors to support catchment-scale status analyses(for example to understand pathways of nutrient loss to water.

For each of the five scenarios described in the Introduction section, there are currently no design frameworks for determining sensor locations in such a way that the data they provide can support such different scales of decision making. Specifically, existing approaches to sensor network design do not simultaneously address three key challenges: designs are typically limited to a single scale of analysis and do not support multiple scales of evaluation; they usually assume that the network, once established at whatever scale, does not change; they require existing information of the process. It also is rare for the network spatial configuration of any network to be static as members leave or join, as new sensors are added as links with other networks are made etc.

In this context the work described in this paper introduces a conceptual framework for optimizing network design across different spatial scales using only surrogate information of the true process of interest. It is predicated on an assumption that surrogate data are available (and increasingly so) to construct a cost surface that approximates the process being monitored by the sensor. The case study allowed for multiple designs for sensing, evaluated over nested spatial scales (field, farm holding and catchment) and cross-scale evaluations were supported by quantifying the information trade-offs for the siting of new sensors and the re-deployment of existing sensors.

The presented design is deliberately taken as a basic situation, where more complicated designs can easily be embedded within the same over-arching framework. This would include, sensing multiple variables concurrently at scale (e.g., soil moisture and soil temperature), using alternative surrogate datasets (e.g., composites for soil type, soil texture; remote sensing products) and alternative search algorithms could replace the p-median approach. The framework supports designs for spatially bounded systems (e.g., field, farm, catchment), but could be extended to systems with fuzzy boundaries. Future work will explore these issues.

In conclusion, the proposed framework is an advance because it suggests network designs to support cross-scale monitoring, it informs on how current sensor coverage could be enhanced, it quantifies the information trade-offs (loss and gain) associated with designs when evaluated at different decision scales, it requires only open surrogate data for its implementation, and it is generic to any monitoring programme and not limited to those in agriculture.

References

1. Balid, W., Tafish, H., Refai, H.H.: Intelligent vehicle counting and classification sensor for real-time traffic surveillance. IEEE Trans. Intell. Transp. Syst. **19**(6), 1784–1794 (2017)
2. Brinkmann, T., Both, R., Scalet, B.M., Roudier, S., Sancho, L.D.: Jrc reference report on monitoring of emissions to air and water from IED installations, p. 155. European IPPC Bureau, European Commission, Joint Research Centre: Ispra, Italy (2018)
3. Brus, D.J.: Statistical approaches for spatial sample survey: persistent misconceptions and new developments. Eur. J. Soil Sci. **72**(2), 686–703 (2021)
4. Brus, D.: Sampling for digital soil mapping: a tutorial supported by R scripts. Geoderma **338**, 464–480 (2019)
5. Burton, L., Jayachandran, K., Bhansali, S.: The "real-time" revolution for in situ soil nutrient sensing. J. Electrochem. Soc. **167**(3), 037569 (2020)
6. Hakimi, S.L.: Optimum locations of switching centers and the absolute centers and medians of a graph. Oper. Res. **12**(3), 450–459 (1964)
7. Kumar, P., et al.: Real-time sensors for indoor air monitoring and challenges ahead in deploying them to urban buildings. Sci. Total Environ. **560**, 150–159 (2016)
8. Lark, R.: Multi-objective optimization of spatial sampling. Spat. Stat. **18**, 412–430 (2016)
9. Maijala, P., Shuyang, Z., Heittola, T., Virtanen, T.: Environmental noise monitoring using source classification in sensors. Appl. Acoust. **129**, 258–267 (2018)
10. Michela, J., et al.: Real-time monitoring of Arundo Donax response to saline stress through the application of in vivo sensing technology. Sci. Rep. **11**(1), 18598 (2021)
11. Paz, A., Silva, T.S., Carnaval, A.C.: A framework for near-real time monitoring of diversity patterns based on indirect remote sensing, with an application in the Brazilian Atlantic rainforest. PeerJ **10**, e13534 (2022)
12. ReVelle, C.S., Swain, R.W.: Central facilities location. Geogr. Anal. **2**(1), 30–42 (1970)
13. Salam, A., Vuran, M.C., Irmak, S.: Di-sense: in situ real-time permittivity estimation and soil moisture sensing using wireless underground communications. Comput. Netw. **151**, 31–41 (2019)
14. Särndal, C.E., Swensson, B., Wretman, J.: Model Assisted Survey Sampling. Springer, Berlin (2003)
15. Webster, R., Lark, M.: Field Sampling for Environmental Science and Management. Routledge, Milton Park (2012)
16. Webster, R., Oliver, M.A.: Geostatistics for Environmental Scientists. John Wiley & Sons, Hoboken (2007)
17. Wikle, C.K., Royle, J.A.: Space: time dynamic design of environmental monitoring networks. J. Agric. Biol. Environ. Stat., 489–507 (1999)
18. Yaroshenko, I., et al.: Real-time water quality monitoring with chemical sensors. Sensors **20**(12), 3432 (2020)

Sensors Networks and Data Steaming

Towards Integration of Spatial Context in Building Energy Demand Assessment Supported by CityGML Energy Extension

Saeid Doodman[1] , Mir Abolfazl Mostafavi[1](✉) , and Raja Sengupta[2]

[1] Center for Research in Geospatial Data and Intelligence, Department of Geomatics Sciences, Université Laval, 1055, Avenue du Séminaire, Quebec City, QC, Canada
mir-abolfazl.mostafavi@scg.ulaval.ca

[2] Department of Geography and Bieler School of Environment, McGill University, 805 Sherbrooke Street West, Montreal, QC, Canada

Abstract. The quality of Building Energy Models (BEMs), as dominant techniques to simulate and analyze building behavior in terms of energy consumption, depends strongly on the weather data that is generally captured by spatially low-resolution weather stations and in 2D. The provided weather data does not satisfy the BEMs requirements in terms of accuracy and spatial details. To address this issue, WSNs (Wireless Sensor Networks) have shown a high potential in offering 3D measurements with desired resolution and quality. However, the optimal deployment of a point-based wireless sensor network in an urban area to capture information on microclimate is a challenging task due to the complexity of the integration and management of diverse affecting factors as well as the 3D nature of the urban environment and its dynamics. This paper proposes to design and develop a workflow based on CityGML-standards to represent and manage the required spatiotemporal information for BEMs and feed a knowledgebase that can be used in WSN deployment optimization algorithms. Finally, the paper presents and discusses a case study to highlight the advantages and limitations of the proposed approach.

Keywords: EnergyADE · Building Energy Model · Microclimate · WSN

1 Introduction

The trend of urbanization is leading to an increase in building energy consumption, making it important to optimize and reduce energy use in cities [1–3]. Hence, the reduction and optimization of energy consumption are increasingly important for more environment-friendly living.

In such a context, there is a growing necessity to simulate the building energy needs on various scales (individual building, neighborhood, and city) demanded by decision-makers from various domains such as urban designing, energy management, etc., to make buildings and cities more energy-efficient and sustainable [4–6]. Making a holistic and accurate energy assessment is a resource-demanding task due to the heterogeneity

© The Author(s), under exclusive license to Springer Nature Switzerland AG 2023
M. A. Mostafavi and G. Del Mondo (Eds.): W2GIS 2023, LNCS 13912, pp. 19–36, 2023.
https://doi.org/10.1007/978-3-031-34612-5_2

and complexity of the exigent information, which requires obtaining, managing, harmonizing, integrating, and exchanging extensive detailed data about the built area and its components [7].

Despite advances in Building Energy Models (BEMs), that simulate the building's behavior in terms of energy consumption, most of them rely on internal building characteristics and envelope, neglecting surrounding land use and its interaction with the building, leading to a discrepancy between actual energy consumption and model-based predictions [5].

The quality of BEMs depends heavily on weather information, which is typically provided by conventional weather stations located mostly in rural or non-urban areas with sparse distribution and low resolution. Numerous studies have shown that current weather measurement methods are insufficient for building energy modeling, as they are inadequate for accurately measuring the impact of surrounding buildings and landscapes on the microclimate [8]. For example, [9] demonstrated that the predicted heating and cooling energy consumption can vary from 2.7% to 11.3% and 10.5% to 82.4%, respectively, when changing the weather dataset used for analysis. The situation becomes more complex with the added effect of Urban Heat Islands (UHI), which increases the sensitivity of urban building energy consumption to temperature changes caused by climate change [10]. Regular weather stations have shortcomings in meeting the current demand for 3D information in BEMs as well.

In such a context, WSNs (Wireless Sensor Networks) increasingly are becoming a highly attractive alternative to offer 3D detailed and accurate data on microclimate conditions in urban areas. Nevertheless, a significant challenge in using WSNs is proper deployment to achieve the desired optimum coverage in complex and dynamic urban environments. This requires prior knowledge of the target field, at the neighborhood scale, mainly in 3D, or at least in 2D. Hence, there will be a mutual dependency between sensor network deployment and knowledge about the target field (microclimate).

To solve this mutual dependency and facilitate the WSN deployment, using urban microclimate models would be an inevitable step in any potential deployment approach for generating preliminary knowledge of target field conditions (e.g. air temperature) and their spatial/temporal variation in the environment. Hence, being compatible with existing urban microclimate models will be necessary. A solving approach, in its initial step, requires a workflow to apply the necessary spatial and non-spatial information for determining the most strategic points in a given neighborhood surrounding the target buildings.

From this viewpoint, the principal research question underpinning this paper is what would be the requirements for an optimal WSN deployment? and how to facilitate the process of preparing these prerequisites. On the other hand, modeling the energy behavior and simulating the microclimate surrounding a building require comprehensive information about that building as well as its neighborhood in terms of morphological and climatological aspects [11, 12]. Hence, the other research question of this paper is how to efficiently manage all required information for both the microclimate simulation and WSN deployment, with a promising and reusable methodology.

To address the aforementioned challenges and research questions, this paper aims to (1) propose a workflow to systematically integrate the contextual information (3D building, land use, etc.) based on the open standard data structure (CityGML), and provide an insight into the target field (e.g., 2D and 3D air temperature variation); (2) propose the incorporation of microclimate-related information on CityGML and its Energy Extension data model (3) create a knowledgebase and set of rules guiding the sensor network deployment approaches to optimize sensor distribution in the future studies.

The rest of the paper is structured as follows. Section 2 briefly reviews the BEMs, and then points out the limitations of CityGML and its Energy Extension in supporting urban microclimate models. Section 3 proposes a context-aware framework to incorporate the microclimate-related concepts into the CityGML data model. To show the feasibility and potential of the proposed framework, a case study carried out on McGill University's campus is presented in Sect. 4. It also includes the obtained results, discussions, and the generated knowledgebase. Finally, Sect. 5 brings the paper to a close through the conclusion and future work.

2 Related Works

Building energy models (BEMs) are techniques to simulate and analyze building energy consumption. For building energy simulation, there are a variety of different types of BEMs available in the market. Each BEM deals with different aspects of building energy performance [13] and has its own requirement in terms of input data and simulation approach. Based on the scale of the simulation, BEMs can be categorized into building and city scales. In the first category, BEMs are used for individual buildings and consider the energy performance of buildings at different levels of detail, including at the level of individual rooms. They include a detailed zone-based model, which allows users to define rooms or spaces within a building and assign specific thermal properties to each zone. Examples are TRNSYS [14], E+ [15]. On the other hand, some BEMs and urban climate models put more emphasis on simulating energy usage and climate behavior at an urban scale, respectively called the Urban Building Energy Models (UBEMs) and Urban Microclimate Models (UMMs). SimStadt [7], CitySim [16], UMI [17], UWG [18], and VCMG [19] are examples of this category. In both cases, 3D geospatial information of buildings and their surroundings are fundamental for efficient energy modeling.

BEMs can also be classified into physics-based and statistical models which the latter depend mainly on the historical energy consumption data. But, the physics-based models apply physical principles of the thermodynamic equation to predict the energy performance of an individual building or a collection of them on a district scale, and are based on real physical characteristics. Therefore, these models are more popular for energy consumption prediction, scenario planning, and decision-making, However, they require comprehensive building-relevant data and weather information to perform the simulation. Hence, the availability of the required building parameters is crucial [11].

Conventional physics-based BEMs overlook the effect of microclimate fluctuation [20] which is affected by the location, configuration, proximity, and height of neighboring buildings and surrounding landscape, leading to changes in a building's energy efficiency through alterations in load, heat transfer, and air infiltration [21].

New generations of BEMs are emerging that couple the existing BEMs with microclimate models. For example, UrBEC [20], couples a multi-zone Urban Microclimate

Model (UMM) with a building energy model (HTB2). The applied UMM uses an inter-connected network of external geospatial thermal zones to assess the microclimate within the canopy layer. The usage of external thermal zone concept has been used in other studies such as [22–24] to generate urban microclimate conditions of open spaces at the scale of streets, and neighborhoods. This approach adds supplementary spatial partition to the urban areas, and needs to be efficiently managed.

In addition, both building energy models and urban microclimate models necessitates strong interoperability between different simulation modules for sharing heterogeneous spatiotemporal data that require highly interoperable data format and standards [20, 25, 26]. These data might have different scales, resolutions, and dimensions (2D or 3D) and be directly related to a building itself or cover their surrounding environments as well.

Among many attempts to solve the complexities caused by heterogeneous data required in energy modeling, a promising solution is to adapt and use open standards for data management. IFC (Industry Foundation Classes), gbXML (Green Building XML), and CityGML are examples of the commonly adopted open standards that can be used in this context [27]. Among them, IFC and gbXML are generally used for individual build-ings. Hence, CityGML is often the preferred option for more comprehensive analysis of neighborhood and urban scale applications. CityGML has been used widely in urban building energy prediction in research works such as [28–30] to name a few. However, the role of CityGML has been mainly in providing building geometry.

In recent years, CityGML Energy Application Domain Extension (EnergyADE) has been particularly developed to provide a unique and standard-based data model for both city-wide bottom-up energy assessment and detailed individual building energy simulation [27]. It is comprehensive in terms of covering the majority of factors that are used in energy assessment, comprising building physics, energy systems, occupant behavior, material and construction, as well as supporting classes such as time series, schedules, and weather data.

Despite these developments, CityGML and EnergyADE are not fully compatible with the requirements of all UBEMs types (such as coupled building energy models) and are not fully adopted for urban microclimate modeling. Only a small number of research works have been conducted in this regard and most of them are not compatible with microclimate modeling, particularly for the WSN deployment applications. For instance, [29] proposed a workflow for the automatic generation of 2.5D urban scenes to simulate the residential building energy from UK mapping datasets. They assigned energy characteristics based on a statistical model, and adopt the CityGML EnergyADE schema to define the energy model information at the city scale. However, their focus is only on the building energy model, and still, the surrounding context and microclimate data are not supported by their schema. Wang [31] proposes mapping tables between the CityGML EnergyADE schema and the simulation parameters of a BEM interface called LadybugTools, to retrieve the information stored in CityGML. Nonetheless, their mapping table doesn't support the surrounding context. Rossknecht & Airaksinen [11] proposed a conceptual method to apply the CityGML EnergyADE schema for heating demand and resulting CO_2 emissions prediction by using the 3D city model of Helsinki City. They extended the simulation environment SimStadt to retrieve the information stored in the energy extension schema and utilize it in simulation recipes. Again, the defined strategy doesn't support the microclimate simulation.

Given these limitations, in the following section, we propose a new approach for the integration of spatial context in building energy demand assessment supported by CityGML Energy ADE.

3   A Conceptual Framework for Context-Aware Building Energy Demand Assessment

This section outlines the aim and conceptual approach of the presented research work. An overview of the proposed framework is illustrated in Fig. 1. This framework is composed of several modules. First, the spatial and non-spatial datasets required for context-aware building energy demand assessment using a point-based WSN are identified. These data are required both for BEM simulators as well as for the optimal point-based WSN deployment. As mentioned in the previous section, these data include not only spatial data from the urban context (3D buildings, vegetation, infrastructure, streets, etc.) but also include field data such as temperature, humidity, solar radiation as well as information on the sensors and the sensor network. In addition, BEM-specific requirements (e.g. thermal zones, etc.) is part of the information to be integrated and managed for our purpose. Hence. We need an efficient way to integrate, represent, manage, and use this information for efficient context-aware building energy demand assessment.

For this purpose, we propose to benefit from the latest advancement in CityGML and its Energy Extension to represent and manage the necessary information for context-aware building energy demand assessment. Hence, this module will allow the integration and representation of building 3D models and additional contextual information using CityGML and the EnergyADE schema and storing them in a relational spatial database. A so-called External_Thermal_Zone and AirNode concept is presented which extends the EnergyADE capability in supporting the outdoor microclimate modeling.

The remaining modules of the framework include the Simulation, Knowledgebase, and Optimization modules. The simulation module is served for preliminary prediction of the target field behavior (e.g., air temperature). This module deals with third-party building energy modeling interfaces and microclimate simulators. The standardized information stored in the EnergyADE-compliant 3D database is retrieved and fed into the simulation recipes defined in this module to generate prior knowledge about the target field. The input data include but are not limited to the thermal zones (and relevant attributes), surrounding vegetation, shading elements (buildings, and tree canopies), and typical meteorological year (TMY[1]) data.

The knowledgebase module takes care of generating the possible knowledge sets based on the available contextual information and the simulation results. It also defines a set of rules and constraints applicable in reasoning engines that serve the WSN deployment optimization modules.

Finally, the WSN deployment optimization module has two key components: the coverage estimator and the distribution engine. The coverage estimator evaluates the

---

[1] A dataset that is designed to represent typical annual meteorological data.

proposed sensor distribution to determine how well it covers the target field, and the distribution engine implements the optimization algorithm that finds the optimal sensor network coverage, taking into account the contextual information and the extracted rules. Developing the context-aware optimization approach is part of the next step of the ongoing research work.

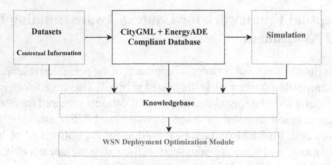

Fig. 1. Overview of the proposed framework

3.1 Identifying the Requisite Contextual Information and Data Preparation

As mentioned before, deploying a point-based wireless sensor network in the urban area to capture the microclimate is a challenging task due to the complexity of affecting factors and the deployment environment as well. A relevant definition of environmental factors in the context of WSNs deployment is called Contextual Information (CI) [32]. From this viewpoint, we use CI to refer to the whole contextual situation, deployment environment, sensor characteristics, sensor network configuration, and the target field (e.g. temperature) as well.

The CI affects the point-based WSN deployment process in two aspects. Firstly, it contains the most driving factors that have a direct impact on the target field (e.g., radiation, vegetation cover rate, etc.). Typically, parts of the prior information about the target field are unavailable or insufficiently detailed/resolved. Therefore, CI can also be applied to generate prior knowledge of the target field by being fed into the simulation engines (i.e. BEMs). CI can also be applied in the deployment algorithms as well, via defining a set of constraints and rules to guide the deployment algorithm (e.g., land use).

The required information for generating the preliminary knowledge of local temperature can be generally classified into building 3D models, tree canopy coverage, land-cover, traffic information, and weather data. The building model should at least include the geometry, building type, building age, and occupation schedule information.

Despite the comprehensiveness of CityGML, there is rarely a city-wide dataset in this format available in open data catalogs. Even if it is accessible, it only includes 3D building geometry and lacks important attributes and other elements of the city. Therefore, conversion from conventional data formats (e.g., ESRI Shapefile) to CityGML format might be too demanding for many required datasets. However, it still presents many advantages (standardisation, multi-scale and multi-resolution, consistency, interoperability, etc.).

3.2   Extending CityGML and EnergyADE Data Model for Building Energy Demand Assessment

The proposed framework highlights the importance of managing the identified contextual information throughout all stages of WSN deployment. While many of the relevant data types can be handled using the classes in CityGML and its Energy Extension data models, as outlined in Table 1, some additional contextual information is not explicitly included in these models (see Table 2). To address this, the GenericCityObject can be employed to support these additional data types.

Table 1. Example list of the predominant contextual information required for generating the prior knowledge of the target field and the corresponding classes in the CityGML and its Energy Extension

Required Contextual Information	Corresponding class in CityGML or EnergyADE
Building 3D models	– CityGML Building:: Building – EnergyADE Building_Physics:: ThermalZone EnergyADE Occupant_Behaviour:: UsageZone
Tree canopy coverage	CityGML Vegetation:: PlantCover
Land-use/Land-cover – street – sidewalk grass area	CityGML Transportation:: TrafficArea
	CityGML Transportation:: AuxiliaryTrafficArea
	CityGML Vegetation:: PlantCover
Additional city elements to define feasible areas constraints; e.g., lanterns/ traffic lights/ traffic signs/ Advertising Columns	CityGML CityFurniture:: CityFurniture
Weather data – Air temperature – Relative humidity – Wind direction/speed Solar direct/normal irradiation	– EnergyADE Supporting_Classes:: IrregularTimeSeriesFile – EnergyADE WeatherData:: WeatherStation EnergyADE Core:: WeatherData

For example, traffic flow information is required to reach a more precise estimation of the air temperature. But, CityGML does not have a specific feature type and attributes that directly represent traffic flow information. In some urban climate models such as UWG (Urban Weather Generator) [18], the traffic information is required as watts_per_area factor. The mechanism to extract such a piece of information can be found in [33].

Using a file-based approach is tedious to do maintenance tasks or update data for the energy demand assessment. Therefore, to homogenize all the procedures and data conversion, and to ensure that all information can be used in the future to conduct different scenarios, a database approach need to be used for data storage, then feeding into the microclimate simulators. The database approach offers significant advantages in ensuring data consistency by implementing constraints and redundancy checks. As a result, only unique features with meaningful attributes that comply with CityGML standards could be written into the database. The open-source geodatabase 3DCityDB [34] is used for this purpose. 3DCityDB, maps object-oriented CityGML data models to the relational database schema. Additionally, 3DCityDB can be enhanced by 3DCityDB_Utility Package which provides an extra schema to store the content of EnergyADE. Additionally, the open-source Importer/Exporter Tool [34] is used to take care of automatically initial writing CityGML files into 3DCityDB with EnergyADE schema.

It is noteworthy that despite various attempts to connect building-oriented standards (such as CityGML, IndoorGML, IFC, etc.) to manage and integrate outdoor and indoor information, their focus has seldom been on the seamless management of volumetric spaces both indoors and outdoors. This need is becoming increasingly important in urban building energy modeling, which will be described further in the next section.

Table 2. Examples of contextual information with no explicit feature type in CityGML. Some of them can be defined as generic city objects.

Required Contextual Information	Corresponding class in CityGML schema
Traffic information	– CityGML Generics:: GenericCityObject
External Thermal Zone	-
Sensor Network configuration	-
Microclimate data	-

Towards Extending the EnergyADE Data Model

Recent urban building energy models (UBEMs) such as [20], couple the building energy models with a simplified urban microclimate model to better estimate the energy performance. In these models, it is common to generate thermal zones for outdoor semi-closed spaces between buildings. Despite the internal thermal zone concept being explained and modeled well by EnergyADE, the concept of external thermal zones used in such UBEMs (see Fig. 2) can be explained by neither the current version of EnergyADE nor the CityGML itself, since CityGML doesn't take care of outdoor spaces, which brings its comprehensiveness to the challenge in managing city-related application.

To overcome this limitation, we propose extending the EnergyADE schema by adding a feature type called _ExternalThermalZone which inherits the EnergyADE:: AbstractThermalZone class and is bounded by EnergyADE:: ThermalBoundary as depicted in Fig. 3.

Moreover, there is a lack of suitable feature types in the EnergyADE schema to deal with microclimate data generated by simulators or measured by in-situ WSNs.

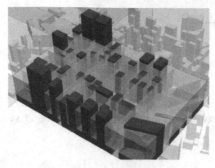

Fig. 2. Outdoor thermal zones represent the semi-enclosed body of air outside the building envelopes to describe the climate in an urban microclimate model (source: Huang et al. 2020)

Although the classes WeatherData and WeatherStation are foreseen in the current version of EnergyADE to combine the energetic model of the building with the meteorological data, there is no explicit class that corresponds to the microclimate data. The microclimate data usually include very high-resolution climate conditions that might be measured by wireless sensor networks or estimated through simulation processes for a set of high-resolution gridded points. To address this issue, we propose to define a feature type specifically for microclimate data, called "AirNode", which represents the sensor network objects or simulation grids. Figure 4 displays the relationship between the suggested feature type and the existing ones in the EnergyADE data model. The blue rectangles correspond to currently existing classes on the EnergyADE data model; the green rectangle corresponds to the "AirNode" feature type; the latte-colored rectangles correspond to the external datasets (via CityGML::ExternalReference) that may provide high-resolution data, but are not explicitly parts of the data model. A schematic view of AirNode in an urban area is demonstrated in Fig. 5. The class AirNode allows the aggregation of various city objects with various energy-related data provided by either simulation approaches or in-situ sensors. It can also be useful for managing the UHI intensity, especially that is known as an "urban heat archipelago," rather than a uniform "island" in recent works [35]. The resolution of AirNodes can be dense enough to generate a 3D grid of them. Hence, the AirNode concept helps to describe the temperature profiles (e.g., as vertical and horizontal cross-sections) at either the neighborhood or the city scale.

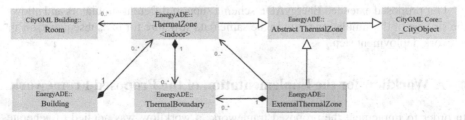

Fig. 3. The UML diagram demonstrating the proposed feature type to support external thermal zones

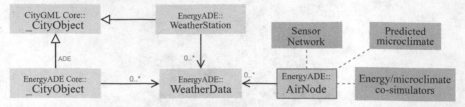

Fig. 4. The relationship between the proposed class AirNode class and weather Data in the EnergyADE schema

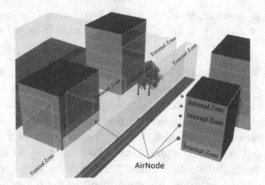

Fig. 5. Demonstration of AirNode in the urban area

3.3 Simulation Module

Having all the required information in CityGML format, it would be possible to feed them into the simulation engines to generate preliminary knowledge about the target field. In this study, the 3D model of mean radiation temperature (MRT) variation is considered as representative of the air temperature variation, allowing these two concepts to be used interchangeably. Figure 6 demonstrates the applied principle to integrate the spatial context and regional climate information to generate finer-scale variations of MRT through simulation engines. Since the air temperature in an urban area is affected by the UHI effect, hence, the UHI intensity calculation is performed using the UWG model.

Our proposed extended EnergyADE schema support different simulators and allows the storage of the simulation result in the same data structure for the subsequent sensor network deployment step.

4 A Workflow for the Implementation of the Proposed Framework

In order to implement the proposed framework, a workflow was applied to generate the required knowledgebase, as shown in Fig. 7. The workflow starts with collecting and preparing the data sources, including 3D building, land use/land-cover datasets

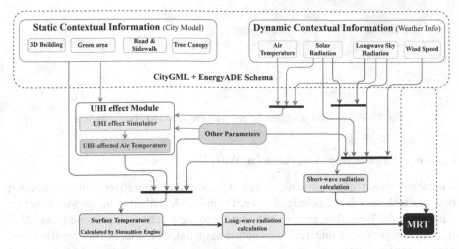

Fig. 6. The principle of mean radiation temperature simulation recipe

(green areas, tree canopies, roads and sidewalks), terrain elevation (relief), and dynamic weather information, as they are known as the major spatial context contributing to the air temperature variation in the urban area.

In our study, green areas, tree canopies, relief, and transport areas (sidewalks, and streets) are added to the model from pre-existing data sources. The green areas are converted to PlantCover Class in CityGML schema, and transport areas such as roads, sidewalks, and paved surfaces are converted to CityGML::TrafficArea class, correspondingly. If building 3D models are not available, LOD1 can be generated by extruding building footprints to the height value obtained from existing digital surface models, which are now more widely available. If a 3D model of the buildings is available in CityGML LoD >1, it should be verified for incorrect geometries such as unclosed solids, duplicated points, or intersecting polygons before being used in the simulation step. These issues can lead to erroneous geometry calculations that are crucial for thermal zone-based calculations.

The next step involves preparing the CityGML-compliant 3D database (3DCityDB) to host all the converted data. Subsequently, a Python script is applied, which has been developed to retrieve the data from the CityGML-compliant database and feed it into the simulation recipes.

The described process generates prior knowledge about the target microclimate. The procedure involves defining different simulation recipes that model the UHI effect in the neighborhood, followed by the simulation of MRT values. By feeding the information into the simulation engine, MRT values are calculated in 3D for a desired period of time. This calculation is performed for each point on a high-resolution 3D grid that corresponds to the AirNode feature type proposed in the previous section. Having almost all relevant CI and the simulated value of the target field as well, it will be possible to generate the expected knowledgebase which is described in the next section.

Fig. 7. The applied workflow to generate the required knowledgebase

4.1 Generating the Knowledgebase for WSN Deployment

Having the AirNode fed by simulation, the last piece of the required requisite information is now available and the knowledgebase (KB) module described in the previous section can play its role. We follow an approach similar to the mechanism proposed by [32] to extract the categories of contextual information in spatial, thematic, and temporal aspects. However, considerations should be taken into account according to the differences in the nature of the target field as well as the characteristics of the sensors that will be used to monitor the field.

In this study, the target field (air temperature) is a continuous space and is defined in 3D. Although the measurements (positions with simulated value) are provided, due to the discreetness of data, an appropriate interpolation method is required to generate the first category of the knowledgebase set that provides the value of air temperature at each desired position of the study area.

To support Building Energy Models (BEMs) with microclimate information, it is important to focus on areas with high rates of temperature change. These areas should be well-covered to ensure accurate modeling. To determine the positions where air temperature changes rapidly, both spatial and temporal variations should be considered. The second derivative of temperature can be used to identify areas with high rates of change, which will form another category in the knowledgebase. It is worth noting that weather data from weather stations includes the global (macro) temporal variation of temperature. Therefore, the aim here is to capture local temporal variations, if any exist.

It is important to note that relying solely on prior knowledge of the target field to run a WSN deployment algorithm may not guarantee an optimal and practical result due to desirability and feasibility constraints. Some areas may be unsuitable for sensor deployment. Examples include water bodies, private buildings, highways, and other locations where the installation of sensors is difficult, useless, or forbidden. We consider them as infeasible areas. If the infeasible space is a 3D solid object, then the whole volume is considered directly for further analysis. In the cases that the infeasible city object is planar, then a CityGML::GenericCityObject is defined as an extrusion of that planar object to perform the volume.

Another point is that sensors should be mounted and secured on already existing physical elements (such as lighting poles, walls, tree trunks, etc.) with minimum effect on their measurements. By incorporating this information into the knowledgebase, the optimization approach can be guided to achieve a more practical and realistic sensor deployment. As a result, the search space homogeneity and the deployment strategy can be adjusted accordingly.

If the boundaries of the external thermal zones are generated in an optimal way, they can be very useful for the sensor deployment step. Because, each thermal zone is defined as a homogenous space in terms of thermal condition (temperature, humidity, air pressure, etc.), therefore, having one-and-only-one sensor per external zone could be a possible constraint.

5 Case Study

5.1 3D Model of the Environment

To conduct the case study, a specific experimental site at McGill University in Montreal, Canada was selected. This site consists of a collection of office buildings and their surrounding neighborhood. Figure 8 provides a 3D representation of the building block in a GIS application, as well as an aerial view.

The campus area is located between a high-density forestry area at the west, and the high-density downtown at the east, comprising high-rise buildings. Given its heterogeneity in land cover, and variation in buildings height, density, and characteristics, the McGill campus is adequate to represent a good case study. The building's 3D model is visualized based on already existing CityGML LoD2 data obtained from open data resources (Canada Government website). Green area, tree canopy, relief, and transport area (sidewalk, and street) were added to the model from other available data sources.

(a)   (b)

Fig. 8. Representing the study area: (a) CityGML buildings in LOD2 + green area, transport area (b) Corresponding view via Google Earth application

5.2 Experimental Results and Discussion

Traditionally, sensor deployment in similar neighborhoods was carried out using a trial-and-error approach, with distance from the target building being the only factor considered in the best case. Such a condition led to several gaps in the network coverage. In addition, the presence of urban elements complexifies the deployment process. Using the proposed framework we aim to facilitate the WSN optimal deployment process and improve the performance of the relevant BEMs as well.

The study used weather data obtained from the nearest weather station, which was selected for its proximity and upwind position relative to the study area. To manage the information, 3DCityDB was utilized based on the CityGML schema and its Energy Extension. The UWG model was applied to consider the UHI effect, and the resulting data was used in the estimation of MRT. A 3D grid was generated and configured as a list of target points, which were then fed into the simulation engine as shown in Fig. 9a.

The simulation engine estimated the MRT value for each target point separately considering surrounding elements, e.g., adjacent buildings, tree canopies, and land-covers. Having the simulation result, it was possible to perform 3D interpolation and create a higher-density 3D MRT. Figure 9(b–d) demonstrate the whole voxelated MRT, two extracted vertical slices, and a horizontal section, respectively. This 3D MRT will serve as the primary data source for calculating the cost function of the desired optimization algorithm. For example, a coverage estimation can be performed using the Kriging method by calculating the interpolation error in any desired set of test points.

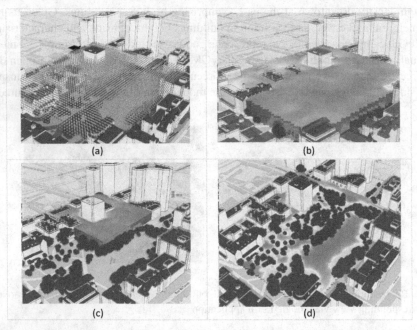

Fig. 9. (a) A 3D grid of the target points fed into the simulation engine; (b): The whole view of voxelated MRT (c) Two vertical slices demonstrate the effect of tree canopy and buildings on MRT (c) The section on the interpolated values shows the spatial variation of the MRT in horizontal dimensions.

We calculated the second derivative (curvature) of the MRT to identify locations with high rates of change in MRT values. The curvature can be calculated in both 2D and 3D, resulting in high-curvature spots in the form of lines and surfaces. These spots indicate potential locations for sensor deployment, provided there are no other factors preventing it (see Fig. 10).

Not all areas with high rates of temperature change may be suitable for sensor deployment. Constructing a base for each sensor is not feasible, so it is important to mount the sensors on existing physical elements (such as street/sidewalk lighting poles, walls, and tree trunks) with minimal impact on their measurements. Therefore, identifying the mountable elements is a crucial step (as shown in Fig. 11), which will be further investigated in future work.

Fig. 10. Extracting the 2D critical spots (red) in which MRT changes with a high rate

Fig. 11. The mountable elements in the case study

6 Conclusion and Future Works

In this paper, we have proposed a new framework based on CityGML Energy ADE for efficient structuring and management of the necessary spatiotemporal information for building energy demand assessment. Building energy models play a critical role in energy engineering and city energy management. BEM's performance has a high dependency on weather information. Currently, the weather data are provided by sparsely-distributed weather stations that do not satisfy the BEM requirement in terms of accuracy and spatial details. Wireless sensor network has shown interesting potential for filling these gaps. However, deploying a point-based wireless sensor network in the urban area to capture the microclimate is a challenging task due to the complexity of affecting factors and their spatial characteristics. Although sensor networks have been used to capture microclimate data in very recent years, the deployment strategies are mainly based on a trial-and-error approach and most of them oversimplify the environment model.

This research is among the first studies that aim to develop a systematic approach to find the optimized distribution of a set of point-based wireless sensors in complex urban areas to capture the microclimate more efficiently. It also suggests a solution to ameliorate the EnergyADE schema to support UBEMs and the microclimate data via defining the concepts of External Thermal Zone and AirNode.

The main sources of information used to generate the knowledgebase for guiding the WSN deployment optimization algorithms are the city model components and the simulated field values. The output knowledgebase includes several key elements, such as the target field values in a continuous space, the locations of high-rate changes in the field values, and general mountable locations extracted from the 3D city model. This paper highlights the development of an ongoing research project. As future work, we plan to integrate contextual information with a deployment optimization algorithm using the proposed framework and validate its effectiveness. In addition, we are preparing a use case to install a set of multi-modal IoT-enabled sensors on Laval University's campus to investigate the efficiency of the framework for sensor network deployment.

References

1. Eremia, M., Toma, L., Sanduleac, M.: The smart city concept in the 21st century. Procedia Eng. **181**, 12–19 (2017). https://doi.org/10.1016/j.proeng.2017.02.357
2. Zubizarreta, I., Seravalli, A., Arrizabalaga, S.: Smart city concept: what it is and what it should be. J. Urban Plan. Dev. **142**, 04015005 (2016). https://doi.org/10.1061/(asce)up.1943-5444. 0000282
3. Kahsay, M.T., Bitsuamlak, G., Tariku, F.: Effect of localized exterior convective heat transfer on high-rise building energy consumption. Build. Simul. **13**(1), 127–139 (2019). https://doi. org/10.1007/s12273-019-0568-7
4. Bahu, J.-M., Koch, A., Kremers, E., Murshed, S.M.: Towards a 3D spatial urban energy modelling approach. Int. J. 3-D Inf. Model. **3**, 1–16 (2015). https://doi.org/10.4018/ij3dim. 2014070101
5. Reinhart, C.F., Cerezo Davila, C.: Urban building energy modeling - A review of a nascent field. Build. Environ. **97**, 196–202 (2016). https://doi.org/10.1016/j.buildenv.2015.12.001
6. Agugiaro, G., Robineau, J.L., Rodrigues, P.: Project ci-nergy: towards an integrated energy urban planning system from a data modelling and system architecture perspective. ISPRS Ann. Photogramm. Remote Sens. Spat. Inf. Sci. **4**, 5–12 (2017). https://doi.org/10.5194/ ISPRS-ANNALS-IV-4-W3-5-2017
7. Nouvel, R., et al.: SimStadt, a new workflow-driven urban energy simulation platform for CityGML city models. In: Proceedings of CISBAT 2015 International Conference on Future Buildings and Districts - Sustainability from Nano to Urban Scale, pp. 889–894 (2015). https:// doi.org/10.5075/EPFL-CISBAT2015-889-894
8. Katal, A., Mortezazadeh, M., Wang, L. (Leon), Yu, H.: Urban building energy and micro-climate modeling – From 3D city generation to dynamic simulations. Energy **251**, 123817 (2022). https://doi.org/10.1016/J.ENERGY.2022.123817
9. Moradi, A., Kavgic, M., Costanzo, V., Evola, G.: Impact of typical and actual weather years on the energy simulation of buildings with different construction features and under different climates. Energy **270**, 126875 (2023). https://doi.org/10.1016/J.ENERGY.2023.126875
10. Ma, Y.X., Yu, C.: Impact of meteorological factors on high-rise office building energy consumption in Hong Kong: From a spatiotemporal perspective. Energy Build. **228**, 110468 (2020). https://doi.org/10.1016/j.enbuild.2020.110468
11. Rossknecht, M., Airaksinen, E.: Concept and evaluation of heating demand prediction based on 3D city models and the CityGML energy ADE-case study Helsinki. ISPRS Int. J. Geo-Inf. **9** (2020). https://doi.org/10.3390/IJGI9100602
12. Lauzet, N., et al.: How building energy models take the local climate into account in an urban context – a review. Renew. Sustain. Energy Rev. **116**, 109390 (2019). https://doi.org/10.1016/ J.RSER.2019.109390
13. Chalal, M.L., Benachir, M., White, M., Shrahily, R.: Energy planning and forecasting approaches for supporting physical improvement strategies in the building sector: a review. Renew. Sustain Energy Rev. 64, 761–776 (2016). https://doi.org/10.1016/j.rser.2016.06.040
14. TRNSYS: Transient System Simulation Tool. http://www.Trnsys.Com/ (2013)
15. U.S. Department of Energy: EnergyPlus|EnergyPlus (2020)

16. Emmanuel, W., Jérôme, K.: A verification of CitySim results using the BESTEST and monitored consumption values. In: Building Simulation Applications, pp. 215–222 (2015)
17. Reinhart, C.F., Dogan, T., Jakubiec, J.A., Rakha, T., Sang, A.: UMI - An urban simulation environment for building energy use, daylighting and walkability. In: Proceedings of BS 2013: 13th Conference of the International Building Performance Simulation Association. pp. 476–483 (2013). https://doi.org/10.26868/25222708.2013.1404
18. Bueno, B., Norford, L., Hidalgo, J., Pigeon, G.: The urban weather generator. J. Build. Perform. Simul. **6**, 269–281 (2013). https://doi.org/10.1080/19401493.2012.718797
19. Moradi, M., et al.: The vertical city weather generator (vcwg v1.3.2). Geosci. Model Dev. **14**, 961–984 (2021). https://doi.org/10.5194/gmd-14-961-2021
20. Huang, J., Jones, P., Zhang, A., Peng, R., Li, X., Chan, P.: Urban Building Energy and Climate (UrBEC) simulation: Example application and field evaluation in Sai Ying Pun. Hong Kong. Energy Build. **207**, 109580 (2020). https://doi.org/10.1016/j.enbuild.2019.109580
21. Gracik, S., Heidarinejad, M., Liu, J., Srebric, J.: Effect of urban neighborhoods on the performance of building cooling systems. Build. Environ. **90**, 15–29 (2015). https://doi.org/10.1016/J.BUILDENV.2015.02.037
22. Yao, R., Luo, Q., Li, B.: A simplified mathematical model for urban microclimate simulation. Build. Environ. **46**, 253–265 (2011). https://doi.org/10.1016/j.buildenv.2010.07.019
23. Liang, W., Huang, J., Jones, P., Wang, Q., Hang, J.: A zonal model for assessing street canyon air temperature of high-density cities. Build. Environ. **132**, 160–169 (2018). https://doi.org/10.1016/J.BUILDENV.2018.01.035
24. Huang, J., Jones, P., Zhang, A., Hou, S.S., Hang, J., Spengler, J.D.: Outdoor airborne transmission of coronavirus among apartments in high-density cities. Front. Built Environ. **7**, 48 (2021). https://doi.org/10.3389/FBUIL.2021.666923
25. Rodler, A., et al.: Urban microclimate and building energy simulation coupling techniques. In: Palme, M., Salvati, A. (eds.) Urban Microclimate Modelling for Comfort and Energy Studies, pp. 317–337. Springer, Cham (2021). https://doi.org/10.1007/978-3-030-65421-4_15
26. Katal, A., Mortezazadeh, M., Wang, L.: (Leon): Modeling building resilience against extreme weather by integrated CityFFD and CityBEM simulations. Appl. Energy. **250**, 1402–1417 (2019). https://doi.org/10.1016/j.apenergy.2019.04.192
27. Agugiaro, G., Benner, J., Cipriano, P., Nouvel, R.: The energy application domain extension for CityGML: enhancing interoperability for urban energy simulations. Open Geospatial Data, Softw. Stand. **3**(1), 1–30 (2018). https://doi.org/10.1186/s40965-018-0042-y
28. Soilán, M., Truong-Hong, L., Riveiro, B., Laefer, D.: Automatic extraction of road features in urban environments using dense ALS data. Int. J. Appl. Earth Obs. Geoinf. **64**, 226–236 (2018). https://doi.org/10.1016/j.jag.2017.09.010
29. Rosser, J.F., Long, G., Zakhary, S., Boyd, D.S., Mao, Y., Robinson, D.: Modelling urban housing stocks for building energy simulation using CityGML energyade. ISPRS Int. J. Geo-Inf. **8**, 163 (2019). https://doi.org/10.3390/ijgi8040163
30. Malhotra, A., Shamovich, M., Frisch, J., van Treeck, C.: Urban energy simulations using open CityGML models: a comparative analysis. Energy Build. **255**, 111658 (2022). https://doi.org/10.1016/J.ENBUILD.2021.111658
31. Wang, X.: Using CityGML EnergyADE Data in Honeybee (2020)
32. Argany, M., Mostafavi, M.A., Gagné, C.: Context-aware local optimization of sensor network deployment. J. Sens. Actuator Netw. **4**, 160–188 (2015). https://doi.org/10.3390/jsan4030160
33. Sailor, D.J., Georgescu, M., Milne, J.M., Hart, M.A.: Development of a national anthropogenic heating database with an extrapolation for international cities. Atmos. Environ. **118**, 7–18 (2015). https://doi.org/10.1016/J.ATMOSENV.2015.07.016

34. Yao, Z., et al.: 3DCityDB - a 3D geodatabase solution for the management, analysis, and visualization of semantic 3D city models based on CityGML. Open Geospatial Data, Softw. Stand. **3**(1), 1–26 (2018). https://doi.org/10.1186/s40965-018-0046-7

35. Cao, J., Zhou, W., Zheng, Z., Ren, T., Wang, W.: Within-city spatial and temporal heterogeneity of air temperature and its relationship with land surface temperature. Landsc. Urban Plan. **206**, 103979 (2021). https://doi.org/10.1016/j.landurbplan.2020.103979

A Three-Stage Framework to Estimate Pedestrian Path by Using Signaling Data and Surveillance Video

Jinlong Cui and Zhixiang Fang[(⊠)]

State Key Laboratory of Information Engineering in Surveying, Mapping and Remote Sensing,
Wuhan University, Wuhan 430072, China
zxfang@whu.edu.cn

Abstract. The estimation of pedestrian path is of great value in the study of crowd dynamics, and various data with location information can be used as the basis for path estimation. In this study, we jointly use the signal data obtained from the pedestrian interaction with the base station and the surveillance video in the study area, and estimate the pedestrian path in the network finally. This paper proposes a three-stage framework for pedestrian path estimation, in the first stage, the video is used to extract the pedestrian's trajectory in the monitoring field of view, and the road segment that the pedestrian certain to pass is determined; in the second stage, the location information contained in signaling data is used to predict the road segments that pedestrian may pass through. In the final stage, the road segments determined by surveillance videos and the road segments inferred from signaling data are integrated, then we use HMM model to determine the combination of road segments with the highest probability, so as to obtain the complete travel path of the pedestrian. To evaluate the framework proposed in this paper, we conducted simulation experiments based on CARLA. The experimental results show that the path of pedestrians in the road network can be estimated effectively through the cooperative application of signaling data and surveillance video. Compared with other methods relying on only one data source, the three-stage framework proposed has higher accuracy in path estimation.

Keywords: Signaling data · Surveillance video · Pedestrian path

1 Introduction

In the study of urban crowd dynamics, it is necessary to restore the path of pedestrians from various data sources, so as to analyze the activities of pedestrians. Extracting the path of pedestrians has many applications in reality. For example, in the prevention and control of the epidemic, it is necessary to analyze the travel path of pedestrians to find potential close contacts [4]. In the field of public security, various data can be used to reconstruct the location information of the target object, so as to track and locate it [5]. In the field of urban planning, the path of pedestrians is an important reference for traffic planning. A large amount of pedestrian path data can help urban management departments analyze the dynamics of crowds in the city [6].

M. A. Mostafavi and G. Del Mondo (Eds.): W2GIS 2023, LNCS 13912, pp. 37–53, 2023.
https://doi.org/10.1007/978-3-031-34612-5_3

The movement of pedestrians can be reflected from various data, and all kinds of data with location information can be used as the basis for reconstructing pedestrian path. For example, GPS track is the most direct and accurate location record, which can reflect the accurate movement path of people [7]. The signaling data represents the communication between the mobile phone and the cellular base station, which can indirectly reflect the location of pedestrians [1]. The monitoring video records the detailed pictures of pedestrian activities, from which the movement trajectory of pedestrians can be extracted [3]. In addition, public transport credit card data and other traffic ride date can also reflect the rough trajectory of people [8].

Using the above data sources independently, the pedestrian's movement information can be restored in different spatial precision and spatial scales, and the pedestrian's movement path can be obtained. Ideally, the accurate trajectory of pedestrians can be extracted through GPS, but due to equipment constraints, the method of using GPS to obtain pedestrian paths is not universal. On the contrary, the mobile phone is a common device, and the signaling data generated during the use of the mobile phone can roughly reflect the location of the user [1]. Therefore, signaling data has the advantage of high coverage, but its spatial accuracy is very low, and it is difficult to accurately reflect the location of people [2]. In cities, surveillance cameras are densely distributed, and high-precision trajectories of pedestrian can be extracted from surveillance videos, but the path of pedestrians in a larger area cannot be extracted only by relying on surveillance videos. For the problem of pedestrian path extraction in the city, each available data source has its unique advantages, but also has insurmountable disadvantages. Better results can be achieved by combining multiple data sources.

In order to extract the complete path of pedestrians and give consideration to both spatial and temporal accuracy, signaling data and surveillance video data can be used together to give full play to the advantages of high temporal sampling rate of signaling data and high spatial accuracy of surveillance video. Therefore, this paper proposes a new pedestrian path extraction method, which uses signaling data and monitoring data to estimate the location information of pedestrians, and maps the location information to the road network, so as to obtain the path of pedestrians in the road network. In order to evaluate the effectiveness of the proposed method, a simulator is constructed in which the pedestrian and environment are simulated and the accuracy of the estimated path of pedestrians is calculated. According to different density of monitoring points and base station we set up four scenarios, and analyzed the effect of path estimation under different parameter settings. In addition, a comparison experiment is designed to compare the proposed method with other two method path estimation only rely on signaling data or Surveillance video.

In this paper, we first clarify some basic concepts and introduce the proposed three-stage framework in stages. Then, we present and discuss the results of a comparative experiment. Finally, we summarize the limitations of this work and discuss the possibility of future improvement.

2   Methodology

2.1   Problem Definition

In this segment, we introduce some preliminary concepts and formulaic the problem of pedestrian path estimation.

Definition 1 (Signaling Data): Signaling data is generated when a cell phone interacts with a nearby cell tower. Typically, signaling data has fields with time stamps, cell ids, user ids, and signaling types. For a particular pedestrian, signaling data can be represented as a sequence of time as bellow:

$$SD_k = \{t_0 : Bs_l, t_1 : Bs_m, \cdots t_i : Bs_n\} \tag{1}$$

where t_i represents the sampling time number of the signaling data, Bs_n represents the number of the base station connected by the pedestrian at time t_i. In this paper, we assume that pedestrians are connected to only one base station at a time of sampling.

Definition 2 (Surveillance Video): For each monitoring point C_i, the spatial range of its monitoring horizon can be represented as Z_i, the video recorded by the monitor in time period $[t_m, t_n]$ can be called $V_i^{t_m, t_n}$.

Definition 3 (Road Network): A road map is typically represented as a graph $G_m = (V, R)$. where the set of vertexes (denoted as V) includes road intersections and other break points on the roadways. A complete road network consists of a collection of road segments (denoted as R).

Definition 4 (Pedestrian Path): The moving path of pedestrians on the road network can be represented as a sequence of road segments, which records the number of road segments passed by pedestrians in chronological order. Pedestrian path can be represented as follows:

$$Pt_k = [s_0, s_1, \cdots s_i] \tag{2}$$

where s_i represents road segment of road that pedestrians passed by. In this paper, we only consider the road segments passed by pedestrians in the road network, and ignore the parts that are not on the road network.

Problem Definition: There are several monitoring points $[C_0, C_1, \cdots C_i]$ in the city. In the research period $[t_m, t_n]$, the set of all surveillance videos is $\left[V_0^{t_m, t_n}, V_1^{t_m, t_n}, \cdots V_i^{t_m, t_n} \right]$. Given the signaling data of pedestrian k and the road network G_m in the research area, our goal is to estimate the pedestrian path Pt_k in the time period $[t_m, t_n]$.

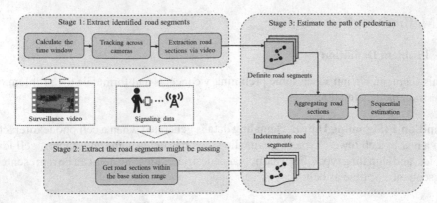

Fig. 1. The framework for pedestrian path estimation

2.2 The Proposed Framework

In order to make comprehensive use of signaling data and surveillance video data, so as to obtain the complete path of pedestrian travel, a framework is proposed in this paper. The overall structure of the framework is shown in Fig. 1.

The framework roughly includes three stages. In the first stage, the road segment of pedestrians is determined by extracting the surveillance video data; in the second stage, the road segment of pedestrians is speculated by signaling data; in the third stage, the complete travel path of pedestrians is estimated. Each phase is described in detail in the following three segments.

Stage 1: Extracting Road Segments that Pedestrian certain to Pass through. At this stage, the first problem is how to find the video clip of pedestrians in the surveillance video. We need to extract the footage of pedestrians in the surveillance video. Signaling data can directly reflect the temporal and spatial information of pedestrians. We can infer whether pedestrians are likely to appear in the monitoring field at a certain moment through the location information contained in signaling data. Here, it is necessary to establish the base station connection relation lookup table of the monitoring view area. According to the base station connection information of the pedestrian at a specific moment, the pedestrian can be judged to enter the monitoring view area if the connection information of the pedestrian and the base station meets certain conditions. We already know the location of each monitoring view, so we can determine the nearby base station, and we can know the possible connection relationship between pedestrians and nearby base stations when they are within a certain range of monitoring view. Once the pedestrian base station connection information conforms to the connection characteristics of a certain monitoring view and lasts for a certain period, we can consider this period as the time window in which the pedestrian appears in the monitoring vision. The problem can be defined as: given the complete signaling connection record SD_k of pedestrian k, we need to obtain the sets of surveillance video clips of pedestrian k appearing in the monitoring field, the sets of surveillance video clips can be represented as follows:

$$V_k^{in} = \left[v_{[t_0, t_1]}^i, v_{[t_2, t_3]}^j, \cdots v_{[t_m, t_n]}^l \right] \tag{3}$$

where, $v^l_{[t_m,t_n]}$ represents each video clip, the superscript represents the number l of the monitoring point C_1, and the subscript represents the time window $[t_m, t_n]$, in which the pedestrian may appear in the monitoring field of view of C_1. The steps to solve the above problems can be summarized as follows:

1) For each monitoring point C_i, its corresponding monitoring view range is Z_i, search for a collection of base stations which can be represented as $L^R_i = [Bs_1, Bs_2, \cdots Bs_n]$ within a certain radius $R(R > r_i)$ near C_i. By traversing each monitoring point, the associated base station lookup table of each monitoring view can be obtained, it can be represented as follows:

$$D^R_{Bs} = \left\{ C_0 : L^R_0, C_1 : L^R_1, \cdots C_n : L^R_n \right\}. \tag{4}$$

Through the base station lookup table, we can find the sequence of base stations near a monitoring point C_i, which can be get by $D^R_{Bs}(C_i)$.

2) The signaling connection record table of pedestrian k is known, which can be represented as SD_k, which records the person's signal data at different times. If a person is within a monitoring horizon Z_i, he will preferentially connect to nearby base stations, which can be found in the base station lookup table. Then, at a certain moment t, if the signaling connection record $SD_k(t)$ of the pedestrian is a member of the associated base station $D^R_{Bs}(C_i)$ of a monitoring horizon Z_i, it can be considered that the person is associated with the monitoring at the current moment, and we can speculate that the person may be in the monitoring horizon. Traversing each signaling sampling time t_i, judging whether the current moment may be associated with any monitoring horizon according to the base station connection relation $SD_k(t_i)$ at time t_i. If there is an association, mark the number C_j of the corresponding monitoring point and record the monitoring association relationship at the current time as $L_k(t_i) = [C_j \ldots]$. If no association exists, it is recorded as $L_k(t_i) = \varnothing$. The process can be expressed as the following formula:

$$L_k(t) = \begin{cases} \phi, & \text{if } cant't \text{ find any } C_j \\ [C_0, C_1, \ldots C_j], & \text{if } SD_k(t) \in D^R_{Bs}(C_j) \end{cases} \tag{5}$$

3) Each time t_i is traversed to obtain the complete monitoring horizon association table of the person in the row, which can be represented as:

$$L_k = \{t_0 : L_k(t_0), t_1 : L_k(t_1), \cdots t_n : L_k(t_n), \} \tag{6}$$

For the moment t_i related to the monitoring range, search forward and backward to find moments with the same base station connection, and expressed in the form of time window $[t_{ini}, t_{end}](t_{ini} \leq t_i \leq t_{end})$. The process of extracting the time window can be summarized as Algorithm 1.

Algorithm 1. Extract the time window in which pedestrian associated with monitoring points

---

1:	**input:** Table of association relation between pedestrian k and monitoring field of view $L_k = \{t_0 : L_k(t_0), t_1 : L_k(t_1), t_2 : L_k(t_2)...\}$
2:	**output:** The time window in which pedestrian k appears in the monitoring view $TW_k = \{C_i : [t_m, t_n], C_j : [t_p, t_q] ...\}$
3:	$TW_k \Leftarrow \varnothing$
4:	**for each** $t_j \in L_k.keys$ **do**
5:	$\quad t_i \Leftarrow t_j.getLastMoment$ // Find the last sampling moment
6:	$\quad t_k \Leftarrow t_j.getNextMoment$ // Find the next sampling moment
7:	$\quad$ **if** $LK(t_i) == LK(t_j)$ **then**
8:	$\quad\quad$ // Look backwards for a moment with the same monitoring association
9:	$\quad\quad t_{ini} \Leftarrow t_i.BackwardJudeg(LK(t_j))$
10:	$\quad$ **end if**
11:	$\quad$ **if** $LK(t_k) == LK(t_j)$ **then**
12:	$\quad\quad$ // Look forward for moments with the same monitoring association
13:	$\quad\quad t_{end} \Leftarrow t_k.ForwardJudeg(LK(t_j))$
14:	$\quad$ **end if**
15:	$\quad c = LK(t_j)$
16:	$\quad$ // $[t_{ini}, t_{end}]$ represents the time window in which pedestrian k appears in the monitoring field of view
17:	$\quad TW_k(c) = [t_{ini}, t_{end}]$
18:	**end for**
19:	**return** TW_k

Through the above methods, we can get the time window of a specific pedestrian k in different monitoring horizons, and then cut out corresponding video clips which can be denoted as $VC^i_{[t_{int}, t_{end}]}$ according to the time window $[t_{ini}, t_{end}]$, where i is the number of the monitoring point corresponding to the video. There may be multiple people in each video clip. Now the problem is how to find the target object from all the pedestrians appeared in the video. Although different people may appear in each surveillance video, the target pedestrian must appear in multiple video clips at the same time, which is the key feature that distinguishes the target pedestrian from other pedestrians. For target pedestrians, the method for object tracking across cameras as Fig. 2 shows can be adopted to find common objects with the same identity from pedestrians in multiple videos. More specifically, we have cropped out multiple video clips, all of which correspond to the same target pedestrian. These video clips may or may not contain the movement of the target pedestrian k, because the surveillance field of view covers a limited area. We can extract all the pedestrian snapshots in each video $VC^i_{[t_{int}, t_{end}]}$ (the target box identified as "Person") through the method of target recognition (Yolo v5), which can be represented as:

$$ST_k = [Cp_0, Cp_1, \ldots Cp_i] \tag{7}$$

$$Cp_n = [st_0, st_1, \ldots st_j] \tag{8}$$

where Cp_i is all pedestrian snapshots extracted from video clip $VC^i_{[t_{int}, t_{end}]}$, st_j is some snapshot in Cp_n.

Then obtain the groups belonging to each independent individual through the similarity of the snapshots, each group represents a pedestrian. The process of extracting groups from all pedestrian snapshots can be represented as follows:

$$[st_0, st_1, \ldots st_n] \Rightarrow Gp_n = \{p_0 : [st_i \ldots], p_1 : [st_j \ldots], \ldots p_m : [st_k \ldots]\} \tag{9}$$

In each group Gp_n, the similarity $Sim(st_i, st_j)$ between any two snapshots is greater than the threshold Tre^{sim}_{high} and the average similarity between different groups is less than the threshold Tre^{sim}_{low}. In this paper, the values of the two thresholds are 0.75 and 0.3. Finally, we calculate the similarity from the independent individuals belonging to different videos. If there are multiple individuals whose similarity is greater than the threshold value, it is considered that this is the tracking object we are looking for. Specifically, find objects that meet the following requirements:

$$Sim\left(Gp_i(p_0), Gp_j(p_1), \ldots Gp_k(p_2)\right) > Tre^{sim}_{high} \tag{10}$$

Accordingly, a record of across cameras tracking is generated, representing the same pedestrian appearing in different monitoring horizons at different times.

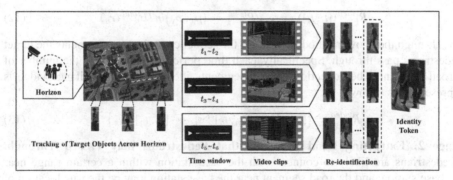

Fig. 2. Schematic diagram of pedestrian tracking across cameras

After getting the snapshot of the target object k, we can track the target pedestrian in each video and extract the complete trajectory tra^i_k of the pedestrian k in the surveillance video V_i. In order to obtain the information of the road segments corresponding to the pedestrian path, we demarcate the scope of each monitoring point according to the road segments' area in the view. Figure 3 shows the sample of the demarcating of the road segment in the monitoring view.

In detail, for specific monitoring horizon Z_i, the correlation table between pixel coordinate boundary and road segment id can be delimited. The correlation table can be represented as follows:

$$Tb_i^{road} = \{r_0: Poly_0, r_1: Poly_1, \ldots r_n: Poly_n\} \tag{11}$$

where, r_n represents the number of road segment and $Poly_n$ represents the list of vertices of the closed polygon made up of pixel coordinates.

Polygons of monitoring horizon   Monitor picture partition   Corresponding road section

Fig. 3. Demarcating road segment in the monitoring view

By demarcating road segment in monitoring view, the correlation between the pedestrian and the road segment can be obtained. In this way, the road segment passed by the pedestrian in a specific period can be determined from the video. If we know the pixel coordinate (p_x, p_y) of a certain pedestrian, we can query the number of the road segment it is in the current monitoring field, which can be represented in the following form:

$$R_k^{video}([t_i, t_j]) = r_n, if P_{id=k}^t = (p_x, p_y) in Tb_i^{road}(r_n) \tag{12}$$

Through the above method, we can get the sequence of the road segments the target pedestrians pass through. Specifically, each time period corresponds to the number of a road segment. The collection of road segments identified by surveillance video is represented as follows:

$$R_k^{video} = \{[t_i, t_j] : s_i, [t_m, t_n] : s_j, \cdots [t_p, t_q] : s_k\} \tag{13}$$

Stage 2: Extracting Road Segments that Pedestrians may Passed Through.
Pedestrians are likely to connect with the base station within a certain range near the base station, and the road segment near the base station may be the true location of pedestrians, because the connection information of each base station will correspond to a nearby candidate road segment set. In this paper, we set the influence radius r_0 of a base station, and the road segments within the radius r_0 are used as the road markings that pedestrians may appear at that time. However, due to the large coverage radius of the base station, more candidate segments are obtained at each moment, and the location corresponding to the signaling data is highly uncertain. In order to reduce the impact of signaling data uncertainty as much as possible, given the invariability of the road segments that pedestrians pass through in a certain period, for a certain signaling sampling

time, the road segments inferred through the base station connection at the current time and the road segments inferred before and after time generally have public segments. The segments that pedestrians actually pass through have the greatest probability of appearing in these public segments. Therefore, the information of the most likely road segment for pedestrians at the current moment can be extracted by considering the road segments that appear together in the preceding and following periods. Figure 4 is a schematic of this approach taking into account of the time before and after.

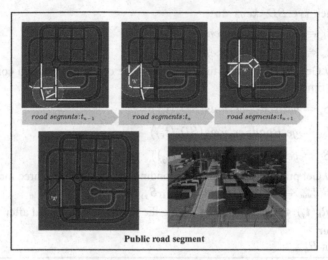

Fig. 4. Estimate the road segment by taking into account of the time before and after

Specifically, three adjacent sampling moments which can be represented as $[t_{n-1}, t_n, t_{n+1}]$ are found in the signaling record of pedestrian k. For each sampling moment t_n, the set of sections within radius r_0 near the corresponding base station $SD_k(t_n)$ is denoted as $S_{t=t_n}$. Similarly, we can also find the set of sections corresponding to the moments before and after t_n, which can be denoted as $S_{t=t_{n-1}}$ and $S_{t=t_{n+1}}$ respectively. The subset $S_{sub} = S_{t=t_{n-1}} \cap S_{t=t_n} \cap S_{t=t_{n+1}}$ of the three sections set is found and updated into the set of candidate sections corresponding to time t_n. By using this method, we calculate the signal sampling record by sliding window, and then we can get the road segments that pedestrian may pass through based on the signaling data at each sampling time.

The above process of extracting the road segment where pedestrians may appear by using signaling data can be aggregated as Algorithm 2:

Algorithm 2. Predict the road segments that pedestrian may pass through based on the signaling data

---

1:   **input:** Signaling data for Pedestrian k (base station connection records) $SD_k = \{t_0:Bs_m, t_1:Bs_n, t_2:Bs_l \dots\}$

2:   **output:** The set of road segments that pedestrian k may appear at each time $R_k = \{t_0:\{s_i, s_j\dots\}, t_1:\{s_m, s_n\dots\} \dots\}$

3:   $R_k \Leftarrow \varnothing$

4:   **for each** $t_j \in SD_k.keys$ **do**

5:      $t_i \Leftarrow t_j.getLastMoment$

6:      $t_k \Leftarrow t_j.getNextMoment$

7:      // Get path set within the coverage range of the base station corresponding to time t_i

8:      $S_i \Leftarrow getRoadSections(SD_k(t_i))$

9:      $S_k \Leftarrow getRoadSections(SD_k(t_k))$

10:     $S_j \Leftarrow getRoadSections(SD_k(t_j))$

11:     // Get public part of the corresponding segments of the three moments

12:     $S_{public}^{i,j,k} \Leftarrow getPublicSections(S_i, S_j, S_k)$

13:     $R_k(t_j) \Leftarrow S_{public}^{i,j,k}$ // Considering the moments before and after

14:   **end for**

15:   **return** R_k

Through the above processing of the base station connected by pedestrians at multiple times, the set sequence of multiple segments can be obtained, and the possible segments of pedestrians can be inferred through the signaling data. The set of segments inferred from signaling data is represented as follows:

$$R_k^{signal} = \{t_0 : [s_i, s_j \cdots], t_1 : [s_m, s_n \cdots], \cdots t_i : [s_p, s_q \cdots]\} \tag{14}$$

Stage 3: Estimate the Complete Path of Pedestrian. After the above two stages, we get two types of road segments, which be represented as R_k^{signal} and R_k^{video}. Before estimating the complete pedestrian path, we aggregate the two types of road segments, the result is R_k^{united}. The road segments determined by signaling data are redundant, and each sampling time point may have more than one road segment. The summary method of aggregate two types of segments is shown in Fig. 5. First, $R_k^{united} = R_k^{signal}$ is initialized with the result of the signaling data estimation. Specifically, for the pedestrian activity information identified by monitoring, if there is no signaling sampling at the corresponding time point t_i, it will be integrated as a time node t_i. And the current time corresponding to the road section information directly written as:

$$R_k^{united}\left(t_i = \frac{t_m + t_n}{2}\right) = R_k^{video}([t_m, t_n]) \tag{15}$$

If there is time overlap between the time window and the signaling sampling point, new sampling information will be added instead.

$$R_k^{united}(t_i) = \phi \text{ then } R_k^{united}(t_i) = R_k^{video}([t_m, t_n]), \ t_i \in [t_m, t_n] \tag{16}$$

The process of aggregating the two segments can be summarized by Algorithm 3.

Algorithm 3. Aggregate the road segments identified by video and the road segments inferred by signaling

---

1:   **input**: Set of road segments identified by surveillance video: $R_k^{video} = \{[t_i, t_j]: s_i, [t_m, t_n]: s_j, \cdots [t_p, t_q]: s_k\}$; Set of segments inferred from signaling data: $R_k^{signal} = \{t_0: [s_i, s_j \cdots], t_1: [s_m, s_n \cdots], \cdots t_i: [s_p, s_q \cdots]\}$

2:   **output**: The aggregated road segments R_k^{united}

3:   $R_k^{united} \Leftarrow R_k^{signal}$
     $T^{signal} \Leftarrow R_k^{signal}.keys$ // Sampling time of signaling sequence

4:   **for each** $[t_i, t_j] \in R_k^{video}.keys$ **do**

5:       // Take the middle moment of the time period as the representative

6        $t_{mid} \Leftarrow Median([t_i, t_j])$

7:       // Determine whether the interval overlaps with the signal sampling time

8:       **If** $Overlap([t_i, t_j], T^{signal}) == True$ **then**

9:           // Overlays overlap moments

10:          $DeleteOverlapMoments(T^{signal})$

11:          // Insert the intermediate moment as a new value

12:          $InsertNewMoments(T^{singnal}, t_{mid})$

13:          // Update road segment information

14:          $R_k^{united}(t_{mid}) \Leftarrow R_k^{video}([t_i, t_j])$

15:      **end if**

16:      **If** $Overlap([t_i, t_j], T^{signal}) == False$ **then**

17:          // Insert the intermediate moment as a new value directly

18:          $InsertNewMoments(T^{singnal}, t_{mid})$

19           $R_k^{united}(t_{mid}) \Leftarrow R_k^{video}([t_i, t_j])$

20:      **end if**

21: **end for**

22: **return** R_k^{united}

The result of road segments aggregation is represented as:

$$R_k^{united} = \{t_0 : [s_i, s_j \cdots], t_1 : [s_m, s_n \cdots], \cdots t_i : [s_p, s_q \cdots]\} \tag{17}$$

where t_i is sampling moment which includes signaling sampling moments and newly added moments through video. $[s_p, s_q \cdots]$ is the set of road segments corresponding to time t_i. If t_i is the signaling sampling moment, there are multiple segments, while for the video sampling moment, only one definite segment is included in the set.

In order to obtain a sequence of segments arranged in chronological order. In this paper, we apply the Hidden Markov Model (HMM) to solve the combination relation of segments, and obtain a path with the maximum probability as the estimated pedestrian path finally. Given certain observations, HMM can be used to find the hidden sequence that produces the observation sequence [10]. In HMM, the observed variable is the sampling time after the segment aggregation, and the hidden state is the segment which the pedestrian pass by. At t_i, there may be one or more candidate segments as vertices in the Markov chain. Observation probability of each candidate road segment can be calculated as:

$$b_{t_i}(k) = \frac{1}{M}(1 \le k \le M) \tag{18}$$

where M is the total of road segments at t_i, k is the number of road segment.

The closer the distance between segments, the greater the probability of state transition between them. The state transition probability can be calculated as:

$$P_i(s, s') = \frac{1}{\beta}e^{\frac{-d_t}{\beta}} \tag{19}$$

where r and r' represents two candidate segments, d_t is the distance between segments, it is the shortest passing distance of the segment center in the road network. β is defined as a coefficient.

Finally, Viterbi algorithm [10] is used to obtain the maximum probability of the road combination, as the estimated path. Pedestrian path can be represented as $Pt_k = [s_0, s_1, \cdots s_i]$, which is a sequence of road segments arranged by time.

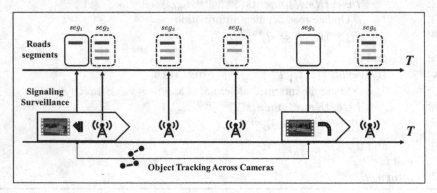

Fig. 5. Schematic diagram of aggregating the two types of road segments

3 Experiment and Result

3.1 Simulation

Limited by the source of data, we cannot get the surveillance video and signaling data in real cities at the same time period at present. Therefore, in order to verify the effectiveness of the framework proposed in this paper, we build an emulator based on CARLA and simulate the urban environment and pedestrians.

CARLA is an Unreal Engine-based autonomous driving simulator that simulates the real world. We simulate the urban environment and pedestrian activities based on CARLA simulator, and simulate the video monitoring point and mobile phone base station. The effect of surveillance video can be simulated through the monitoring point, and the connection between pedestrians and base stations can be simulated through the mobile phone base station, so as to generate signaling data. The Settings and parameters of the simulation experiment are shown in Table 1:

Table 1. Parameter setting of simulation

Map		Spatial range
		$600m \times 600m$
Total of pedestrians		45
Duration of simulation		1200s

In reality, users connect with the base station every certain time, and signaling data has temporal and spatial uncertainty [1]. The temporal uncertainty comes from users' irregular frequency of use, such as phone calls, Internet access, or mobile APP grade data usage. In this paper, we can simulate the uncertainty of sampling time by referring to the distribution of sampling interval of real signaling data sets. The spatial uncertainty shows that the user may interact with any nearby base station. Therefore, in order to simulate the spatial uncertainty of signaling data, the strategy is set as follows: at each sampling moment, the user chooses one of the nearest k base stations to establish a connection.

3.2 Scenarios and Analysis

In order to explore the effect of the distribution of base stations and monitoring points on the results, we set up four scenarios, which are the combination of high and low monitoring density and high and low base station density. Table 2 shows the parameter settings in different scenarios.

In different scenarios, we have simulated the activities of pedestrians, and their real moving trajectories can be known. Pedestrian path estimation results can be obtained by

Table 2. Parameter settings of different scenarios

	Distribution of monitoring points		Distribution of base stations	
Density	high	low	high	low
Total	16	9	16	10
Distribution				

using the path estimation framework proposed in this paper. Under the premise that the real track of pedestrians is known, the correctness of each segment in the path can be judged by artificial comparison, and the accuracy of the estimated path can be calculated. After multiple rounds of simulation tests, we selected 20 paths in four different scenarios respectively, and calculated the overall accuracy according to the difference between the simulated path and the estimated path. The results are shown in Table 3.

Table 3. The accuracy of pedestrian path estimation in different scenarios

Monitoring point	Base station	
	High density	Low density
High density	59%	47%
Low density	32%	28%

Table 3 shows the accuracy of path estimation in different scenarios. In the four scenarios, the best result is 59% for two high density parameter combinations. It can be seen that relatively high density of monitoring points and base station can promote the accuracy of path estimation results. In the scenario of high monitoring density, the accuracy of path estimation can reach 47% even if the base station density is reduced. However, in the scenario with low monitoring density, the impact of changing the base station density on the results is relatively small, and the accuracy rate cannot exceed 32%. The experimental results show that the density of the monitoring point and the density of the base station have different effects on the path estimation results.

In the three-stage framework, the road segment where pedestrians are at a specific moment can be directly judged through surveillance video. The higher the density of monitoring points, the higher the coverage rate of monitoring view area, and therefore, the more accurate the pedestrian track extracted through video. In the framework proposed in this paper, the role of the base station is to provide the basis for location estimation, and it plays an auxiliary role. Therefore, the density of base stations mainly affects the accuracy of path estimation between two monitoring points, and the distribution of monitoring points affects the complete path estimation. The experimental results confirm the above analysis. In the scenario where the density of monitoring points is low, it is difficult to effectively improve the accuracy of path estimation by increasing the density of base stations. In summary, using the three-stage framework proposed in this paper, the path estimation results are affected by both base station and monitoring point density, but the monitoring point density contributes more to the results.

3.3 Comparison and Evaluation

To further evaluate the performance of the proposed method, two other methods were also used for comparison.

Method 1: Path estimation only based on signaling data. Under the premise of the three-stage framework proposed in this paper, if pedestrian activity information in surveillance video is not taken into account. Then the road segment that pedestrians may pass through is directly estimated based on signaling data, and the route estimation is carried out according to HMM method (referring to step 3 in 2.2).

Method 2: Extract the road segments that pedestrians pass by based on video (referring to step 1 in 2.2), and obtain a complete path through the shortest path estimation method in the road network.

For the same group of pedestrians, the path is estimated by Method 1, Method 2 and the three-stage framework proposed in this paper, the results are shown in Table 4.

Table 4. Comparison of path estimation results obtained by different methods

Method	Total of paths	Total of road segments	Total of correct road segments	Accuracy rate
Method 1 (Only based on signaling data)	20	166	42	25%
Method 2 (Only based on video)	20	141	49	34%
Three-stage framework	20	147	87	59%

Experimental results show that the three-stage framework proposed in this paper achieves higher accuracy than path estimation methods using only one data source. Figure 6 shows a set of comparison results. It is observed that the path estimated by the signaling data has the largest deviation from the true path. The path estimated by the video is relatively accurate locally, but the accuracy of the overall path is low, because only the pedestrian activity trajectory in the local range can be extracted through the video. The three-stage framework proposed in this paper can not only extract accurate local information in the video, but also take into account the possibility of road segments in a larger spatial range through signaling data, therefore, it achieves the best results.

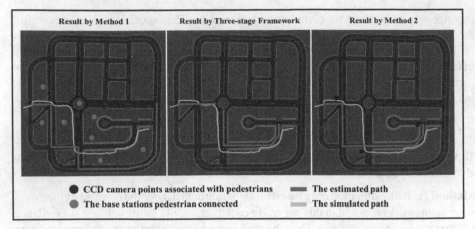

Fig. 6. Comparison of different path estimation methods

4   Conclusion

In this paper, we propose a path estimation framework, which combines the signaling data generated by the communication between pedestrians and base stations with the surveillance video data in the city to realize the purpose of estimating the pedestrian path. The framework proposed in this paper has three stages. Firstly, the video is used to extract the pedestrian's trajectory in the monitoring field of view, and the road segment that the pedestrian certain to pass is determined. Secondly, the road segments that pedestrians may pass by are inferred through signaling records. Finally, the two types of road segments are aggregated and a most likely path is estimated. We constructed the simulation environment through CARLA and set up different scenarios. The experimental results show that the path estimation results are affected by both base station density and monitoring point density, but the monitoring point density contributes more to the results.

In current work, We do not consider the complexity of the relationship between the pedestrian path and the road network, but assuming that that the path passed by the pedestrian must be on the road network, which may lead to the deviation between the estimated path and the actual path. In the follow-up work, we will continue to improve the structure of the road network and give more consideration to the particularity of pedestrian walkways. We will also improve the path estimation method and introduce some space-time constraints to improve the accuracy of pedestrian path estimation.

References

1. Song, Y., et al.: MIFF: human mobility extractions with cellular signaling data under spatio-temporal uncertainty. Proc. ACM Interact. Mob. Wearable Ubiquit. Technol. **4**(4), 1–19 (2020)
2. Bonnetain, L., et al.: TRANSIT: fine-grained human mobility trajectory inference at scale with mobile network signaling data. Transp. Res. Part C Emerg. Technol. **130**, 103257 (2021)
3. Li, Y., et al.: Pedestrian origin–destination estimation based on multi-camera person re-identification. Sensors **22**(19), 7429 (2022)

4. Wesolowski, A., et al.: Quantifying the impact of human mobility on malaria. Science **338**(6104), 267–270 (2012)
5. Johansson, A., et al.: From crowd dynamics to crowd safety: a video-based analysis. Adv. Complex Syst. **11**(04), 497–527 (2008)
6. Hillier, B., et al.: Metric and topo-geometric properties of urban street networks: some convergences, divergences and new results. J. Space Syntax Stud. (2009)
7. Zhu, X., Qun L., Chen, G.: APT: accurate outdoor pedestrian tracking with smartphones. In: 2013 Proceedings IEEE INFOCOM. IEEE (2013)
8. Zhang, L.: Study on the method of constructing bus stops OD matrix based on IC card data. In: 2007 International Conference on Wireless Communications, Networking and Mobile Computing. IEEE (2007)
9. Janecek, A., et al.: The cellular network as a sensor: from mobile phone data to real-time road traffic monitoring. IEEE Trans. Intell. Transp. Syst. **16**(5), 2551–2572 (2015)
10. Ren, M., Karimi, H.A.: A hidden Markov model-based map-matching algorithm for wheelchair navigation. J. Navig. **62**(3), 383–395 (2009)

Mobility and Navigation

Investigating the Navigational Behavior of Wheelchair Users in Urban Environments Using Eye Movement Data

Sanaz Azimi[1] (iD), Mir Abolfazl Mostafavi[1](✉) (iD), Krista Lynn Best[2] (iD),
and Aurélie Dommes[3] (iD)

[1] Center for Research in Geospatial Information and Intelligence, Department of Geomatics
Sciences, Université Laval, 1055, Avenue du Séminaire, Québec, Canada
mir-abolfazl.mostafavi@scg.ulaval.ca
[2] Interdisciplinary Research Center for Rehabilitation and Social Integration, Université Laval,
Québec, QC, Canada
[3] Laboratoire de Psychologie Et d'Ergonomie Appliquées (LaPEA), Université Gustave Eiffel,
Paris, France

Abstract. People with mobility disabilities (PWMD) often struggle with challenges in getting around independently for their daily activities. Mobility is one of the most important life habits which might be constrained by diverse environmental and social obstacles, limiting the social participation of PWMD. Upgrading the social integration of these people is a major challenge in Canada and internationally. Even though the advent of assistive navigation technologies improves the interaction of PWMD with their environments during their mobility, these tools mostly ignore the capabilities, capacities, and specific needs of this population. It is required to better understand PWMD's navigational behavior in the environment to make these navigation tools adapted to their profile and specific needs. Hence, this research aims at using state-of-the-art technology (i.e., eye-tracking glasses) to explore the navigational behavior of PWMD. To do so, we designed and carried out an experiment in which a wheelchair user wearing eye-tracking glasses navigated a route following the instructions given by Google Maps. Several eye-tracking metrics for the collected eye movement data were computed and analyzed to explore the participant's visual and mental activities while performing the navigation task. Artificial intelligence was used to automatically assign eye movement data to specific features in the environment during navigation. The preliminary findings of this research show that the highest level of fixation was assigned to the cell phone for receiving the route instructions, distracting thus the participant from his surroundings. In this sense, we have noticed that these route instructions were not sufficient and clear for wheelchair users in some situations. In addition, fixations on sidewalks and crosswalks were the second-highest amount because of the low accessibility level of several parts of the route. Some buildings as landmarks were also eye-catching for the wheelchair user during exploring the environment, and searching for the route, particularly when the route was accessible. In this way, it is required to help the wheelchair user to become aware of information on the accessibility of routes and salient environmental objects in advance to draw more attention to the environment, better orient in the environment, and make

M. A. Mostafavi and G. Del Mondo (Eds.): W2GIS 2023, LNCS 13912, pp. 57–75, 2023.
https://doi.org/10.1007/978-3-031-34612-5_4

sure of following the correct route, therefore, upgrading wheelchair users' spatial learning and being autonomous.

Keywords: Wheelchair users' mobility · Eye tracking · Artificial intelligence

1 Introduction

Social participation can be defined as the engagement of a person in activities in interaction with others in a society or community [1]. It contributes to the well-being of people and their life quality [2, 3]. Mobility is fundamental for the social participation of PWMD[1]. These individuals often struggle with different accessibility issues and many social and physical obstacles in their daily activities (e.g. going to work, school, and attending social activities) that restrict their mobility [4–6]. Indeed, even though PWMD are likely to be functionally limited, their engagement with their social and physical environments can shape their disability. According to the DCP model[2], the interactions between personal factors of PWMD and environmental factors influence their life habits including their mobility [7, 8]. A recent Canadian Survey (2020) on mobility disability actually indicated that 2.7 million Canadians aged 15 years and older suffer from mobility disability, and over half of a million Canadian people with disabilities regard themselves as housebound. One percent of the Canadian population are community-dwelling wheelchair and scooter users [9], including 197,560 manual wheelchair users, 42,360 powered wheelchair users, and 108,550 scooter users.

The advent of assistive navigational technologies can significantly change and enhance the navigational behavior of the general population and PWMD. However, the special requirements, capacities, and capabilities of motor-disabled people are often taken for granted in these technologies. In this sense, it is required to enrich these navigation tools with pertinent information on accessibility information, security information, and landmarks. Adapted navigation tools might have several benefits for these people, the very epitomes of which are upgrading the likelihood of their social participation and integration in communities, their well-being, and their spatial learning.

To acquire and process information from the environment, human beings mainly use their eyes, rather than other senses [10]. Human beings' eyes allow information processing activities from their observation of surroundings, but also the interpretation of their interaction with the environment. Hence, visual and attentional behavior during interaction with the environment can pave the path for analyzing human beings' navigational behavior efficiently, rather than the traditional means of gathering information on navigation like interviews [6, 11], questionnaires [12], walking behind users, and documenting their behavior [13]. Indeed, the advent of state-of-the-art eye-tracking technology opens doors for measuring the navigational behavior of people since this technology can capture the visual attention of people to reveal their interaction with their surroundings [14]. Eye trackers are increasingly applicable in navigation scenarios

---

[1] People with mobility disabilities.
[2] Disability Creation Process model.

due to their capability to measure the gaze behavior of travelers in the real world [15, 16].

There are several studies performed on the application of eye-tracking technology in pedestrian navigation for the general population, not PWMD. Some examples of which are research work like [17–20] that analyzed eye-tacking data to investigate the wayfinders' gaze behavior to upgrade the navigation of people in environments. However, there have been limited studies that investigate and measure the interaction of PWMD with their surrounding environments using this technology. Indeed, PWMD interacts differently with their environment during their mobility. They experience diverse problems during their navigation, that adversely impact their execution of navigation tasks including orientation and heading [6].

In this paper, we propose to benefit from eye-tracking technology to semantically explore and analyze different features which attract PWMD's (i.e., a wheelchair user) attention while interacting with the environment during their navigation tasks. We want to answer questions such as what are a wheelchair user's visual and mental activities (e.g., confusion) while performing different navigation tasks (e.g., decision-making, orientation, street crossing, and route searching)? where, when, how many times, and how long do and in which sequence a wheelchair user looks at certain features/or objects in the environment? How does a wheelchair user visually scan the environment to avoid obstacles and make sure of his/her safety? How does a wheelchair user interact with the surroundings while getting route instructions from assistive navigational technology from her/his mobile phone? In addition, we also propose to use artificial intelligence to automatically assign eye movement data to the specific feature in the environment that would facilitate their interpretation. Ultimately, this information will be used to adapt and enrich assistive navigation tools for the navigation of PWMD. Besides, this information may help city designers and planners to upgrade the accessibility of the urban environment for wheelchair users.

The remainder of this paper is organized as follows. In Sect. 2, we will investigate the potential of using eye movement data for analyzing navigational behavior. In Sect. 3, we present our methodology for investigating the navigational behavior of wheelchair users in urban environments using eye movement data. In Sect. 4, we will explain our experiment for collecting a wheelchair user's eye movement data, its analysis, and data preparation using a deep learning approach. Then we will present the results and discussion in Sect. 5. We provide a conclusion and future works in the last section.

2 Background on the Potential of Eye-Tracking Technology for Navigation

People use their eyes to select and process the relevant information in their surrounding environment at various distances with a better resolution compared to other senses [21, 22]. Visual attention can be captured directly by the eye-tracking method. Indeed, gaze data can be gathered through a mobile (head-mounted) eye tracker or a remote (table-mounted) eye tracker. The users wearing a mobile eye tracker can look around their 3D environment for measuring mobile gaze-based interaction, while the environment of a remote eye tracker is generally restricted to the computer monitor [15, 23].

In general, the eye movement data comprises two initial components which are fixations (when peoples' eyes remain focused on an object spatiotemporally) and saccades (i.e., the reposition of gaze between fixations) [24]. Fixations have several metrics and indicators such as fixation duration and count, density, and time to the first fixation [25, 26]. A long fixation duration on one object can be interpreted as how appealing it is [25]. Some instances of saccades metrics and indicators are saccadic duration, velocity, and count [25, 26]. In cognitive psychology, saccades indicate the searching process [25]. Furthermore, other eye measurements including human pupil size and blinks (e.g., blink rates, duration, and velocity) can be investigated to better understand the cognitive activities of wayfinders (e.g., the mental efforts used working memory resources while conducting cognitive tasks, i.e. cognitive load) [24, 25].

Eye-tracking sensors allow for measuring visual activities, cognitive processing, and perception during wayfinding [15, 27]. One example of visual activities can be what are the interesting and useful environmental objects, features, and information for them and their task. There are some examples of cognitive activities such as cognitive load during performing navigational tasks [21]. Studies like [24, 25] indicated that the extraction of information and cognitive processing corresponds to the level of fixation duration. Indeed, the high amount of fixation duration refers to mental efforts during performing tasks and so the complexity of tasks [28]. The efficiency in the process of information is related to fixation frequency (i.e., the ratio of fixation count to navigation duration)[29]. In addition, the frequency and duration of fixation on objects can be interpreted as how appealing they are [21]. Also, the demanding searching process may increase the fixation and saccade count [30, 31]. In this way, the analysis of eye movements of wayfinders makes it possible to get insight into their interactions with their surrounding environment while they conduct navigation tasks (e.g., decision-making, self-localization, route following, and search targets).

Various studies concentrate on the potential of eye-tracking sensors in different aspects of pedestrian navigation for the general population. In terms of the gaze behavior of wayfinders, Wiener and Condappa (2011) [19] examined the influence of mobile eye-tracking data on analyzing pedestrians' map usage in an urban environment, Schwarzkopf et al. (2017) studied eye-tracking data to investigate attentional behavior in the case of individual and collaborative navigation [17], and Dong et al. (2020) compared the visual behavior of male and female wayfinders [18]. The findings of the study of [18] reveal that, in general, the environmental features like bicycles, cars, buildings, and vegetation were eye-catching for the wayfinders. For probing navigation tasks (e.g., self-localization and orientation) in pedestrian navigation, Liao et al. (2018) performed a field-based experiment while participants were equipped with eye-tracking glasses [32]. Furthermore, eye-tracking technology has been used to detect landmarks for assisting people's wayfinding in different research works [33–35]. For an instance, Wenczel et al. (2017) examined the role of gaze behavior in extracting landmarks, their saliency, and acquiring spatial knowledge in the real world [36]. As for addressing the challenges of the existing navigation tools, Giannopoulos et al. (2015) [37] proposed a gaze-based pedestrian navigation system, named GazeNav, that used human gaze data in the interaction of the user with the environment during navigation to improve users' performance during navigation. Furthermore, regarding the assessment of the proposed design for pedestrian navigation tools, Brügger et al. (2019) used eye-tracking sensors to examine the effects of several levels of automation of navigation systems on the navigational behavior of people [13].

Despite the numerous research work on examining the navigation of the general population by taking advantage of eye movement data, the PWMD were mostly taken for granted. As suggested by Prescott et al. [6], the interactions of PWMD with their environment are different from those of the general population. Indeed, PWMD are more likely to face diverse challenges (e.g., accessibility challenges) while performing navigation tasks (e.g., orientation and heading) that can limit their mobility. Hence, in the next section, we propose a methodology to investigate the navigational behavior of PWMD using eye movement data during their navigation.

3 Methodology

Here, we propose and present a new methodology to investigate PWMD's navigational behavior (i.e., the visual and mental activities of PWMD during their navigation) based on the use of eye-tracking data acquired through an experiment with a wheelchair user in an urban environment. To do so, we need to detect things and objects in urban environments that catch the attention resources of a wheelchair user while navigating in a given urban environment. The proposed methodology is composed of several steps (Fig. 1). Initially, for data collection, we need to perform a field-based experiment with a wheelchair user equipped with Tobii Pro Glasses 3[3] to navigate a route while getting the route instructions from a navigation application such as Google Maps. It is important to note that Tobii Pro Glasses 3 with a sampling rate of 50 Hz can capture eye movement data with 4 sensors (2 per eye), and they are lightweight (i.e., 76.5 g including cable) to collect the natural human attentional behavior.

Next, it is necessary to compute the wheelchair user's fixation points and eye-tracking metrics (e.g., fixation duration and count). To do so, we propose to use iMotion software which is generally used in biometric research to study and analyze human behavior. It provides an interesting function (velocity-based algorithm (i.e., IVT filter) with a minimum duration of 100 ms) to automatically determine the user's eye movement fixations and saccades.

After that, it is required to annotate and segment the eye movement data of the wheelchair user based on different parts of the route (i.e., sidewalks and crosswalks) in iMotion software.

The next crucial requirement for eye movement data analysis necessities the annotation of features (e.g., people and buildings) on different parts of the route of the wheelchair user. This will allow map fixation points to the corresponding real-world objects. Nevertheless, the data captured by Tobii pro-eye-tracking glasses 3 are not georeferenced and so there are some challenges with the detection of the eye-catching objects in the environment (i.e., generally called AOI[4]). This is specifically related to matching eye-tracking records with the corresponding objects in the real world. Manual

---

[3] https://imotions.com/hardware/Tobi-pro-glasses-3/
[4] Areas of interest.

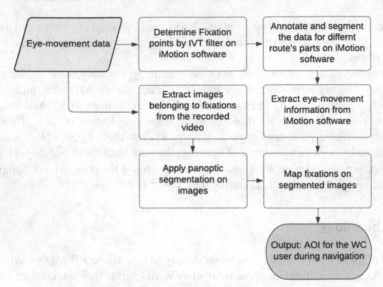

Fig. 1. The proposed methodology for semantically determining attention-grabbing features for a wheelchair user

matching of this information is very time-consuming and not efficient as conducted in several previous studies such as [13, 23].

To tackle this problem, it is required to use a deep learning method for automatically performing the semantic segmentation of the navigation scene. To do so, we initially need to extract images related to the wheelchair user's fixation points from eye movement video captured by the eye-tracking glasses. After that, we propose to use pan-optic image segmentation in the Detectron 2[5] tool. Indeed, Detectron 2 is based on Mask R-CNN[6] which is an extension of Faster R-CNN that considers the segmentation mask branch on ROI[7] in addition to the existing classification branch and bounding box regression [38]. Detectron 2 tool provides the opportunity for applying panoptic segmentation on images. In fact, panoptic segmentation engages instance and semantic segmentation, meaning that panoptic segmentation considers background elements that were ignored in the instance segmentation [39]. In other words, in semantic segmentation, a pixel-wise classification is applied to images and the same label is assigned to pixels related to the same class although instance segmentation allows distinctly identifying the objects of the same class [39]. In this research work, the Detectron 2 panoptic segmentation model needs to be trained with a couple of datasets including COCO[8] and LVIS datasets, leading to determining object classes in the images.

---

[5] https://github.com/facebookresearch/detectron2.
[6] Region-based Convolutional Neural Networks.
[7] Regions of Interest.
[8] Common Objects in Context.

Finally, following the extraction of the eye movement information including gazes' coordinates, time, fixations' coordinates, duration, and count, annotations, etc. from the iMotion software, the fixation points can be mapped on the determined object classes in the images.

4 Case Study

4.1 Data Collection

4.1.1 Participant

As mentioned, the navigation experiment with the eye-tracking glasses was performed by a manual wheelchair user. He was 48 years old and able to propel his manual wheelchair for about 1 km. In addition, he had approximately one year of manual wheelchair-using experience. He had self-reported normal vision, and he was unfamiliar with the study area. He also had the experience of using navigational technologies on a cell phone (e.g., Google maps) for about one year.

4.1.2 Procedure

The experiment took place in the Saint-Roch district in Quebec City (see Fig. 2). The selected route had approximately 1-km length and consisted of different obstacles and barriers (e.g., curbs, steep slopes, cracked and uneven sidewalks, crosswalks without traffic lights) and facilitators (e.g., ramps, and curb cuts) and the combination of simple and complex configurations (e.g., a couple of T-intersections and two five-way intersections). Figure 2 shows the selected route on Google Maps. For this experiment, one wheelchair user who was unfamiliar with the route was recruited following ethical approval. In the experiment, we met the participant at Café Van Houtte in the Saint-Roch district. The participant was led to the starting point of the pre-determined route, and he was equipped with Tobii pro glasses 3. After calibrating the glasses, a thigh band for keeping a cell phone was fixed on the participant's thigh and so he had his hands free to maneuver his wheelchair during navigation. The participant received visual and vocal route guidance from Google Maps through a headphone. Then, the participant was asked to follow the route using Google Maps' route instructions (i.e., turn-by-turn route instructions) on the cell phone. The researchers intervened if the participant was in danger. After carrying out the navigation task, the participant took off the eye-tracking glasses.

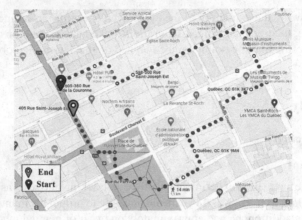

Fig. 2. Study site in St-Roch district in Quebec City

4.2 Data Preparation and Assessment Using Deep Learning Approach

Following the data collection step, according to the proposed methodology in Sect. 3, detectron2 panoptic segmentation was implemented in Python and it was performed on images extracted from the participant's eye movement video captured by the eye-tracking glasses in order to segment the images to different object classes with high accuracy. In this way, 22 object classes such as the road, pavement, buildings, the cell phone, trees, etc. were presented in the training data sets. One example of the panoptic image segmentation model which was performed for determining object classes for the participant is demonstrated in Fig. 3.

(a) An image recorded by eye-tracking glasses   (b) The semantically segmented image

Fig. 3. The segmentation of eye-tracking recording of the participant while navigating

Next, we integrated several object classes to lead to seven AOI categories (see Table. 1). The initial AOI category is Route, which consists of sidewalks and crosswalks that the wheelchair user interacted with while navigating. The second one is Cell phone which the wheelchair user looks at when he got a new route instruction to make a navigational decision, etc. The third AOI is Building which can include landmarks that attract the wheelchair user's attention. The fourth and fifth categories are Car and Person. The person can be himself or other people that he looked at. Green area is the sixth AOI category. The last category is Other objects that can be POI[9] and obstacles for the wheelchair user in some situations. After the segmentation process, the fixations were overlaid on the determined object classes to annotate them.

Table 1. The link between the AOIs category and corresponding segmentation objects.

AOIs Category	Segmentation objects
1-Route	Pavement and road
2-Cellphone	Cell phone
3-Building	Wall and building (e.g., Cafe, Restaurant, Store, and Church)
4-Car	Car, bus, and truck
5-Person	Person
6-Green area	Tree and grass
7-Other objects	Orange barrel, pole, bicycle, trash can, fireplug, bench, and traffic light

5   Results and Discussion

After applying panoptic segmentation on the images, the fixation points were mapped on the AOI categories. The preliminary results indicate that the participant had significant amount of fixation on his cell phone to find the route using Google Maps' route instructions (see Fig. 4). This indicates that the instructions were confusing for the participant led to several navigational errors in complex situations. The fixation duration (i.e., about 158867 ms) and count (i.e., 578) on Cell phone reveal that this AOI was the first biggest target of attention for the participant rather than other AOIs categories. The second most attention-grabbing AOI was the Route itself, indicating that the participant paid attention to the sidewalks and crosswalks to avoid obstacles and barriers and make sure of his safety and security (see Fig. 5). While the third AOIs category that got the participant's attention in terms of fixation duration is the Person category, the fixation frequency for the Building class is higher than that of the Person category. Car, Green area, and Other objects categories are the last categories in terms of fixation duration and frequency. The participant mostly fixated on cars when he crossed the crosswalk. These preliminary results show the differences between the navigational behavior of a wheelchair user and the general population; the former prefer to pay attention to the roads, sidewalks, and crosswalk rather than the buildings and objects in the environment (e.g., bicycles, cars, and vegetation) which are favorable for the later one as investigated in several research works like [18].

---

[9] Points of interest.

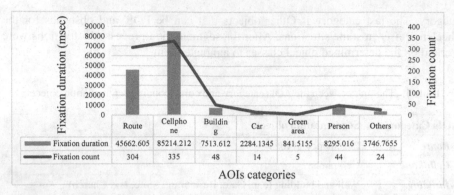

Fig. 4. Fixation duration and count on AOIs categories

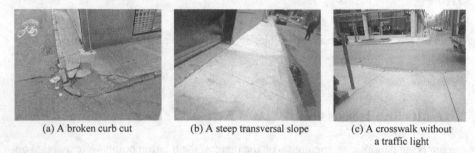

(a) A broken curb cut   (b) A steep transversal slope   (c) A crosswalk without a traffic light

Fig. 5. Examples of the obstacle and barriers that the participant faced while navigating the route

Two examples of the distribution of gazes of the wheelchair user, named a heatmap, during performing navigation tasks are represented in Fig. 6. Green, yellow, and red areas demonstrate the number of gaze points that are allocated to features in ascending order. Figure 6(a) shows the huge level of fixation on the cell phone to find the route. In Fig. 6 (b), the wheelchair user was crossing the street and he paid plenty of attention to the broken curb for entering the next sidewalk.

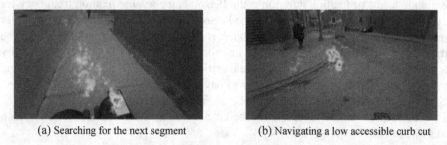

(a) Searching for the next segment   (b) Navigating a low accessible curb cut

Fig. 6. The heat map of the navigational behavior of the participant

The following paragraphs present some of the results on the attentional behavior of the participant. Figure 7 represents the different parts of the route navigated by the participant (i.e., the sidewalks with S and the crosswalks with C). The mean fixation duration on each AOI at each part of the route (i.e., the ratio of fixation duration on each AOI in each part of the route to the time duration of navigating that part) as well as fixation frequency on AOI at each part of the route (i.e., the ratio of fixation count on each AOI at each part of the route to the time duration of navigating that part) are shown in Fig. 8 and 9, respectively. The changing pattern of mean fixation duration and frequency for each AOI category in different parts of the route is approximately similar. Totally, regarding these figures, the level of fixation on Route for crosswalks is higher than that for sidewalks. In addition, Fig. 10 demonstrates the sequence and frequency of switches between fixations (i.e., the ratio of the number of switches between fixations on AOI for each part of the route to the time duration of navigating that part). Switches are regarded as a change of fixation points.

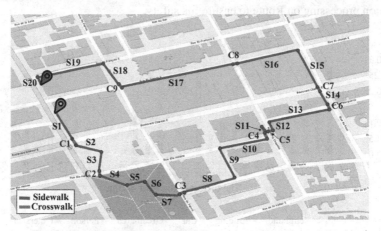

Fig. 7. The sidewalks and crosswalks navigated by the participant

As illustrated in Fig. 7, 8, and 9, there were some accessibility challenges for the wheelchair user while navigating from the start point to the park "Jardin Jean Paul-L'Allier" particularly on sidewalks S2, S6 and S7 as well as crosswalks C1 and C2. Indeed, C1 with a traffic light had cracks and an upward curb cut with a steep slope to enter the park. The participant continuously looked at C1 to go through it immediately and make sure of his safety. In this way, the complexity of crossing C1 results in an increase in the mean fixation duration and frequency on Route compared to those of S1. Figure 10. Also confirms that there were attention switches on the route for C1. After entering the park, S2 was uneven, its' surface was concrete, and also its' width was limited which resulted in a high level of fixation duration on Route. At the same time, he needed to find the next part of the route through the route instructions of Google Maps and so he continuously looked at his cell phone. This is also demonstrated on Fig. 10 as fixation shifts on Route and between route and cell phone. On C2 which has a traffic light, he faced a curb that was difficult to pass, and he searched for a part of the curb cut with a better slope to follow. He was in a hurry to pass the crosswalk in the limited time duration and so he faced mental effort. The mean fixation duration on this crosswalk were higher than those of the previous parts of the route. Then, he entered the park "Jardin Jean Paul-L'Allier". While there were a few cracks on the surface of S6, the participant received the route instruction for the next sidewalk which was going up an upward steep slope (incline $> 5°$). At that time, he became worried and confused, and he searched for finding an alternative path instead of navigating an upward steep slope. That is the reason for an increase in the frequency of switches on the route along S6 as shown in Fig. 10. Unfortunately, during the above-mentioned searching process, the other paths were impossible to follow because of stairs, etc. and so these conditions made him go through the suggested sidewalk on Google Maps not independently but with our help. Indeed, Google Maps led him to the part of the environment which was inaccessible to him. Hence, this task was complex for the participant and so the significant mean fixation duration on Route is assigned to S7. On this sidewalk, the greatest level of fixation frequency on Route for the whole route took place as he struggled with information processing on Route to ensure his safety.

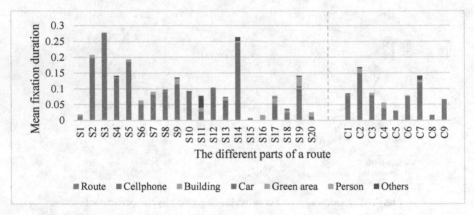

Fig. 8. The participant's mean fixation duration on AOI while navigating the route

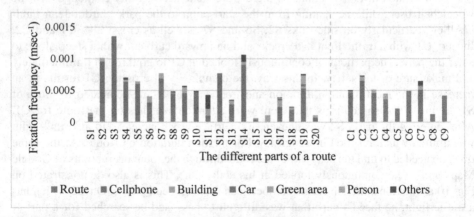

Fig. 9. The participant's fixation frequency on AOI while navigating the route

After leaving the park, he faced some problems in terms of the accessibility level of the route until arriving at Boulevard Charest Est, particularly at C3, C4, C5, S12, and C6. The participant passed the third crosswalk (i.e., C3) with no traffic light. He wanted to take this crosswalk which has a broken curb cut. He needed to navigate the crosswalk immediately until there were not any cars. Hence, he increasingly fixated on C3. Also, C4 had a curb cut with cracks that made him allocate his attention to it. Subsequently, he took S11, but he understood that he could not cross the street to follow S13 because of the street's curb. He returned to cross C5 which had no traffic light and was near an indoor parking lot. Then he followed S12 while he fixated on Route to ensure his safety as its' surface was unlevel and he verified the route with Google Maps. The most remarkable amount of mean fixation duration and frequency on Route was assigned to C6 among other crosswalks. The reason is the lack of traffic lights and also a broken curb which was difficult to pass and so he experienced mental effort as demonstrated in Fig. 6(b). C6 also has the highest number of shifts on Route regarding Fig. 10.

In terms of route accessibility in the remaining part of the route, the most challenging sidewalk was S19 and the crosswalks C7 and C9 were also problematic as shown on Fig. 8, 9, and 10. In fact, when he arrived at C7, he pushed the crosswalk button and waited for crossing it and so he had time to check the accessibility level of the route. This crosswalk's surface was bricked. The switches on the route on C7 are also remarkable. The level of attention on Route for C9 was considerable due to the curb cut with an upward steep slope. The most amount of mean fixation duration on Route was assigned to S19 because of its' steep transversal slope that made following S19 very complex. One of the highest numbers of switches on Route is also allocated to this sidewalk.

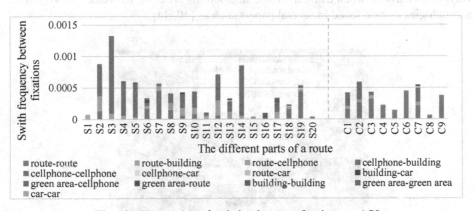

Fig. 10. The number of switches between fixations on AOI

As for Google Maps' route instructions, visual and vocal route guidance were considered in our experiment. The vocal route instructions were used to avoid distracting the participant from the environment and the route. The cell phone was fixed on the thigh of the participant for his use. However, Fig. 4, 8, 9, and 10 reveal the remarkable level of attention on Cell phone on different parts of the route. As shown in Fig. 8 and 9, the significant mean fixation duration and frequency on Cell phone took place on sidewalks S2-S5, S8, S9, S12, and S14 as well as crosswalks C2, and C7. The participant made navigational errors on S2 and C2 due to the insufficiency and the lack of clarity of route instructions. The challenging route instructions for finding S2 and C2 are represented on Fig. 11. Hence, these route instructions increased the participants' mental effort for finding his route. Actually, the participant made a mistake and followed the wrong route instead of S2, but he understood his mistake by paying a high level of attention to the Google Map application on his cell phone and then came back to the correct route. For finding C2, he kept looking at his cell phone on S3, but he followed the wrong route. Figure 10 also demonstrates the high level of fixation switches on the cell phone and between the cell phone and the route for S2, S3, and C2, depicting a searching process for finding the route by visually connecting the objects on Google Maps with the real-world corresponding ones. S4, S9, S10, and S14 were accessible to the participant, and he searched for the following parts of the route on Cell phone which was the reason for the growing mean fixation duration and frequency on this AOI. The same happened for S5 as he stopped for taking a rest and finding his route. On S8, the route instruction led him to turn left to a small park between two buildings which was confusing for him and resulted in putting fixation on Cell phone for verifying the route and he made considerable switches between the route and cell phone. On S12, Cell phone was a target of attention because the participant wanted to verify the route. As he waited to cross C7, he had time to fixate on Cell phone for confirming his route. Indeed, there were switches on the cell phone, between the cell phone and route, and also between the cell phone and building for justifying this. These preliminary findings highlighted several challenges (e.g., the distraction of wayfinders from the environment, lack of clarity of the route instructions, and lack of information components in the route instructions for wayfinders) arising when using the route instructions provided by assistive navigation technologies as mentioned in several papers such as [40–44].

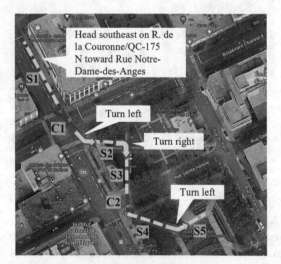

Fig. 11. The route instructions led to the participants' confusion.

In this experiment, as mentioned previously, the participant was unfamiliar with the study area and so the experiment was an exploratory trip that returns the participant to a familiar starting point. As indicated in [45], the wayfinder may pay attention to landmarks and recall them to organize his mental map of unfamiliar space in the exploration of the environment. In this sense, Building was a target of attention on S16 and S17 as illustrated in Fig. 8, 9, and 10, partly because these sidewalks were accessible for the participant but also because there were eye-catching and appealing commercial buildings, cafes, restaurants, and stores (i.e., Benjo and Denis Musique) and a historical church (Église Saint-Roch) near S16 and S17. On S16, there were many switches between Buildings, indicating the exploration process of the surrounding environments. In addition, as for S17, the participant also switched his fixation between Route and Building. The attentional shifts between Route and Building are more likely to be due to make sure of his safety on the route continuously and then paying attention back to Building for the exploration.

Supplementary to this, landmarks can be used in performing navigational tasks such as self-localization, orienting wayfinders to make sure whether they follow the correct path, and finding destinations [45, 46]. Regarding Fig. 8, 9, and 10, on S11, as the participant wanted to look for and confirm his route by shifting his attention between cell phone and buildings near the route, the mean fixation duration and frequency on Building for S11 are considerable. Similarly, Building on S13 was a target of attention partly because the participant geolocated and oriented himself to verify and find his route.

Fixations on the remaining AOI including Car, Green area, Person, and Other are lower. On S4, S5, and S6, the participant fixated shortly on Grean area because these parts of the route are located in the park. He was likely to select the parks as landmarks in his exploratory navigation for his future travel. As for Other AOI, the highest values of mean fixation duration and frequency were assigned to S11. The pole on S11 took his attention. Indeed, when the participant went back on S11, he faced the pole as an obstacle on his way and he passed by it.

The participants' saccade frequency on the environmental objects along different parts of the route is demonstrated in Fig. 12. The highly considerable saccade frequency was computed for sidewalks S2, S4, S7, S8, S12 as well as crosswalks C4 and C6. This can justify the search process on different AOI in these parts of the route.

These preliminary findings on the navigational behavior of the wheelchair user in the environment indicate the challenge of a considerable level of fixations on the cell phone for getting route instructions that need to be addressed by increasing the clarity of route instructions and enriching them with sufficient information. In this way, it is required to make wheelchair users aware of the accessibility level of the route and its obstacles, as well as salient objects in the environment (for geo-locating themselves and making sure of navigating the correct route in advance) to decrease their mental effort while navigating and enable them to pay more attention to their environment, to help them improve their spatial learning and thus allow them to become more autonomous. It is important to note that we still require confirming these preliminary results by studying more navigational behaviors among several other wheelchair users' information. We will

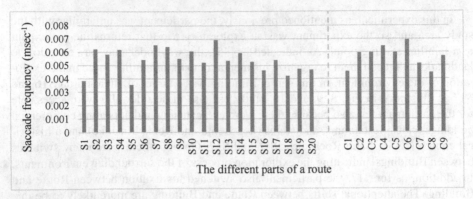

Fig. 12. The participant's saccade frequency on objects while navigating the route

then need to integrate these findings into assistive navigation tools to sufficiently enrich them for wheelchair users once all the empirical data has been gathered.

6   Conclusions and Future Works

In this paper, we have investigated the navigational behavior of a wheelchair user based on eye-tracking data collected during his navigation in an urban environment. In doing so, a navigation experiment with the wheelchair user was considered. In addition to computing eye-tracking metrics for the captured eye movement data of the participant, the objects and information taking up the attention of the wheelchair user were semantically determined and analyzed. According to the preliminary outcomes of this research, the most attention-grabbing feature was *Cell phone*. The Cell phone was mainly used for getting route instructions and was visually consulted when the route instructions were confusing. A highly considerable level of attention was assigned to *Route* (i.e., crosswalk, and sidewalk) while navigating on the predetermined route particularly on the crosswalks for safety and security reasons. The wheelchair user paid more attention to *Buildings* when he felt safe on the route, and when he needed to look for or confirm the route and explore his environment. Hence, according to our results, enriching route instructions through the provision of information on the accessibility level of routes and landmarks is more likely to help wheelchair users efficiently perform navigation tasks in urban environments. As a perspective, we plan to perform this experiment with the participation of more wheelchair users with different capabilities and preferences. This will ultimately help us to provide more adapted route instructions to wheelchair users.

References

1. Levasseur, M., Richard, L., Gauvin, L., Raymond, É.: Inventory and analysis of definitions of social participation found in the aging literature: proposed taxonomy of social activities. Soc. Sci. Med. **71**, 2141–2149 (2010). https://doi.org/10.1016/J.SOCSCIMED.2010.09.041
2. Rimmer, J., Riley, B., Wang, E., Rauworth, A.: Physical activity participation among persons with disabilities: barriers and facilitators. Elsevier (2004)

3. Ding, D., Parmanto, B., Karimi, H.: Design considerations for a personalized wheelchair navigation system (2007)
4. Bennett, S., Lee Kirby, R., MacDonald, B.: Wheelchair accessibility: descriptive survey of curb ramps in an urban area. Disabil. Rehabil. Assist. Technol. **4**, 17–23 (2009). https://doi.org/10.1080/17483100802542603
5. Giesbrecht, E., Ripat, J., Cooper, J., Quanbury, A.: Experiences with using a pushrim-activated power-assisted wheelchair for community-based occupations: a qualitative exploration. Can. J. Occup. Therapy **78**, 127–136 (2011). https://doi.org/10.2182/cjot.2011.78.2.8
6. Prescott, M., et al.: An exploration of the navigational behaviours of people who use wheeled mobility devices in unfamiliar pedestrian environments. J. Transp. Heal. **20**, 100975 (2021). https://doi.org/10.1016/j.jth.2020.100975
7. Fougeyrollas, P., Cloutier, R., Bergeron, H., St-Michel, G.: The Quebec classification: Disability creation process (1998)
8. Matthews, H., Beale, L., Picton, P., Briggs, D.: Modelling access with GIS in urban systems (MAGUS): capturing the experiences of wheelchair users. Area **35**, 34–45 (2003). https://doi.org/10.1111/1475-4762.00108
9. Smith, E.M., Giesbrecht, E.M., Ben Mortenson, W., Miller, W.C.: Prevalence of wheelchair and scooter use among community-dwelling Canadians. Phys. Ther. **96**, 1135–1142 (2016). https://doi.org/10.2522/PTJ.20150574
10. Just, M.A., Carpenter, P.A.: A theory of reading: From eye fixations to comprehension. Psychol. Rev. **87**, 329–354 (1980). https://doi.org/10.1037/0033-295X.87.4.329
11. Gupta, M., et al.: towards more universal wayfinding technologies: navigation preferences across disabilities (2020). https://doi.org/10.1145/3313831.3376581
12. Mirri, S., Prandi, C., Salomoni, P.: Personalizing Pedestrian Accessible way-finding with mPASS. In: 2016 13th IEEE Annual Consumer Communications Network Conference CCNC 2016, pp. 1119–1124 (2016). https://doi.org/10.1109/CCNC.2016.7444946
13. Brügger, A., Richter, K.-F., Fabrikant, S.I.: How does navigation system behavior influence human behavior? Cognit. Res.: Principles Implications **4**(1), 1–22 (2019). https://doi.org/10.1186/s41235-019-0156-5
14. Giannopoulos, I., Kiefer, P., Raubal, M.: GazeNav: Gaze-Based Pedestrian Navigation (2015). https://doi.org/10.1145/2785830
15. Giannopoulos, I., Kiefer, P., Raubal, M.: GeoGazemarks: Providing gaze history for the orientation on small display maps. In: ICMI'12 - Proceedings of the ACM International Conference on Multimodal Interaction, pp. 165–172 (2012). https://doi.org/10.1145/2388676.2388711
16. Kiefer, P., Giannopoulos, I., Duchowski, A., Raubal, M.: Measuring cognitive load for map tasks through pupil diameter. In: Miller, J.A., O'Sullivan, D., Wiegand, N. (eds.) GIScience 2016. LNCS, vol. 9927, pp. 323–337. Springer, Cham (2016). https://doi.org/10.1007/978-3-319-45738-3_21
17. Schwarzkopf, S., Büchner, S.J., Hölscher, C., Konieczny, L.: Perspective tracking in the real world: Gaze angle analysis in a collaborative wayfinding task. Spat. Cogn. Comput. **17**, 143–162 (2017). https://doi.org/10.1080/13875868.2016.1226841
18. Dong, W., Zhan, Z., Liao, H., Meng, L., Liu, J.: Assessing similarities and differences between males and females in visual behaviors in spatial orientation tasks. ISPRS Int. J. Geo-Inf. **9**, 115 (2020). https://doi.org/10.3390/ijgi9020115
19. Wiener, J., Condappa, O.: Do you have to look where you go? Gaze behaviour during spatial decision making (2011)
20. Liao, H., Dong, W., Huang, H., Gartner, G., Liu, H.: Inferring user tasks in pedestrian navigation from eye movement data in real-world environments. Int. J. Geogr. Inf. Sci. **33**, 739–763 (2019). https://doi.org/10.1080/13658816.2018.1482554

21. Coutrot, A., Hsiao, J.H., Chan, A.B.: Scanpath modeling and classification with hidden Markov models. Behav. Res. Methods **50**, 362–379 (2018). https://doi.org/10.3758/S13428-017-0876-8/TABLES/1
22. Kiefer, P., Giannopoulos, I., Raubal, M., Duchowski, A.: Eye tracking for spatial research: cognition, computation, challenges. Spatial Cognit. Comput. **17**, 1–19 (2017). https://doi.org/10.1080/13875868.2016.1254634
23. Jacob, R.J.K., Karn, K.S.: Eye tracking in human-computer interaction and usability research. ready to deliver the promises. In: The Mind's Eye: Cognitive and Applied Aspects of Eye Movement Research, pp. 531–553 (2003). https://doi.org/10.1016/B978-044451020-4/50031-1
24. Zagermann, J., Pfeil, U., Reiterer, H.: Measuring cognitive load using eye tracking technology in visual computing. ACM Int. Conf. Proc. Ser. 78–85 (2016)
25. Joseph, A.W., Murugesh, R.: Potential eye tracking metrics and indicators to measure cognitive load in human-computer interaction research. J. Sci. Res. **64**(1), 168–175 (2020). https://doi.org/10.37398/JSR.2020.640137
26. Tullis, T., Albert, B.: Measuring the User Experience: Collecting, Analyzing, and Presenting Usability Metrics, Second Edn (2013). https://doi.org/10.1016/C2011-0-00016-9
27. Clay, V., König, P., König, S.: Eye Tracking in Virtual Reality. J. Eye Mov. Res. 12 (2019)
28. Chen, F., et al.: Robust Multimodal Cognitive Load Measurement. Springer, Cham (2016). https://doi.org/10.1007/978-3-319-31700-7
29. Ooms, K., Maeyer, P.D., Fack, V., Assche, E.V., Witlox, F.: Investigating the effectiveness of an efficient label placement method using eye movement data. Cartograph. J. **49**(3), 234–246 (2012). https://doi.org/10.1179/1743277412Y.0000000010
30. Goldberg, J., Kotval, X.P.: Eye movement based evaluation of human-computer interfaces (1998)
31. Holmqvist, K., Nyström, M., Andersson, R., Dewhurst, R.: Eye tracking: a comprehensive guide to methods and measures (2011)
32. Liao, H., Dong, W., Huang, H., Gartner, G.: Inferring user tasks in pedestrian navigation from eye movement data in real-world environments. Taylor Fr. **33**, 739–763 (2018). https://doi.org/10.1080/13658816.2018.1482554
33. Ohm, C., Müller, M., Ludwig, B., Bienk, S.: Where is the Landmark? Eye Tracking Studies in Large-Scale Indoor Environments (2014)
34. Schrom-Feiertag, H., Settgast, V., Seer, S.: Evaluation of indoor guidance systems using eye tracking in an immersive virtual environment. Spat. Cognit. Comput. **17**, 163–183 (2017)
35. Wang, J., Li, R.: Reassessing Underlying Spatial Relations in Pedestrian Navigation (2018). https://doi.org/10.4018/978-1-5225-5396-0.ch003
36. Wenczel, F., Hepperle, L., von Stülpnagel, R.: Gaze behavior during incidental and intentional navigation in an outdoor environment. Spat. Cognit. Comput. **17**, 121–142 (2017). https://doi.org/10.1080/13875868.2016.1226838
37. Giannopoulos, I., Kiefer, P., Raubal, M.: Gaze nav: Gaze-based pedestrian navigation. In: MobileHCI 2015 - Proceedings of the 17th International Conference on Human-Computer Interaction with Mobile Devices and Services, pp. 337–346. Association for Computing Machinery (2015). https://doi.org/10.1145/2785830.2785873
38. He, K., Gkioxari, G., Dollár, P., Girshick, R.: Mask R-CNN. IEEE Trans. Pattern Anal. Mach. Intell. **42**, 386–397 (2017). https://doi.org/10.48550/arxiv.1703.06870
39. de Carvalho, O.L.F., et al.: Panoptic segmentation meets remote sensing. Remote Sens. **14**, 965 (2021). https://doi.org/10.3390/rs14040965
40. Götze, J., Boye, J.: Resolving Spatial References using Crowdsourced Geographical Data. In: Proceedings of the 20th Nordic Conference of Computational Linguistics, pp. 61–68 (2015)

41. Ishikawa, T., Fujiwara, H., Imai, O., Okabe, A.: Wayfinding with a GPS-based mobile navigation system: a comparison with maps and direct experience. J. Environ. Psychol. **28**, 74–82 (2008). https://doi.org/10.1016/j.jenvp.2007.09.002

42. Dahmani, L., Bohbot, V.: Habitual use of GPS negatively impacts spatial memory during self-guided navigation. Sci. Rep. **10**(1), 6310 (2020)

43. Schwering, A., Krukar, J., Li, R., Anacta, V.J., Fuest, S.: Wayfinding through orientation. Spat. Cogn. Comput. **17**, 273–303 (2017). https://doi.org/10.1080/13875868.2017.1322597

44. Anacta, V.J.A., Schwering, A., Li, R., Muenzer, S.: Orientation information in wayfinding instructions: evidences from human verbal and visual instructions. GeoJournal **82**(3), 567–583 (2016). https://doi.org/10.1007/s10708-016-9703-5

45. Yesiltepe, D., Conroy Dalton, R., Ozbil Torun, A.: Landmarks in wayfinding: a review of the existing literature. Cogn. Process. **22**(3), 369–410 (2021). https://doi.org/10.1007/s10339-021-01012-x

46. Michon, P.-E., Denis, M.: When and why are visual landmarks used in giving directions? In: Montello, D.R. (ed.) COSIT 2001. LNCS, vol. 2205, pp. 292–305. Springer, Heidelberg (2001). https://doi.org/10.1007/3-540-45424-1_20

A New Approach for Accessibility Assessment of Sidewalks for Wheelchair Users Considering the Sidewalk Traffic

Maryam Naghdizadegan Jahromi[1,2] (iD), Najmeh Neysani Samany[2(✉)] (iD),
Mir Abolfazl Mostafavi[1(✉)] (iD), and Meysam Argany[2]

[1] Center for Research in Geospatial Data and Intelligence, Department of Geomatics Sciences,
Université Laval, 1055, Avenue du Séminaire, Québec, QC, Canada
`mir-abolfazl.mostafavi@scg.ulaval.ca`
[2] Department of Remote Sensing and GIS, Faculty of Geography, University of Tehran,
Zarrinkoob Alley, Vesal-Shirazi Street, Tehran, Iran
`nneysani@ut.ac.ir`

Abstract. Independent mobility of people with motor disabilities is fundamental for their daily activities. However, the mobility of these people is often restricted by diverse environmental and social factors. In addition to static factors, temporal factors such as the presence of the crowd could reduce the accessibility on the sidewalk. Hence, in this paper, we focus on the accessibility of sidewalks for people with mobility impairment, specifically for manual wheelchair users, in the presence of crowd. The paper aims at understanding how environmental factors, including temporal factors such as crowd density, affect the independent mobility of individuals with mobility impairments. The proposed method evaluates each user's confidence level in navigating different sidewalk components in the presence of different population densities and uses a fuzzy-based model for accessibility assessment. Besides the accessible maps for different population densities, a similarity index has been applied to compare the impact of crowd on the accessibility of sidewalk components. The findings suggest that, the direction of the movement of people have a significant effect on the level of accessibility of each segment. Moreover, while the presence of crowds is discouraging in some situations, it improves accessibility in others.

Keywords: Accessibility · Crowd · Wheelchair users' mobility

1 Introduction

Social participation of people with disabilities is of great importance for their quality of life. Independent mobility of these people as for other citizens in their daily activities is very important [1]. But social participation of these people is constrained by diverse social and physical barriers. In fact, built-up environments are not designed in a way that considers people with mobility impairment [2–4]. So, their mobility is restricted not only by their disabilities but also by the existing obstacles in the urban space. This could affect the quality of their life which is the interaction of their personal factor and social and physical factors in the environment [1]. Social and physical barriers could limit their daily activities, and lead to their isolation and exclusion from society. [1, 3, 5].

© The Author(s), under exclusive license to Springer Nature Switzerland AG 2023
M. A. Mostafavi and G. Del Mondo (Eds.): W2GIS 2023, LNCS 13912, pp. 76–92, 2023.
https://doi.org/10.1007/978-3-031-34612-5_5

Despite, many efforts dedicated to the improvement of urban environments, people with mobility impairments still have limited access to urban infrastructure and services. This could be due to improper universal design standards or inappropriate management [6]. Hence, being aware of the existing obstacles and the level of sidewalk accessibility would be essential for their safety and could improve their social participation [6, 7]. Indeed, providing information about the location of obstacles and their characteristics would be very assistive for the navigation of these people.

Recent advancements in geospatial technologies such as GIS (Geographic Information System), GPS (Global Positioning System), wireless networks, and devices could provide useful tools for collecting, analyzing, and communicating information on the accessibility of the environment. Using these technologies and developing services and applications adapted to the needs of wheelchair users could facilitate their mobility. But, despite many efforts, the available navigation technologies are not adapted to the specific needs of people with mobility impairment [5, 8, 9]. According to a recent study on the usability of the geospatial mobility assistive technologies [10], information content on the routes is very important to wheelchair users. However, information on the accessibility of sidewalks, the presence of curb cuts, and ramps are usually absent in the available navigation tools, and online resources. Most navigation services like Google Maps, do not provide information on the slope of pedestrian routing [11]. Besides information on the obstacles and facilitators on the sidewalks, the navigation applications must provide proper accessibility information on sidewalk segments to guarantee safe and easy trips [5].

To overcome these limitations, many investigations are dedicated to evaluate the effects of different factors on the sidewalk accessibility. Physical factors affecting the accessibility of sidewalks have been subject to intensive studies during the past few years compared to the social factors [6, 7, 12–17]. According to these investigations, the physical factors are either static or dynamic. Slope, width, surface type, quality, and height changes are static factors, and precipitation, crowd, and lighting are dynamic factors that could change over time. The majority of the previous studies have considered the static factors for the evaluation of the accessibility of sidewalks and dynamic factors are omitted due to the complexities of data collection [18]. However, dynamic factors might significantly affect the accessibility of sidewalks and their consideration is very important in the mobility of wheelchair users.

This paper proposes a fuzzy-based method for the assessment of the accessibility of the pedestrian network by considering the presence of crowd on the sidewalks and how the dynamics of the crowd impact its accessibility. To fulfill our aim, we investigated the effective static physical parameters for the accessibility of sidewalks for wheelchair users. Then, the effects of crowd density on these factors have been evaluated based on a user confidence approach. The proposed method was implemented in a case study and the results were presented and discussed.

The remainder of the paper is organized as follows: Sect. 2 provides information on related research works regarding the accessibility of pedestrian networks for wheelchair users and the role of crowds. Section 3, describes the proposed methodology for accessibility assessment. Section 4 presents the details of our experiment. In Sect. 5, the results of the implemented approach for a manual wheelchair user have been discussed using a similarity index, and the personalized routes are presented and finally, the conclusion of the research is presented in the last section.

2 Related Research Works

Different frameworks were developed for evaluating the accessibility of pedestrian networks and routing for people with disabilities in recent years [3, 6, 15–17, 19–21]. While some researchers used participants' experience and feedback for routing, some others used sidewalk physical barriers for evaluating the accessibility [6, 12–15]. Other studies have designed and developed methods and software tools for the assessment of the accessibility of the pedestrian networks [16, 18, 20, 22, 23].

Despite fruitful results and outcomes of these studies, the accessibility maps in these researches are mostly based on static factors without considering the impact of the dynamic factors on the accessibility of sidewalks based on the users' perception. Dynamic factors are very important to wheelchair users as they might significantly affect the accessibility of a rout. For example, navigating through a crowd for wheelchair users is always a challenging factor. In fact, mobility in the presence of the crowd has been recognized as one of the most difficult situations for wheelchair users [24]. The way people cope with wheelchair users is very important, and how impaired people deal with the crowd despite the presence of other obstacles is crucial [25]. So, it is essential to model the effect of a crowd on the mobility of the wheelchair users.

Some researchers analyzed the interaction of crowds with people with mobility impairment in indoor environments, especially during evacuation operations [26–32]. But, most of these studies neglect the needs and preferences of mobility-impaired people moving through a crowd. They only explored the perception of other pedestrians interacting with these people.

Only few researchers have considered the preferences of wheelchair users encountering the crowd [25, 33]. Stuart et al. (2019), investigated the movement behaviors of people with mobility impairment in a crowd and how these differences could affect pedestrian interaction. A method has been developed that explains how pedestrians adjust their movement behaviors based on the changes formed by people with mobility impairments [25]. Zhang et al. (2022), analyzed the interaction of participants with their smart wheelchairs and also between the participants and the crowd. Using a semi-structured interview, they assessed wheelchair users' needs and challenges while navigating through a crowd. They concluded that to be efficient, the smart wheelchair must be adaptable to different indoor and outdoor situations while considering the wheelchair users' preferences at the same time. Moreover, it must give proper information on different obstacles and crowds at an appropriate time using different modes of communication [33].

The above-mentioned studies evaluated the interaction of wheelchair users with crowds according to their movement and behavior, but as it is explained, the movement of people is not only affected by interactions with one another but also by the physical environment. These studies did not analyze the effects of the crowds on the physical factors that are vital to the accessibility of sidewalks and wheelchair users' wayfinding. The presence of crowds on the itinerary components (sidewalk segments, bridges, ramps, etc.) could change their accessibility. Hence, in this research, we consider the effects of crowds on the accessibility of sidewalks. More specifically, our objective is to evaluate the accessibility of sidewalks for people moving with a manual wheelchair.

3 The Proposed Method for Accessibility Assessment in the Presence of a Crowd

Our method for the accessibility assessment of sidewalks for people with mobility impairment is based on the DCP (Disability Creation Process) model, according to which, disability is the result of the interaction between personal factors (ex. Identity, capacity, …) and environmental factors (slop, step, ramp, …). Environmental factors could be either static or dynamic [34]. While the majority of the previous works are dedicated to the role of static factors on the mobility of wheelchair users, few research works consider the role of dynamic factors in the accessibility of side-walks. Our method for the assessment of the accessibility of sidewalks in the presence of a crowd is composed of three main steps: 1) identification of sidewalk physical factors in the presence of a crowd based on users' confidence, 2) quantification of these factors, and 3) accessibility assessment.

Based on the previous works [8, 18], confidence-based methods can help to measure the perception of a wheelchair user to carry out a mobility task in the presence of a specific physical factor. The first step consists on the measurement of the level of confidence of wheelchair users. This needs the identification of physical factors affecting the mobility of wheelchair users in the presence of a crowd. Hence, we need to capture the level of the confidence of the users to carry out a mobility action in the presence of a physical factor as well as a crowd with a specific level of density. Then, the accessibility level of each segment is determined by combining the capabilities of users with regard to various physical factors related to each segment of a rout and the data measured data both on physical factors and on the crowd.

Different algorithms such as linear model, AHP, MMT-MCW, and fuzzy logic were applied in different studies [13, 35, 36] for computing accessibility index. These algorithms, although helpful, have limitations for accessibility assessment due to their oversimplifications. Fuzzy-TOPSIS has been recently used by Gharebaghi et al. (2018) [3]. This algorithm takes into consideration the importance of the user's confidence for each criterion in the predefined context by calculating its distance to the best and worst confidence level for that criterion. This algorithm, although simple, is still very efficient in computing the accessibility index. The proposed approach has been illustrated in Fig. 1.

3.1 Determination of Effective Sidewalks' Physical Factors on the Mobility of Wheelchair Users in the Presence of a Crowd

The most important physical factors affecting the mobility of wheelchair users have been investigated in different studies [8, 13, 37, 38]. However, the norms and standards for the design of sidewalks are different from a country to another. The present study has been conducted in Tehran, the capital of Iran. Although most of the relevant physical factors affecting the mobility of wheelchair users are similar to other cities. However, there are some differences in the norms and standards applied for design and implementation of sidewalks which are specific to Tehran. For instance, there is a drainage separating the

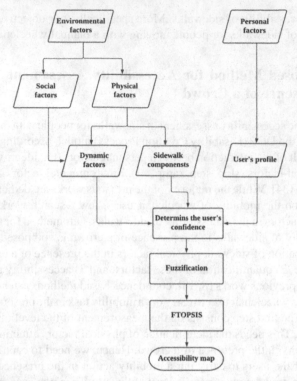

Fig. 1. Proposed approach for the assessment of the accessibility of the sidewalks in the presence of a crowd for the mobility of wheelchair users

street and sidewalks in many streets and hence there are many small bridges that links sidewalks to the street that might be used by the wheelchair users during their mobility. Hence, we had to adapt our list of physical factors affecting the mobility of wheelchair users to the specificity of sidewalks in Tehran. Hence in addition to sidewalks and curb cuts, bridges are very important in connecting sidewalks to streets (Fig. 2).

Fig. 2. An example of a bridge connecting a sidewalk and a street in Tehran

Moreover, some sidewalks have a cobblestone pavement which is common in Tehran. Hence, this type of texture also needs to be considered in the accessibility assessment.

Besides these, texture change along an itinerary is also very common and it is essential to be considered in our evaluation (Fig. 3).

(a)   (b)

Fig. 3. a) cobblestone, b) texture change

Considering the above-mentioned factors, to evaluate sidewalk accessibility, the main physical factors affecting the navigation of wheelchair users on their daily trips have been determined. In particular, different physical factors including width, length, slope, surface coverage, cracks, texture, and height changes are considered as permanent properties for four different components of an itinerary including sidewalk, curb-cut, ramps, and bridges. An instance of the set of factors affecting sidewalk accessibility has been presented in Table 1.

Iranian standards of urban planning and architecture for people with mobility impairment have been then used to retrieve the range values for each physical factor. These values were categorized into different criteria using the mentioned standard and experts.

Finally, we have considered the impact of the crowed on the accessibility assessment. To do so, sidewalk traffic was considered as a temporal factor (Table 2) and has been categorized to three classes according to Nicolas et al. (2019) [39]. Each category has been defined based on the density of population in each square meter on the sidewalk.

3.2 Fuzzifying Physical Factors

People often use a qualitative approach to characterize environmental factors that affect the mobility of people with mobility impairments. This is because precise quantitative values may not accurately depict real-life situations. To address this issue, fuzzy logic is used to convert crisp values into non-crisp values, a process called fuzzification. This is done by defining membership functions, which are mathematical functions that map a given value to a set of values between 0 and 1. In this study, the membership functions for all physical factors are described as trapezoidal fuzzy values and are classified into fuzzy set classes. The membership functions of each physical factor (Width, Slope, type, and change), for each segment component, are defined based on the values determined by the Iranian standards of urban planning and architecture for wheelchair users. The membership functions for the physical factors of each component would be different from

Table 1. An instance of the set of factors affecting sidewalk accessibility

Sidewalk	Width	Wide	> 120cm
		Medium	90–120 cm
		Narrow	70–90 cm
	Slope	Cross Slope	< 1%
			1%-3%
			> 3%
		Longitudinal Slope	< 2%
			2%-5%
			> 5%
	Type	Non-slippery	Asphalt, Brick, Gravel, Concrete, Cobblestone
		Slippery	Marble, Granit
	Texture change	Without texture change	0
		With texture change	1
	Crack	Without crack	0
		With crack	1
	Height change	Up the Height	< 2%
		Down the Height	
	Length		

Table 2. Sidewalk traffic categories.

	Low dense	Fairly dense	very dense
Population(ped/m^2)	2.5	3.5	6

the other components. For example, while the slope values for curb cut are classified into five different sets, the slope values for ramps have three sets.

A membership function has been also defined for a crowd. Population density has been classified into three sets, low, medium, and high.

This fuzzification could be represented mathematically. A fuzzy set A within the context of a universe X is characterized by a membership function, denoted as $\mu_A(x_i)$, such that the domain of X is within the range of [0,1]. The membership value of x_i within set A denoted as $\mu_A(x_i)$, is defined by Eq. 1 in accordance with the seminal work of Zadeh et al. (1965) [40]. Here, set A is represented as a trapezoidal fuzzy number, denoted as A = (a,b,c,d), and x_i serves as a criterion that belongs to the set X

$$= [x_1, x_2, \ldots x_n].$$

$$\mu_A(\text{xi}) = \begin{cases} 0, & x_i \leq a \\ \frac{x_i - a}{b - a}, & a \leq x_i \leq b \\ 1, & b \leq x_i \leq c \\ \frac{d - x_i}{d - c}, & c \leq x_i \leq d \\ 0, & d \leq x_i \end{cases} \tag{1}$$

For each physical factor of a segment, membership values are derived for each criterion and crowd density concerning the direction of movement.

3.3 Constructing Confidence-Based Fuzzy Vectors in the Presence of the Crowd

The level of accessibility of the sidewalk component as a function of the different criteria in each crowd density varies from a person to another. Therefore, the role of the user's confidence in computing the accessibility of the sidewalk in the presence of a crowd is crucial [6].

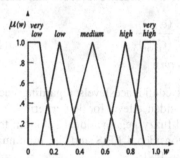

Fuzzy set	Fuzzy numbers
Very low	(0, 0, 0.1, 0.2)
Low	(0.1, 0.25, 0.25, 0.4)
Medium	(0.3, 0.5, 0.5, 0.7)
High	(0.6, 0.75, 0.75, 0.9)
Very high	(0.8, 0.9, 1, 1)

Fig. 4. Membership function, fuzzy sets, and fuzzy values of user's confidence

In this study, users are expressing their confidence using linguistic terms such as very low, low, medium, high, and very high. So, we used a membership function proposed by Malczewski(1999) [41] to demonstrate different confidence levels. The membership function, fuzzy sets, and values have been demonstrated in Fig. 4.

Using this membership function, a confidence level is assigned to each criterion according to the membership values derived in the previous section. For example, a curb cut with a slope of 3%, and crowd density of 2 ped/m^2 belongs to fuzzy set gentle with the membership value of 0.92 and fuzzy set low with the membership value of 0.87 respectively. The confidence level very high is assigned to this criterion while the user is moving in the same direction as the crowd.

3.4 Accessibility Indices

In this research, the accessibility index for each segment is computed based on the user's confidence while encountering different physical factors along a segment in the presence of a crowd. Accessibility levels are assigned to segments, which are in turn calculated by aggregating user confidence with respect to multiple factors of each segment in each crowd. In this study, the accessibility index is computed using the Fuzzy TOPSIS method. Fuzzy-TOPSIS is an extension of the TOPSIS approach within a fuzzy logic environment [42]. This method is based on the distance of each segment from the fuzzy positive ideal condition (FPIC) and the fuzzy negative ideal condition (FNIC).

3.4.1 Fuzzy-TOPSIS

Fuzzy-TOPSIS which is developed by Chen (2000), is a Technique for Order Preference by Similarity to Ideal Situation. This method is based on the nearest distance to the FPIS (Fuzzy Positive Ideal solution) and the farthest distance to FNIS (Fuzzy negative ideal solution) [42]. The relevant steps of Fuzzy-TOPSIS in each crowd density are presented below:

1. Creating normalized fuzzy vectors(r_i): this stage aims to adjust the user's confidence values for physical factors to a consistent scale, allowing for calculations and comparisons to be performed. The normalized value is identified by the user's confidence level for each factor concerning the user's maximum confidence level for that factor.

$$r_i = \frac{(a_{con})_i}{(c^*_{coni})}, \frac{(b_{con})_i}{(c^*_{coni})}, \frac{(c_{con})_i}{(c^*_{coni})}$$

$$(c\_con)i* = \max(c\_con)i \tag{2}$$

where (a_con, b_con, c_con) are the user's confidence levels regarding each criterion and ($c\_con^*_i$) is the user's maximum confidence level for that criterion.

2. Computing the fuzzy positive ideal solution and fuzzy negative ideal solution: the maximum confidence level for each factor is considered FPIS and the minimum confidence level for the same factor is identified as FNIS.

$$FPIS = [r^*_1, r^*_2, \ldots r^*_8] \text{ where } r^*_i = \max\{r_{i5}\}$$
$$FNIS = [r^*_1, r^*_2, \ldots r^*_8] \text{ where } r^*_i = \min\{r_{i1}\} \tag{3}$$

3. Computing the distance from each normalized value to the FPIS and FNIS: the distance of each confidence value for each factor is calculated to both FPIS and FNIS.

$$d^*_i = \sqrt{\frac{1}{5}\sum_{i=1}^{8}(r_i-r^*_i)^2} \quad d^-_i = \sqrt{\frac{1}{5}\sum_{i=1}^{8}(r_i-r^-_i)^2} \tag{4}$$

4. Calculating the closeness coefficient: closeness coefficient is calculated for each physical factor as follows:

$$CC_i = \frac{d^-_i}{d^-_i + d^*_i} \tag{5}$$

5. Ranking of the closeness coefficient: considering the user's confidence in these calculations, the segment with the higher closeness coefficient is supposed to be more
   accessible.

This coefficient is considered as the primary accessibility index and is classified into
four classes that represent the cost value in the specified context for each segment.

3.5 Similarity Index

The effects of crowd density on a user's confidence of different physical factors of
a sidewalk are of great importance. Moreover, the direction of crowd movement can
change the user's confidence. The Similarity Index (SI) can help to analyze these effects
more precisely.

For each movement direction (same and opposite direction with the crowd), the
similarity index is a measure of the similarity of a user's confidence in different crowd
densities. It is defined as the ratio of the number of confidence levels that are equal in
different crowd densities to the total [43].

The value of SI ranges between 0 and 1, where 0 indicates that there are no similarities
between the user's confidences and 1 indicates that the user's confidence values are
identical in different population densities.

4 The Experiment

We propose a framework for assessing the accessibility of sidewalks based on the participants' perceptions of physical factors on their trajectories (Fig. 1). The proposed framework seeks to understand how people with mobility impairments, specifically wheelchair
users, perceive and interact with various environmental barriers in different crowd densities. To accomplish this, an experiment was conducted with the participation of three
middle-aged (35–55 years old) wheelchair users in three districts of Tehran. For each
participant, three routes were selected - two familiar routes (one easy and one difficult)
and one chosen by a specialist that had specific characteristics such as being a major
street with various land cover and having main transportation. The study was carried out
according to a specific protocol, and participants' confidence levels of different factors
in each crowd density were recorded. Due to the Covid-19 pandemic, it was not possible
for participants to physically navigate through their designated routes. To overcome this
issue, videos were recorded for each route, with a focus on the physical factors of the
sidewalks. Participants were asked to watch the videos and provide their confidence
levels for each factor in every segment of the route, with options for expressing their
confidence as very low, low, medium, high, and very high, during a semi-structured
interview. A questionnaire was also used to gather additional information on some physical factors of the sidewalks which are not included in the three predefined routes. Each
route was then segmented based on its properties and observed physical barriers, and
the attributes were stored in a database. The confidence level of the user for each physical factor in different crowd densities was imported and analyzed for each participant
using the Fuzzy-TOPSIS algorithm. The accessibility index (AI) was calculated, and
results were presented in the form of an accessibility map, with segments classified as

very accessible, accessible, low accessible, and not accessible for each user and in each context domain. The results were analyzed using AIs and similarity indices for different population densities and in both directions.

5 Results and Discussion

Here, we present the impact of population density on four components of a pedestrian route (sidewalks, bridges, curb-cuts, and ramps) for one of our participants. The accessibility index and similarity index have been calculated to analyze the results in more detail.

According to the results, different population densities could affect the mobility of a wheelchair user in dissimilar ways. The user's confidence varies in moving through a crowd while passing through a sidewalk, curb cut, bridge, and ramp. The effects of three population densities (high, medium, and low populations) in two different directions (same and opposite directions) on these components have been analyzed precisely. Figure 5 illustrates the user's confidence level in passing through the four components in three population densities in the same and opposite directions as a crowd.

Our findings show that (Fig. 5a), the user's confidence in passing through most sidewalk factors decreases when there is a high population density moving in the same direction as the participant except for some factors. His confidence increases when he is passing a sidewalk with a longitudinal slope of less than 5% or a sidewalk covered by slippery textures like marble and granite in high population density. This is due to the fact that the presence of the crowd helps him to feel safe, and this could facilitate his mobility.

It can be seen from the results that when the user is moving against the flow of the crowd along a sidewalk, his confidence decreases in areas with high crowd density. However, certain factors such as cracks, non-slippery surfaces, and cross slopes greater than 3% do not appear to be affected by crowd density, as shown by the similarity index is equal to 1 for these factors. Regardless of the population density, the user's confidence is moderate when passing through areas with cracks or non-slippery surfaces, but low when passing through slippery sidewalks. These findings are important for urban designers and managers to consider when assessing sidewalk accessibility.

When going through a curb cut (Fig. 5b), the participant's confidence level remains relatively similar regardless of whether they are moving in the same or opposite direction as the crowd. However, there are slight variations in confidence. For example, the participant feels more confident when going through a curb cut with a texture that differs from the sidewalk when moving in the same direction as the crowd. Additionally, their confidence level is higher when going down a curb cut while moving in the opposite direction of the crowd. However, the presence of a crowd does not seem to have a significant impact on the participant's mobility when going up a curb cut with a slope greater than 8% in either direction.

In passing through a bridge (Fig. 5c), the results demonstrate that the participant is more confident while he is moving in the same direction as crowed. However, the effects of crowd density on most factors are not significant except for moderate width in both directions and cracks and slippery surfaces in the same direction (Fig. 6). It is

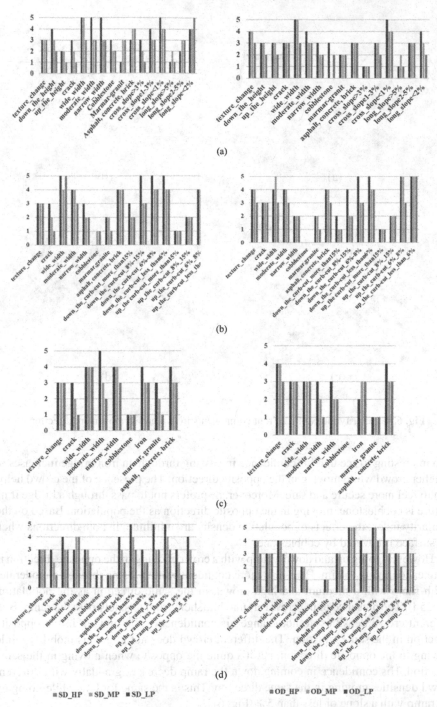

Fig. 5. User's confidence levels while navigating through a crowd a) sidewalk, b) curb cut, c) bridge, d) ramp, in the same direction (SD) and opposite direction (OD) as the population.

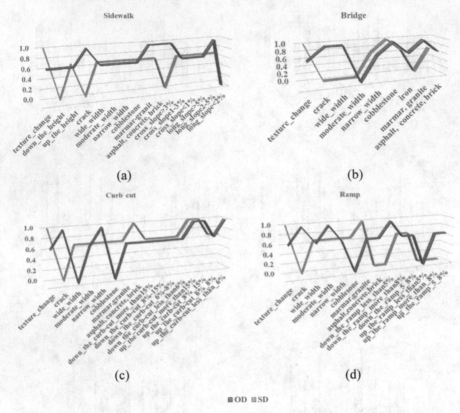

Fig. 6. Similarity index of four rout components in two crowd movement directions

also interesting to see that his confidence in passing through an iron bridge increases in a higher crowd while moving in the opposite direction. The presence of the crowd helps him to feel more secure and safe. Moreover, he prefers not to pass through a bridge if its texture is cobblestone, moving in the opposite direction as the population. Based on the similarity index, the effects of population density are minimum in both directions when the surface is covered by cobblestone.

However, going up and down a ramp with a crowd moving in the opposite direction is more encouraging to him. He is also more confident while passing through a moderate-width ramp with a medium and high crowd, in the same direction as the population (Fig. 5d). The presence of the crowd around him, helps him to safely pass the ramp. But, different crowd densities do not change his confidence while moving in the opposite direction in the same situation. The different crowd does not affect his mobility while moving in the opposite direction, but it's quite the opposite when moving in the same direction. His confidence in coming down the ramp decreases gradually with different crowd densities moving in the same direction. This is the same for him while going up the ramp with a slope of less than 5% (Fig. 6).

However, investigating the similarity index indicates that different population densities do not change his confidence when there is a texture change in any of the four components of a segment in the same direction as the population, but it can change his confidence in the opposite direction. Moreover, the calculation of the accessibility index for each segment has been carried out based on the user's confidence for each criterion of the available physical factors and three crowd densities in the study area. These values have been computed using the Fuzzy-TOPSIS algorithm. This index is used for accessibility assessment of each segment according to different user profiles within the routes with a different crowd.

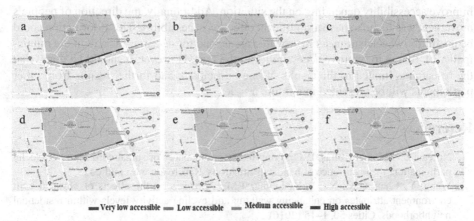

━ Very low accessible ━ Low accessible ━ Medium accessible ━ High accessible

Fig. 7. Accessibility maps (a: low crowded, b: medium crowded, c: highly crowded, in the same direction; d: low crowded, e: medium crowded, f: highly crowded, in the opposite direction)

Figure 7 illustrates the accessibility of a sidewalk located on Keshavarz Boulevard. In this Figure "Very low Accessible" segments are shown in red, "Low Accessible" segments are represented in orange, " Medium Accessible" segments are shown in yellow, and "High Accessible" are in Green. According to the map, this sidewalk is more accessible in the western parts and less accessible in the eastern part. Lower accessibility in this part is due to a narrow sidewalk and the presence of cracks and texture changes which is as a result of some constructions in that region. Moreover, as it is obvious the accessibility of sidewalks varies depending on both the density of the population and the direction of crowd movement. The results show that most segments are moderate to highly accessible when the crowd is moving in the same direction and there is a low to medium population density. However, when the crowd is moving in the opposite direction, most segments are only moderately accessible. Additionally, highly crowded situations tend to have a higher level of accessibility when the crowd is moving in the same direction, compared to when the crowd is moving in the opposite direction. These variations in accessibility when encountering physical factors on sidewalks are crucial and should be considered by those involved in urban design and management.

6 Conclusion

In this paper, a new approach was developed for the accessibility assessment of sidewalks based on wheelchair users' perceptions in the presence of a crowd. The study assessed users' perceptions of their surroundings in the presence of a crowd with different levels of densities based on their mobility experiences. The obtained results from the first participant showed that the crowd has a significant impact on the accessibility of different segments of sidewalks and that the presence of crowds can both hinder and improve accessibility depending on the situation. Additionally, the direction of people's movement was found to have a significant effect on accessibility. This information could be useful for wheelchair users in crowded areas, and for decision-makers in the municipality of Tehran to improve accessibility in the area. However, it should be noted that the research is limited to the results of one participant, and further results from other participants will be presented in a future article.

References

1. Noreau, L.O., Fougeyrollas, P. O.: Long-term consequences of spinal cord injury on social participation: the occurrence of handicap situations. Repéré à www.tandf.co
2. Wang, Y., Chau, C.K., Ng, W.Y., Leung, T.M.: A review on the effects of physical built environment attributes on enhancing walking and cycling activity levels within residential neighborhoods. Cities **50**, 1–15 (2016)
3. Gharebaghi, A., Mostafavi, M.-A., Chavoshi, S., Edwards, G., Fougeyrollas, P.: The role of social factors in the accessibility of urban areas for people with motor disabilities. ISPRS Int. J. Geo-Inf. **7**(4), 131 (2018). https://doi.org/10.3390/ijgi7040131
4. Orellana, D., Bustos, M.E., MarínPalacios, M., Cabrerarara, N., Hermida, M.A.: Walk 'n' roll: mapping street-level accessibility for different mobility conditions in Cuenca Ecuador. J. Transp. Health **16**, 100821 (2020). https://doi.org/10.1016/j.jth.2020.100821
5. Wheeler, B., Syzdykbayev, M., Karimi, H.A., Gurewitsch, R., Wang, Y.: Personalized accessible wayfinding for people with disabilities through standards and open geospatial platforms in smart cities. Open Geosp. Data Softw. Stand. **5**(1), 1–15 (2020). https://doi.org/10.1186/s40965-020-00075-5
6. (Revue Développement Humain, Handicap et Changement Social Journal of Human Development, Disability, and Social Change ACTES DU COLLOQUE-Pour Une Ville Inclusive : Innovations et Partenariats. Proceedings of the Colloquium-For an Inclusive City: Innovations and Partnership, n.d.)
7. Gharebaghi, A., et al.: Integration of the social environment in a mobility ontology for people with motor disabilities. Disabil. Rehabil. Assist. Technol. **13**(6), 540–551 (2018). https://doi.org/10.1080/17483107.2017.1344887
8. Gharebaghi, A., et al.: A confidence-based approach for the assessment of accessibility of pedestrian network for manual wheelchair users. In: Peterson, M.P. (ed.) Advances in Cartography and GIScience. LNGC, pp. 463–477. Springer, Cham (2017a). https://doi.org/10.1007/978-3-319-57336-6_32
9. Hara, K., Chan, C., Froehlich, J.E.: The design of assistive location-based technologies for people with ambulatory disabilities: a formative study. In: Conference on Human Factors in Computing Systems - Proceedings, pp. 1757–1768 (2016)
10. Prémont, M.É., Vincent, C., Mostafavi, M.A.: Geospatial assistive technologies: potential usability criteria identified from manual wheelchair users. Disabil. Rehabil. Assist. Technol. **15**(8), 844–855 (2020)

11. Bolten, N., Mukherjee, S., Sipeeva, V., Tanweer, A., Caspi, A.: A pedestrian-centered data approach for equitable access to urban infrastructure environments. IBM J. Res. Dev. **61**(6), 101–1012 (2017)
12. Naude, A., de Jong, T., van Teefelen, P.: Measuring accessibility with GIS-tools: a case study of the wild coast of South Africa. Trans. GIS **3**(4), 381–395 (1999)
13. Kasemsuppakorn, P., Karimi, H.A.: Personalised routing for wheelchair navigation. J. Loc. Based Serv. **3**(1), 24–54 (2009). https://doi.org/10.1080/17489720902837936
14. PérezDelhoyo, R., GarcíaMayor, C., Mora, H., GilartIglesias, V., AndújarMontoya, M.D.: Improving urban accessibility: a methodology for urban dynamics analysis in smart, sustainable and inclusive cities. Int. J. Sustain. Dev. Plan. **12**(3), 357–367 (2017). https://doi.org/10.2495/SDP-V12-N3-357-367
15. Tajgardoon, M., Karimi, H.A.: Simulating and visualizing sidewalk accessibility for wayfinding of people with disabilities. Int. J. Cartogr. **1**(1), 79–93 (2015)
16. Menkens, C., et al.: EasyWheel-A Mobile Social Navigation and Support System for Wheelchair Users
17. Mostafavi, M.A., et al.: Urban Accessibility in Action: Development of a Geospatial assistive technology for navigation of people with motor disabilities. Géocongrès, October 2014
18. Gharebaghi, A., et al.: A confidence-based approach for the assessment of accessibility of pedestrian network for manual wheelchair users. In: Peterson, M.P. (ed.) Advances in Cartography and GIScience. LNGC, pp. 463–477. Springer, Cham (2017b). https://doi.org/10.1007/978-3-319-57336-6_32
19. Mackett, R.L., Achuthan, K., Titheridge, H.: AMELIA: making streets more accessible for people with mobility difficulties. URBAN Des. Int. **13**, 80–89 (2008)
20. Sobek, A.D., Miller, H.J.: U-Access: a web-based system for routing pedestrians of differing abilities. J. Geogr. Syst. **8**(3), 269–287 (2006)
21. Volker, T., Weber, G.:RouteChecker: Personalized multicriteria routing for mobility impaired pedestrians. In The 10th international A CM SIGACCESS conference on computers and accessibility, pp. 185–192. ACM, Halifax, NS (2008)
22. Matthews, H., Beale, L., Picton, P., Briggs, D.: Modelling access with GIS in urban systems MAGUS): capturing the experiences of wheelchair users. Area **35**(1), 34–45 (2003)
23. Mobasheri, A., Deister, J., Dieterich, H.: Wheelmap: the wheelchair accessibility crowdsourcing platform. Open Geosp. Data Softw. Stand. **2**(1), 1–7 (2017). https://doi.org/10.1186/s40965-017-0040-5
24. Wang, R.H., Korotchenko, A., Clarke, L.H., Mortenson, W.B., Mihailidis, A.: Power mobility with collision avoidance for older adults: user, caregiver and prescriber perspectives. J. Rehabil. Res. Dev. **50**(9), 1287 (2013)
25. Stuart, D.S., Sharifi, M.S., Christensen, K.M., Chen, A., Kim, Y.S., Chen, Y.: Crowds involving individuals with disabilities: modeling heterogeneity using fractional order potential fields and the social force model. Physica A **514**, 244–258 (2019)
26. Shields, T.J., Boyce, K.E., Silcock, G.W.H., Dunne, B.: The Impact of a Wheelchair Bound Evacuee on the Speed and Flow of Evacuees in a Stairway During an Uncontrolled Unannounced Evacuation. In: DeCicco, P., DeCicco, P.R. (eds.) Evacuation from Fires, pp. 139–150. Routledge (2019). https://doi.org/10.4324/9781315228006-9
27. Geoerg, P., Schumann, J., Holl, S., Boltes, M., Hofmann, A.: The influence of individual impairments on crowd dynamics. In: 15th International Conference and Exhibition on Fire Science and Engineering (No. FZJ-2019–05680). Zivile Sicherheitsforschung (2019)
28. Gupta, M., et al.: Towards more universal wayfinding technologies: navigation preferences across disabilities. In Proceedings of the 2020 CHI Conference on Human Factors in Computing Systems, pp. 1–13, April 2020
29. Pan, H., Zhang, J., Song, W.: Experimental study of pedestrian flow mixed with wheelchair users through funnel-shaped bottlenecks. J. Stat. Mech. Theory Exp. **2020**(3), 033401 (2020)

30. Asha, A.Z., et al.: Co-designing interactions between pedestrians in wheelchairs and autonomous vehicles. In: Designing Interactive Systems Conference 2021, pp. 339–351, June 2021

31. Bennett, C., Ackerman, E., Fan, B., Bigham, J., Carrington, P., Fox, S.: Accessibility and the crowded sidewalk: micromobility's impact on public space. In: Designing Interactive Systems Conference 2021, pp. 365–380, June 2021

32. Hata, J., Yu, H., Raychoudhury, V., Saha, S., Quang, H.T.: Study of heterogeneous user behavior in crowd evacuation in presence of wheelchair users. In: Dignum, F., Mathieu, P., Corchado, J.M., De La Prieta, F. (eds.) Advances in Practical Applications of Agents, Multi-Agent Systems, and Complex Systems Simulation. The PAAMS Collection: 20th International Conference, PAAMS 2022, L'Aquila, Italy, July 13–15, 2022, Proceedings, pp. 229–241. Springer International Publishing, Cham (2022). https://doi.org/10.1007/978-3-031-18192-4_19

33. Zhang, B., Barbareschi, G., Ramirez Herrera, R., Carlson, T., Holloway, C.: Understanding interactions for smart wheelchair navigation in crowds. In: Proceedings of the 2022 CHI Conference on Human Factors in Computing Systems, pp. 1–16, April 2022

34. Fougeyrollas, P.: L'évolution conceptuelle internationale dans le champ du handicap : enjeux socio-politiques et contributions québécoises. Perspectives Interdisciplinaires Sur Le Travail et La Santé, 4–2 (2002).https://doi.org/10.4000/pistes.3663

35. Socharoentum, M., Karimi, H.A.: Multi-modal transportation with multi-criteria walking (MMT-MCW): Personalized route recommender. Comput. Environ. Urban Syst. **55**, 44–54 (2016). https://doi.org/10.1016/j.compenvurbsys.2015.10.005

36. Karimi, H.A., Zhang, L., Benner, J.G.: Personalized accessibility map (PAM): a novel assisted wayfinding approach for people with disabilities. Ann. GIS **20**(2), 99–108 (2014). https://doi.org/10.1080/19475683.2014.904438

37. Rushton, P.W., Miller, W.C., Lee Kirby, R., Eng, J.J., Yip, J.: Development and content validation of the Wheelchair Use Confidence Scale: a mixed-methods study. Disabil. Rehabil. Assist. Technol. **6**(1), 57–66 (2011)

38. Neis, P.: Measuring the reliability of wheelchair user route planning based on volunteered geographic information. Trans. GIS **19**(2), 188–201 (2015)

39. Nicolas, A., Kuperman, M., Ibañez, S., Bouzat, S., AppertRolland, C.: Mechanical response of dense pedestrian crowds to the crossing of intruders. Sci. Rep. **9**(1), 105 (2019)

40. Zadeh, L.A., Introduction, I., Navy, U.S.: Fuzzy Sets **353**, 338–353 (1965)

41. Malczewski, J.: GIS and Multicriteria Decision Analysis. John Wiley & Sons (1999)

42. Chen, C.T.: Extensions of the TOPSIS for group decision-making under fuzzy environment. Fuzzy Sets Syst. **114**(1), 1–9 (2000)

43. Li, D., Li: A survey of image retrieval with high-level semantics. Pattern Recogn. **42**(9), 1857–1881 (2009)

AI for Mobility Data Analytics

Mobility Data Analytics with KNOT: The KNime mObility Toolkit

Sergio Di Martino⬥, Nicola Mazzocca⬥, Franca Rocco Di Torrepadula⬥, and Luigi Libero Lucio Starace(✉)⬥

Università degli Studi di Napoli Federico II, Dipartimento di Ingegneria Elettrica e Tecnologie dell'Informazione (DIETI), Via Claudio 21, Naples 80125, Italy
{sergio.dimartino,nicola.mazzocca,franca.roccoditorrepadula,
luigiliberolucio.starace}@unina.it

Abstract. Developments in Web and Wireless technologies have enabled the diffusion of large volumes of geospatial mobility data, and new challenges and opportunities have emerged for the GIScience research community, interested in extracting knowledge from these data.

In most data analytics scenarios, well-known analytics platforms, such as KNIME or RapidMiner, offer practical general-purpose tools to data analysts. However, when dealing with mobility data, these platforms provide only limited support to some peculiar geospatial data manipulation tasks, thus forcing researchers and practitioners to manually implement significant portions of their pipelines, hindering productivity and replicability of the results.

This paper presents a solution we are currently working on to support mobility data analysis. Our prototype, which we called KNOT (KNime mObility Toolkit), extends the KNIME Analytics Platform with a collection of new components specifically designed to support processing steps typical of mobility data, including map-matching, trajectory partitioning, and road network coverage analysis. To show the effectiveness of these components, we report also on how we applied them to perform a realistic analytical task on a real-world massive mobility dataset.

Keywords: Mobility Data Analytics · Knowledge Discovery · Intelligent Trasportation Systems

1 Introduction and Context

In recent years, the continuous technological improvements in connected vehicles and in the number of on-board sensors integrated in most modern cars have made available huge amounts of mobility data, typically in the form of (eXtended) Floating Car Data (XFCD) [18]. This has enabled a massive amount of research in the Intelligent Transportation Systems (ITS) community, aimed towards the extraction of new knowledge on (spatio-temporal) phenomena of interest from these XFCD, allowing for the implementation of a number of novel services and solutions [10,15]. Many new exciting use cases have been proposed, leveraging

M. A. Mostafavi and G. Del Mondo (Eds.): W2GIS 2023, LNCS 13912, pp. 95–104, 2023.
https://doi.org/10.1007/978-3-031-34612-5_6

knowledge extracted from these XFCD, like for example more accurate traffic predictions, real-time on-street parking availability [2,16,22], air quality monitoring [6], better surveillance of urban scenarios [12], and so on.

Broadly speaking, extracting new knowledge from massive datasets is an issue widely addressed by a number of methodologies and technologies falling within the Data Science domain [21] and in the Knowledge Discovery from Data (KDD) process [9]. KDD includes a broader set of different activities, involving data storage and retrieval, preprocessing, transformation, etc., to handle massive datasets and interpreter results. Many very effective general-purpose data analytics platforms, such as KNIME[1], RapidMiner[2], IBM Watson Studio[3], etc., have been developed to support data analyst implementing KDD pipelines. Some of these platform are based on a visual programming paradigm, where a KDD pipeline is composed by connecting data manipulation/visualization components. Thus, with these tools, it is possible to visually assemble and execute KDD pipelines without the need of writing a single line of code.

Nevertheless, instantiating a KDD process on XFCD datasets presents some peculiar challenges. Due to the nature and quality of the spatio-temporal information, some very domain specific preprocessing steps are required, such as *map matching*, i.e., aligning raw positions collected from inherently inaccurate Global Navigation Satellite Systems to the underlying road network, handling macroscopic positioning errors, reconstructing coherent vehicular trajectories, even in presence of low XFCD sampling rates, and so on.

In our industrial and academic experience, these tasks are practically not supported by the above mentioned general-purpose analytics platforms. Consequently, scientists and practitioners working with XFCD are forced to either use extremely specialized and expensive commercial solutions, or to deal with the time-consuming task of manually implementing the code required for these preprocessing steps. In both the cases, this results in highly specialized and/or hard-to-reproduce preprocessing scripts, significantly hindering the replicability of research results. The situation is further complicated when an analytic procedure is based on multiple mobility datasets, featuring possibly different characteristics, which is a pretty common scenario (e.g.: [2]).

In this paper, we present a solution we are currently working on to support ITS scientists and practitioners in creating KDD pipelines, by enriching the well-known KNIME Analytics Platform with advanced preprocessing, transformation and analysis capabilities specifically meant for XFCD. In particular, we implemented a set of components providing standard ITS-related tasks, such as map-matching, trajectory partitioning and manipulation, as well as segment coverage analysis, etc. The components we developed can be seamlessly integrated with the default KNIME ones, to visually compose KDD pipelines based on XFCD.

---

[1] https://www.knime.com/.

[2] https://rapidminer.com/.

[3] https://www.ibm.com/cloud/watson-studio.

To show how the proposed components can be easily assembled into an effective KDD pipeline, we describe a usage example based on real-world analytical task on a massive FCD dataset. Finally, we made all the developed software freely available on a dedicated GitHub repository[4]. In our opinion, the free availability of these components for the ITS community could significantly simplify the implementation of KDD pipelines to conduct data analytics investigations.

The remainder of the paper is structured as follows: in Sect. 2, we first present in detail the KNIME platform, and then describe each of the new components we developed. In Sect. 3, we show how the proposed components can be easily assembled into an effective KDD pipeline, by describing a usage example based on real-world analytical task on a massive FCD dataset. Some final remarks and future research directions conclude the paper.

2   KNOT: The KNime mObility Toolkit

In this section, we first briefly describe the KNIME Analytics Platform, and then we present the key features of KNOT, the solution we propose.

2.1   Overview of the KNIME Analytics Platform

KNIME is an open-source solution based on a graphical workbench, enabling visual assembly and interactive execution of KDD pipelines. An example of its graphical user interface is shown in Fig. 1. As we can notice from the figure, the core element of the KNIME interface is the *workflow frame*, which is used to visually compose the intended KDD pipeline. The tasks composing these pipelines are represented by *nodes*, which can be selected from a palette frame on the bottom-left of Fig. 1. Each node is displayed in the workbench as a colored box whose external interfaces are *input* and *output ports*. The platform offers nodes to perform many standard KDD tasks, such as reading/writing files, transforming data, training and evaluating models based on many different machine learning techniques, creating interactive visualization reports, and so on. A knowledge discovery pipeline can thus be assembled by connecting the output port of a node with the input port of other nodes representing subsequent tasks (or steps) of the pipeline. In addition to the large number of nodes provided out-of-the-box, KNIME is designed to be easily extended, as it enables the integration of new, custom nodes, that can be used to offer new and/or specialized algorithms and tools.

2.2   The KNOT Components

Trajectory Partitioner. Many mobility datasets (e.g.: [3,17]) consist of a single stream of Floating Car Data (FCD), collected from a number of distinct vehicles over time. Each data entry in such datasets typically contains a reference

---

[4] https://github.com/luistar/knot.

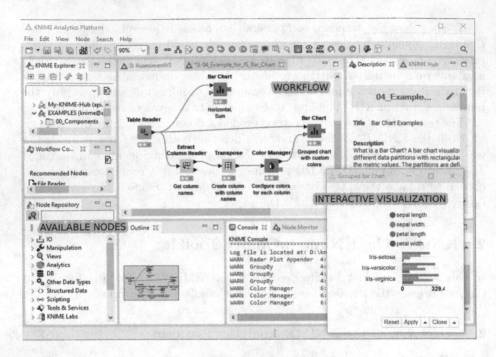

Fig. 1. The KNIME workbench

to the source vehicle, a timestamp, a GPS position, and additional data (e.g.: speed, occupancy status, external temperature, etc.). The Trajectory Partitioner node takes care of the task of splitting (or grouping) such massive datasets of FCD into a set of independent vehicular trajectories (intended as sequences of FCD), according to heuristics that can be customized by users using the node's GUI. The node produces as output a set of trajectories encoded as WKT linestrings, in which each vertex is the GPS position of a FCD.

Map Matcher. This node performs the map matching of raw vehicular trajectories (such as the ones produced in output by the Trajectory Partitioner node) to a logical Open Street Map (OSM) representation of the underlying road network. More in detail, the node takes as inputs a sequence of raw mobility trajectories encoded as WKT linestrings, and produces in output, for each input trajectory, a sequence of traversed OSM road segments. In our implementation, the map matching is performed leveraging the well-known Open Source Routing Machine (OSRM) [14], largely used in a number of scientific studies (e.g.: [11,19]). Moreover, the node is designed to be easily extended, and an interested user could easily implement additional map-matching strategies.

Route Calculator. In a number of analytical scenarios, raw trajectories collected from vehicles might need to be processed in different ways before carrying out the intended analyses. For example, in presence of significant GPS errors or particularly low sampling rates, trajectory restoration approaches [13] might need to be put in place to reconstruct the original trajectory. The Route Calculator node is intended to support these scenarios. The node takes as input a set of raw trajectories, and processes each of them according to a customizable strategy, producing a new set of trajectories in output. In the current implementation, the node offers a single processing strategy, namely "shortest-path", which replaces each trajectory with the shortest possible trajectory between the original source and destination points. Nonetheless, the node has been designed to be easily extended, and interested users can provide additional strategies.

Segment Coverage Analyzer. In many analytical scenarios, such as in the Vehicular Crowd-Sensing (VCS) domain (e.g. [1,7,8,23]), computing the frequency with which each segment of a road network is visited by a set of considered vehicles is a common task. The Segment Coverage Analyzer aims at supporting this kind of analysis. The node takes as input a set of map-matched trajectories, such as the one produced in output by the Map Matcher node, and computes, for each road segment in the considered road network, two key coverage metrics: (1) the number of times that segment was visited by one of the vehicles, and (2) the average timegap between subsequent visits.

Grid Coverage Analyzer. Similarly to the Segment Coverage Analyzer, the Grid Coverage analyzer takes as input a set of map-matched trajectories and computes spatio-temporal coverage metrics, but does so at a coarser-grained scale of entire city areas rather than single road segments. Indeed, this node allows users to define a custom grid over an area and then computes coverage metrics (number of visits and average timegaps between visits) for each cell of such grid.

Bounding-Box Filter. When working with mobility data, researchers and practitioners often need to restrict their analyses to a particular subset of data based on spatial constraints. The *Bounding-Box Filter* utility node allows users to filter data based on whether a given spatial feature, encoded in WKT format, belongs to a customizable bounding box, and can be used to directly refine the output of any of the KNOT nodes.

3   Using KNOT

In this section, we give an usage example of our solution by performing a KDD process on a massive real-world dataset of FCD. More in detail, we simulate a data analytics scenario where the Decision Maker of a Smart City has to decide whether a fleet of high-mileage vehicles (e.g., taxis) can provide enough spatio-temporal coverage of the road network to enable potential use cases leveraging crowd-sensed data (e.g.: air quality monitoring, pothole monitoring, etc.). This is a pretty common scenario, investigated in a number of works [4,5,20]. The analysis is based on a massive, publicly available dataset of real-world taxi trajectories recorded in the city of Rome [3]. In detail, this dataset contains mobility traces of 315 taxis collected over 30 days, corresponding to about 22 millions FCD points. For the KDD task at hand, we defined the KNIME workflow depicted in Fig. 2.

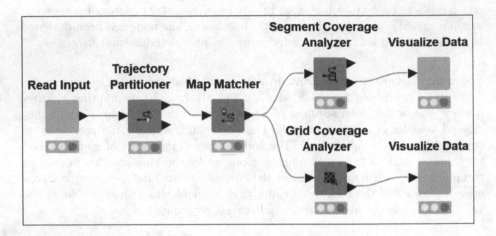

Fig. 2. A KNIME Workflow for spatio-temporal coverage analysis.

In our workflow, we first use standard KNIME components to read the CSV file containing the dataset, and then we leverage the Trajectory Partitioner node to split the original stream of FCD into subsets, each corresponding to a distinct vehicular trajectory. In particular, we configured our route splitting heuristic using a threshold of 3 min between subsequent FCD to determine the beginning of a new trajectory, and obtained 67,482 trajectories. After partitioning the original FCD stream into trajectories, we used the Map Matcher node to match those trajectories to OSM road segments. After this phase, each trajectory was matched, on average, to approximately 387 OSM road segments. With the Map Matching in place, we used the Segment Coverage Analyzer to compute spatio-temporal coverage metrics at road segment level.

Thanks to the Segment Coverage Analyzer, a Decision Maker can compute, at a fine-grained level of road segment, the spatio-temporal road-network coverage obtained by the considered trajectories. Moreover, since the node encodes road segments as WKT linestrings, its output can be easily visualized, as we did, on an interactive map using the existing KNIME node "*View Geometries as Map*". An example of such visualization is shown in Fig. 3, in which each visited segment is highlighted on the map and colored based on the number of times it was traversed by a taxi during the 30-days considered timespan, with blue segments being visited less frequently and red segments being the most traversed.

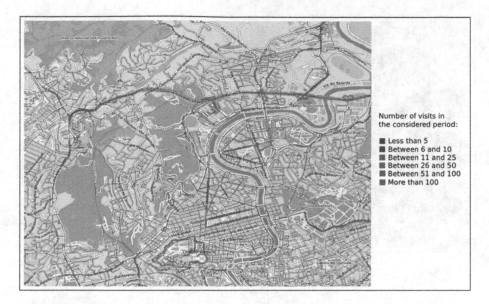

Fig. 3. Segments visited by the taxis, detail of the norther part of the Municipality of Rome.

Subsequently, we performed a coarser-grained spatio-temporal coverage analysis using the "Grid Coverage Analyzer" node. In this analysis, we configured the node to consider an area of about $600 \, km^2$ over the City of Rome, and to split it in a 10 by 10 grid of blocks, each with a surface of approximately $6 \, km^2$. Moreover, since this is a coarse-grained analysis at city block level, we configured the node to count a new sensing of an area only after at least 10 min had passed from the last sensing. As with the road segment-level coverage analysis, also in this case we visualized the coverage information on an interactive map using existing KNIME nodes. The result of this visualization, in which each block is colored based on the number of visits during the 30-days timespan, is shown in Fig. 4.

To highlight the potential productivity boost that analytical platforms, equipped with proper components, can provide to practitioners, let us note that the above described processing pipeline can be implemented with just a few clicks on the KNIME interface, without the need to write a single line of code. To put this in perspective, one of the authors of the current paper dealt with a similar scenario in the study presented in [2], which was aimed at investigating the suitability of a fleet of taxis to monitor on-street parking space availability in San Francisco. In that work, the implementation from scratch of the KDD pipeline to compute the spatio-temporal coverage obtained by the taxis took months of (error-prone) work of two research fellows.

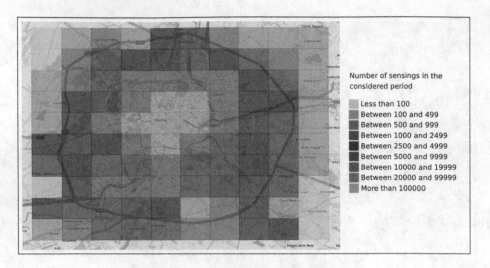

Fig. 4. Grid Coverage achieved by the taxis.

The workflow we developed, as well as data and supplementary materials to replicate our usage example are available at the public doi: https://doi.org/10. 5281/zenodo.7554341.

4   Conclusions

With the continuous technological improvements in connected vehicles, huge amounts of (eXtended) Floating Car Data are being made available, enabling a number of data-driven research in the ITS community. Nevertheless, the implementation of a typical KDD process on these mobility datasets, requires ITS practitioners either to use commercial solutions, or to create highly specialized and hard-to-reproduce scripts. This because current analytical platforms, such as KNIME or RapidMiner lacks of primitives to orchestrate individual software fragments and cover the peculiar steps of a mobility dataset analysis, including trajectory reconstruction and map matching.

To address these issues and support ITS scientists and practitioners in more effectively performing KDD tasks, we developed an extension of the KNIME Analytics Platform to support advanced preprocessing, transformation and analysis of for (eXtended) Floating Car Data. In particular, we implemented a set of components providing standard ITS-related tasks, such as map-matching, trajectory partitioning and manipulation, as well as Segment coverage analysis, etc. We showed also the effectiveness of our solution by performing a spatio-temporal coverage analysis on a real-world massive FCD dataset, which required just a few clicks.

It is worth pointing out that we made our solution and its source code publicly available on a dedicated repository[5]. We hope this can help the ITS community in conducting data-driven experiments more effectively, as well as to improve the replicability of the experiments across different institutions.

In future works, we plan to further extend our solution to support the inference of vehicular trajectories from additional data sources, such as General Transit Feed Specification (GTFS) files, and to introduce built-in spatial filtering nodes allowing users to easily restrict their analyses to a particular area. Moreover, we are studying the feasibility of integrating Micro- and Macro-simulators, such as SUMO, within the KDD pipeline, also to investigate what-if scenarios.

References

1. Asprone, D., Di Martino, S., Festa, P., Starace, L.L.L.: Vehicular crowd-sensing: a parametric routing algorithm to increase spatio-temporal road network coverage. Int. J. Geogr. Inf. Sci. (2021). https://doi.org/10.1080/13658816.2021.1893737
2. Bock, F., Di Martino, S., Origlia, A.: Smart parking: using a crowd of taxis to sense on-street parking space availability. IEEE Trans. Intell. Transp. Syst. **21**(02), 496–508 (2020). https://doi.org/10.1109/TITS.2019.2899149
3. Bracciale, L., Bonola, M., Loreti, P., Bianchi, G., Amici, R., Rabuffi, A.: CRAW-DAD dataset roma/taxi (v. 2014-07-17), July 2014. https://doi.org/10.15783/C7QC7M, https://crawdad.org/roma/taxi/20140717
4. Chuah, S.P., Wu, H., Lu, Y., Yu, L., Bressan, S.: Bus routes design and optimization via taxi data analytics. In: Proceedings of the 25th ACM International on Conference on Information and Knowledge Management, pp. 2417–2420 (2016)
5. Cussigh, M., Straub, T., Frey, M., Hamacher, T., Gauterin, F.: An all-electric alpine crossing: time-optimal strategy calculation via fleet-based vehicle data. IEEE Open J. Intell. Transport. Syst. **1**, 134–146 (2020)
6. Devarakonda, S., Sevusu, P., Liu, H., Liu, R., Iftode, L., Nath, B.: Real-time air quality monitoring through mobile sensing in metropolitan areas. In: Proceedings of the 2nd ACM SIGKDD International Workshop on Urban Computing, p. 15. ACM (2013)
7. Di Martino, S., Starace, L.L.L.: Towards uniform urban map coverage in vehicular crowd-sensing: a decentralized incentivization solution. .IEEE Open J. Intell. Transport. Systems **3**, 695–708 (2022)
8. Di Martino, S., Starace, L.L.L.: Vehicular crowd-sensing on complex urban road networks: a case study in the city of porto. Transport. Res. Proc. **62**, 350–357 (2022)
9. Fayyad, U., Piatetsky-Shapiro, G., Smyth, P.: From data mining to knowledge discovery in databases. AI Mag. **17**(3), 37–37 (1996)
10. Guo, B., et al.: Mobile crowd sensing and computing: the review of an emerging human-powered sensing paradigm. ACM Comput. Surv. (CSUR) **48**(1), 1–31 (2015)
11. Kaurav, R.S., Rout, R.R., Vemireddy, S.: Blockchain for emergency vehicle routing in healthcare services: an integrated secure and trustworthy system. In: 2021 International Conference on COMmunication Systems NETworkS (COMSNETS), pp. 623–628 (2021). https://doi.org/10.1109/COMSNETS51098.2021.9352903

---

[5] https://github.com/luistar/knot.

12. Lee, U., Zhou, B., Gerla, M., Magistretti, E., Bellavista, P., Corradi, A.: Mobeyes: smart mobs for urban monitoring with a vehicular sensor network. IEEE Wirel. Commun. **13**(5), 52–57 (2006)
13. Li, B., et al.: A trajectory restoration algorithm for low-sampling-rate floating car data and complex urban road networks. Int. J. Geogr. Inf. Sci. 1–24 (2020)
14. Luxen, D., Vetter, C.: Real-time routing with openstreetmap data. In: Proceedings of the 19th ACM SIGSPATIAL International Conference on Advances in Geographic Information Systems, pp. 513–516. GIS 2011, ACM, New York, NY, USA (2011). https://doi.org/10.1145/2093973.2094062, http://doi.acm.org/10.1145/2093973.2094062
15. Ma, H., Zhao, D., Yuan, P.: Opportunities in mobile crowd sensing. IEEE Commun. Mag. **52**(8), 29–35 (2014)
16. Mathur, S., et al.: ParkNet: drive-by sensing of road-side parking statistics. In: Proceedings of 8th International Conference on Mobile Systems, Applications, and Services, pp. 123–136. ACM, New York, NY, USA (2010). https://doi.org/10.1145/1814433.1814448
17. Piorkowski, M., Sarafijanovic-Djukic, N., Grossglauser, M.: CRAWDAD dataset epfl/mobility (v. 2009–02–24), February 2009. http://crawdad.org/epfl/mobility/20090224, https://doi.org/10.15783/C7J010
18. Shi, Q., Abdel-Aty, M.: Big data applications in real-time traffic operation and safety monitoring and improvement on urban expressways. Transport. Res. Part C. Emerg. Technol. **58**, 380–394 (2015)
19. Singh, A.D., Wu, W., Xiang, S., Krishnaswamy, S.: Taxi trip time prediction using similar trips and road network data. In: 2015 IEEE International Conference on Big Data (Big Data), pp. 2892–2894. IEEE (2015)
20. Tu, W., Li, Q., Fang, Z., Shaw, S.l., Zhou, B., Chang, X.: Optimizing the locations of electric taxi charging stations: a spatial-temporal demand coverage approach. Transport. Res. Part C. Emerg. Technol. **65**, 172–189 (2016)
21. Aalst, Wil: Data science in action. In: Process Mining, pp. 3–23. Springer, Heidelberg (2016). https://doi.org/10.1007/978-3-662-49851-4_1
22. Wan, J., Liu, J., Shao, Z., Vasilakos, A.V., Imran, M., Zhou, K.: Mobile crowd sensing for traffic prediction in internet of vehicles. Sensors **16**(1), 88 (2016)
23. Xu, S., Chen, X., Pi, X., Joe-Wong, C., Zhang, P., Noh, H.Y.: ilocus: incentivizing vehicle mobility to optimize sensing distribution in crowd sensing. IEEE Trans. Mobile Comput. **19**, 1831–1847 (2019)

Bus Journey Time Prediction with Machine Learning: An Empirical Experience in Two Cities

Laura Dunne[1]([envelope]) [ID], Franca Rocco Di Torrepadula[2] [ID], Sergio Di Martino[2] [ID], Gavin McArdle[1] [ID], and Davide Nardone[3] [ID]

[1] School of Computer Science, University College Dublin, Belfield, Dublin, Ireland
laura.dunne2@ucdconnect.ie, gavin.mcardle@ucd.ie
[2] DIETI, University of Naples Federico II, via Claudio 21, Naples, Italy
{franca.roccoditorrepadula,sergio.dimartino}@unina.it
[3] Hitachi Rail, via Argine 425, Naples, Italy
davide.nardone@hitachirail.com

Abstract. With increasing urbanisation, and a growing population, transport within cities has never been more important. Buses are the most widespread form of transport worldwide, often being cheaper and more flexible than rail, but also less reliable. Long term bus journey time predictions are important for advanced journey planning and scheduling of bus services. For this reason, several machine/deep learning techniques have been defined to predict bus journey time. Still, due to the number of involved factors, such as complexity and noise in bus data, road network topology, etc., accurate predictions remain elusive. In this paper we aim at validating some Machine Learning methods recently shown to be effective in the literature, on new bus datasets from Dublin and Genoa. The analysis of the results shows some interesting insights into bus networks, highlighting that the accuracy of the predictions is strongly related to the standard deviation of the whole journey times. It emerges that some bus routes show consistency in the prediction error across methods, and for these routes it makes sense to use methods that are fast and computationally efficient, as there is no benefit to applying more complex algorithms. We use features of the route data distribution to develop an explanatory model for the consistency of the route across methods, with a coefficient of determination (R^2) of 0.94. Finally, we identify a systematic anomaly in the data in Dublin that alters the performance of the methods.

Keywords: Bus journey time prediction · Bus travel time prediction · Machine Learning · Random Forest · Intelligent Transportation Systems

1   Introduction and Related Work

The world's population reached 8 billion for the first time in November 2022 and is expected to reach 9 billion in 2037 [19]. Alongside a growing population,

M. A. Mostafavi and G. Del Mondo (Eds.): W2GIS 2023, LNCS 13912, pp. 105–120, 2023.
https://doi.org/10.1007/978-3-031-34612-5_7

urbanisation is also increasing; 55% of the world's population live in urban areas now, and this is expected to increase to 68% by 2050 [18]. Many urban centres are rapidly expanding and have exceeded the road and parking infrastructure for every inhabitant to have a private car [10]. Solving the human transport problem will require many facets, increased infrastructure of active transport, hybrid working, car sharing and improving public transport. In particular, buses are the most widespread form of transport, not requiring an extensive infrastructure. They are flexible and can be redeployed or rerouted as required, being also cost-effective compared to rail [1]. However, buses are not without limitations and often lack reliability [5]. Indeed, punctuality and accurately predicted journey times are synonymous and are among the most frequently requested improvements by bus passengers [3,6]. Accurate journey time predictions can significantly reduce waiting time and encourage greater use of public transport. Cats et al. found that the potential waiting time gains associated with a prediction scheme are equivalent to the gains when introducing a 60% increase in service frequency [2].

As a consequence, many statistical and Machine Learning (ML) methods have been proposed to address bus journey time prediction, but being a highly complex problem, machine learning methods are usually superior [17]. Regardless of the prediction method involved, the existing literature in this area has several deficiencies; the studies tend to be small, many of the commonly used ML models are not scalable to an entire bus network, and there is also no standard dataset, so results of different methods are not comparable between studies, which often give conflicting results on the most accurate ML algorithm to use. Studies predicting bus journey time are usually small, often involving only one or two bus routes, for example, these recent studies [15,20,21]. This is likely because bus data is very large, and at least weeks, but ideally, months of data are required, and many of the ML methods employed are resource intensive. Lack of scalability to an entire bus network is another common issue. Jeong et al. examined an Artificial Neural Network (ANN) with fourteen different training functions, and researchers chose to use the second-best training function, due to excessive running time on their small experimental dataset of 340 unique trips [11]. Cristobal et al. reported that an ANN took over two hours to train on bus data from Gran Canaria [4]. Complex ML models do not always seem to give improved results. Maiti et al. demonstrated comparable levels of error with differences in training time of ten times between ANN, Support Vector Machine (SVM) and Historical Average (HA) approaches on one bus route in Chennai, India [13]. Dunne et al. found HA approaches to be superior to Random Forest (RF) on 25% of bus routes tested in Dublin, Ireland [9]. ML has a significant environmental impact [12] so it is important to carefully select the most efficient method that will have the desired accuracy.

There is robust evidence in the literature that bus routes should not be treated as a homogenous population for journey time prediction. For instance, on 253 routes in Dublin, using a HA method, R^2 scores ranged from 0.95 for routes with many thousands of unique trips to -0.75 for infrequent routes [8].

Dunne et al. found that of four methods tested, one performed best on at least one of 16 bus routes [9]. On a large dataset from Warsaw, four Radial Basis Function Network (RBFN) architectures were compared to five MultiLayer Perception (MLP) network architectures on categories of routes. Two layer MLP architectures with 12 and 32 neurons performed best on many of the categories, but seven different architectures performed best on at least one category of route [14]. Bus routes are not even homogenous within a route. A recent paper evaluates a three-layer architecture for the prediction of bus arrival times on bus route, but analyse the 72 consecutive stop pair segments on that route individually. They show an impactful visual representation of the thirteen methods that produce the best result on at least one segment [15].

The transferability of methods, therefore, cannot be assumed between bus routes or networks, and it is important to replicate methods in diverse geographical areas. Previous works have shown the impact of geographical factors on bus journey time and reliability [16]. Urban location, especially retail land use, has the greatest negative impact on bus reliability, followed by secondary roads, increased length of the route, and the presence of traffic lights [7]. It is likely that poor reliability leads to less accurate predictions, and thus routes with poor reliability may need to be managed differently to reliable routes.

In this paper, we compare four different methods for predicting bus journey times, including two techniques that were recently published, in [9]. These methods are employed on a new dataset of eight bus routes from Dublin, Ireland, and Genoa, Italy. We choose such cities since they present a number of differences in terms of urban plan, road network topology, and bus network structure. This allows us to conduct a deep investigation on the generalisability and transferability of the methods. Summarizing, the present paper makes the following contributions:

- We have reproduced and verified recently published methods on a new dataset, including two diverse geographical locations.
- We have gained insights into how bus journey time prediction methods can be customised to the route, including when simple methods are likely to outperform complex methods.
- We present previously unreported systematic issues with bus data.

2   Data

In this paper, we compare the results of different ML methods on two datasets. The first one consists of data acquired in Dublin (Ireland) in 2018, whereas the second one is from Genoa (Italy), collected in 2021. We chose these cities since they present a number of differences which are useful to better understand the generalisability of the methods. In particular, the two considered scenarios are characterized by significantly different urban planning. On one hand, Dublin is mostly flat, with a road network developed in a radial fashion from the centre. On the other hand, Genoa is compressed between mountains in the north and the sea in the south. Also, the bus networks are designed and managed differently, with routes in Dublin being much longer than those in Genoa. Further details about the data are provided in the following subsections.

2.1   Dublin Data

Dublin is the capital city of Ireland, and in 2018 had a population of approximately 1.2 million inhabitants and is shown in Fig. 1a. It is a coastal, historical city, factors which have greatly influenced its development and led to the proliferation of narrow and windy roads in the city centre, unlike the grid layout of planned urban centres. The urban bus network in Dublin, in 2018, was operated entirely by Dublin Bus, and the data in this study was provided by the National Transport Authority (NTA) in Ireland. The data spans from the 1st of January until the 31st December 2018 and includes all the unique trips on a route on days from Monday to Sunday inclusive. Short routes are quite unusual in Dublin, where policy has favoured long routes. Many routes start in a remote suburb, travel through the city centre and continue to another remote suburb. Of the 253 routes that existed in Dublin in 2018, the average number of stops was 50. The two bus routes (routes 26 and 59, in both directions) chosen for this study were selected because they contain relatively few stops, to most closely match the Genoa data. Route 26_1 shown in Fig. 2a is an outbound route that starts in the city centre, travels along the quays to a remote suburb where there is a large shopping centre. Route 26_2 is the return journey inbound. Route 59_1 shown in Fig. 2b connects a coastal part of South Dublin where there is a light rail station, with a nearby suburb, and route 59_2 is the return journey. Summary statistics for these routes are shown in Table 1.

The buses in Dublin are typically double-decker buses, this is potentially relevant to our study as it may impact the number of people that can board, and the dwell time required. Fare payment is by prepaid travel card or by cash, and in 2018, most passengers completed payment by interacting with the driver. Importantly, in Dublin, there is no timetable for intermediate stops. There is only a departure time from the origin stop, and even if a bus is running faster than usual, it will not pause at stops to maintain even headway between buses.

2.2   Genoa Data

Genoa is an Italian city of 558,805 inhabitants, depicted in Fig. 1b. It is the largest city of the Liguria region, and the sixth-largest city of Italy. The geography of the region and the historic formation of the settlement have influenced the development of the infrastructure. As a result, the city is compressed by both the sea and the mountains, and extended only widthwise.

The city is served by a metropolitan route and a wide urban bus network. The latter consists of 139 routes and 2,634 stops, with a total network length of about 1,000 km. Differently from the Dublin bus network, here most of the routes do not span from one suburb to another, but typically cover specific areas of the city, resulting in fewer stops. Another important difference lies in the payment

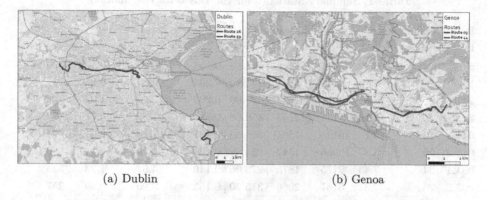

(a) Dublin   (b) Genoa

Fig. 1. The considered routes, w.r.t. the considered urban areas

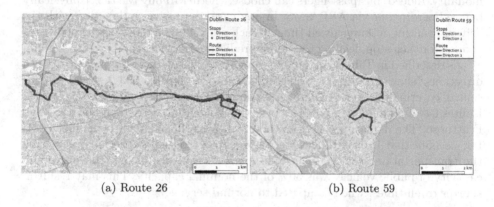

(a) Route 26   (b) Route 59

Fig. 2. Dublin routes

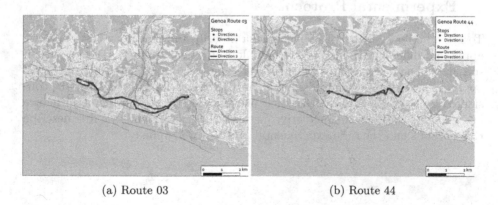

(a) Route 03   (b) Route 44

Fig. 3. Genoa routes

Table 1. Summary Statistics for the Bus Data Distribution.

Route ID	Number Stops	Len (km)	Number Trips	Mean (sec)	SD (sec)	Variance	Kurtosis	Skew	Last Seg Max(sec)
59_1	23	6.80	3743	1194	188.83	0.158	−0.28	0.152	390
59_2	26	6.79	3940	1183	241.14	0.204	0.837	0.654	1237
26_1	29	13.81	6316	2104	431.06	0.205	1.91	1.020	1728
26_2	25	12.16	5134	2133	458.59	0.215	1.85	0.776	872
044_1	19	5.7	16125	1591	208.60	0.131	1.13	−0.012	924
044_2	20	5.4	10966	1517	223.88	0.148	1.24	−0.14	590
003_1	24	7.43	9175	1875	273.06	0.146	4.07	1.23	525
003_2	26	7.31	5167	2066	315.20	0.153	3.20	0.89	257

modality. Indeed, bus passengers can choose whether to buy the ticket physically before boarding, or via APP/SMS. In any case, there is no interaction with the driver, resulting in lower dwell time at each stop. Furthermore, the timetable is defined for each stop, leading to a more predictable service, compared to Dublin.

As described in Table 1, in our experiment we consider two bus routes, in both directions (shown in Fig. 3). Routes 003_1 and its inverse 003_2 serve the city centre, covering the area of Sampierdarena and Sestri, just behind the port area; Routes 044_1 and its inverse 044_2 cover the residential districts of Foce and San Fruttuoso. The dataset spans from the 22nd of April to 31st of December 2021. Let us note that in this timeframe there were Covid-19 restrictions impacting the transportation system. Indeed, to ensure social distancing, the maximum capacity of public vehicles was 50% of the nominal capacity. This may result in shorter dwell times, when compared to normal service.

3   Evaluating Bus Journey Prediction Methods: Experimental Protocol

To get a better insight on the phenomena described in Sect. 1, in this paper we apply four different ML methods for Bus Journey Time Prediction, to two urban scenarios. The four methods we chose were employed in a related paper [9]. We apply them on two new datasets, with the aim of investigating whether the considered geospatial scenarios, with their peculiarities, impact on the performance and generalisability of the predictive methods. In the following, we first describe the methods and then the experimental protocol we applied.

3.1   The Considered Bus Journey Time Prediction Techniques

Historical Averages (HA). As a first naive baseline, we consider the Historical Averages (HA) method, which estimates passenger Partial Trip Time (PTT). The input of HA is a table containing the mean journey time for each consecutive stop pair segment and day/time combination (calculated from the historical data). The HA estimates the PTT as the sum of the historical average time of each of the n segments in the trip ($\bar{T}_{i,d,t}$), for the day of week d and time of day t the partial trip occurs. Such a method is formalized in Eq. 1.

$$PTT = \sum_{i=1}^{n} \bar{T}_{i,d,t} \tag{1}$$

Whole Journey Prediction with Calculated Proportion (WJP-C). The Whole Journey Prediction with Calculated Proportion (WJP-C) method takes as input a similar table as HA, but containing the mean proportion of the total, or whole, journey time. Then, it calculates the proportion of the partial journey made by the passenger, w.r.t the whole journey made by the bus. This is a ratio between 0 and 1, indicating how much of the whole journey the passenger travels, based on the historical average of the journey segments. The proportion is estimated as the sum, on the n segments of the partial journey, of the historical average proportion of each segment (at the time t and day d the trip occurs), namely $\bar{P}_{i,d,t}$. The ratio is multiplied by the second input of the WJP-C, which is the whole journey time predicted by a Random Forest (RF) model (i.e. $\hat{W}$). The RF is trained on the historical whole journey times, for each day and time. We chose RF as it is scalable and needs minimal hyperparameter tuning. The WJP-C method is described in Eq. 2.

$$PTT = \hat{W} \cdot (\sum_{i=1}^{n} \bar{P}_{i,d,t}) \tag{2}$$

Whole Journey Prediction with Predicted Proportion (WJP-P). The Whole Journey Prediction with Predicted Proportion (WJP-P) method operates similarly to the WJP-C. It multiplies the whole journey time, predicted through the aforementioned RF, by the proportion of the partial trip. The only difference is that, for each segment i, the WJP-P estimates the predicted proportion of the occurred segment (i.e. $\hat{P}_i$), w.r.t the whole journey, through RF models. More specifically, a different RF model is trained separately for each stop pair segment of the route, based on the historical journey time of the considered segment. This leads to $L-1$ models (where L is the number of stops of the route). The WJP-P model is described in Eq. 3.

$$PTT = \hat{W} \cdot (\sum_{i=1}^{n} \hat{P}_i) \tag{3}$$

Segment Prediction (SP). The Segment Prediction (SP) method is the most common approach in the literature and operates similarly to the WJP-P, but it predicts directly the segment journey time (S_i), for each segment i, rather than its proportion. Again, the prediction on each segment is made by a different RF, trained on the specific stop pair segment, resulting in $L-1$ RF models (as in the WJP-P method). The PTT is then calculated as the sum of the n segments of the predicted times S_i.

$$PTT = \sum_{i=1}^{n} \hat{S}_i \tag{4}$$

3.2   Experimental Setting

The ML methods above presented are employed to perform Bus Journey Time prediction on two different datasets, namely the one of Dublin and the one of Genoa, described in Sect. 2. The Dublin and Genoa datasets are split into training (80%) and testing (20%) data. The training data is used as described in the four methods above. The same data is used to calculate the mean journey times and mean proportions w.r.t the whole journey time as is used to train the RF models. During testing, a random partial journey is selected from each journey in the reserved testing data, and the PTT is predicted with each of the four methods. The results obtained from the four methods, on the two cities, are then examined from different perspectives. Firstly, we look at the magnitude of the errors for all routes and discuss any patterns that emerge. Secondly, we look at the consistency of the results for the four methods on each route. This is important because if a route is very consistent across methods, using the fastest and least resource intense method makes sense. Two of the methods, HA and WJP-C, are fast, use very little computational power and require minimal storage space, whereas SP and WJP-P are more complex. We will explain why a given route is consistent or inconsistent across methods. Finally, we explore some differences between the datasets, assessing if methods that use whole journey time (WJP-P and WJP-C) or methods that use only the segment data (HA and SP) perform best.

4   Results and Discussion

In this section, we discuss the results of our experiments in terms of both magnitude of errors and consistency between methods.

4.1   Magnitude of Errors

The full error metrics results in Dublin and Genoa are shown in Table 2 and 3 respectively. The results of the individual routes in Dublin and Genoa are shown in Figs. 4a and 4b respectively. The overall results in Dublin have higher error across all metrics, with values between 102 and 118 s MAE for the four methods tested, compared to values between 96 and 98 s in Genoa.

Table 2. Dublin Full Results.

	HA	SP	WJP-C	WJP-P
MAE/s	114.32	102.34	117.579	**101.93**
MAPE	0.157	0.153	0.162	**0.152**
RMSE/s	196.11	163.52	195.62	**159.80**

Table 3. Genoa Full Results.

	HA	SP	WJP-C	WJP-P
MAE/s	97.91	96.56	**96.01**	96.79
MAPE	0.143	0.143	**0.141**	0.142
RMSE/s	144.03	**141.74**	142.46	143.34

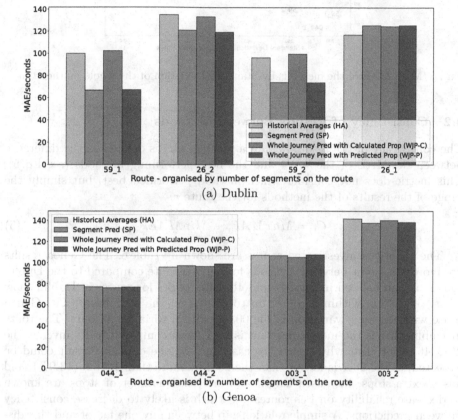

(a) Dublin

(b) Genoa

Fig. 4. MAE of the four methods per route

The average MAE of the methods within a route in both cities increases linearly with the standard deviation of the whole journey time, as shown in Fig. 5. In Dublin, route 26 has a higher standard deviation of journey time than route 59. This is likely because route 26 passes through the urban centre, but route 59 does not. In Genoa, route 003_2 deviates further from the line of best fit than the other routes shown in Fig. 5, which could be because there is less data available for this route as shown in Fig. 1.

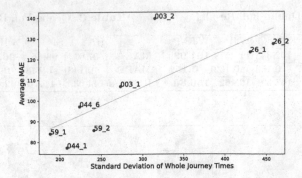

Fig. 5. Mean MAE of the methods by Standard Deviation of the whole journey times.

4.2 Consistency of Results Between Methods

The consistency of the results within a route r (C_r) is defined as the difference between the MAE of the worst and the best performing methods (see Eq. 5). This metric does not consider which method performed best, but simply the range of the results of the methods for the route r.

$$C_r = MaxMAE_r - MinMAE_r \tag{5}$$

The C_r of the investigated routes are shown in Table 6. The Genoa results are more consistent between methods for a given route compared to the Dublin routes, as can be seen in Figs. 4a and 4b. The results for routes in Dublin show a large variation within a route, up to 35.52 s on the 59_1 route. The Genoa route with the most variation is the 003_2, with a variation of 3.9 s. The route in Dublin that is the most consistent is 26_1, even compared to its inverse, the 26_2. It is not clear why this is the case. In fact, the opposite result could be expected, as the 26_1 is longer than the 26_2 by more than 1.7 km (13.9%), and has 4 extra stops. Increased length and increased number of stops are known to decrease reliability on bus routes [8], which is likely to decrease consistency between predictions. A simple relationship between any one factor and this discrepancy could not be found, or to explain the significant difference between the consistency of the results in the Genoa routes versus the Dublin routes. A visual examination of the data distributions of the whole journey time suggested a relationship between high kurtosis and the consistency of the results. There was also a possible relationship between skew of the data distribution and consistency. To demonstrate this, some samples of the data distributions of an inconsistent route (Dublin route 59_1) and a consistent route (Genoa route 003_1) are shown in Figs. 6a and 6b. The whole journey times of the 59_1 have a kurtosis of -0.23, a skew of 0.15 and has large C_r, whereas the 003_1 data has a kurtosis of 4.07 a skew of 1.23 and a small C_r.

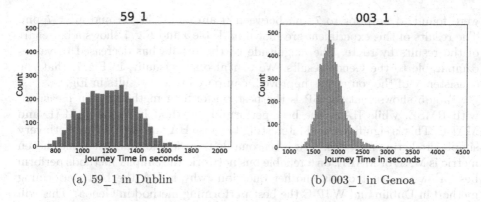

(a) 59_1 in Dublin   (b) 003_1 in Genoa

Fig. 6. Data distribution of two routes to show disparity.

An Ordinary Least Squares (OLS) linear regression analysis was performed with features from the whole journey time data distribution (skew, kurtosis, etc.) as the independent variables and C_r as the dependent variable. The coefficients of the best combination of independent variables are shown in Table 4. This model has an R^2 of 0.94 and an adjusted R^2 of 0.85, indicating that the model has very good explanatory power. The condition number is low, 5.23, which means there is unlikely to be significant correlation between the features impacting the result. The model is stable to small changes, for example substituting the standard deviation of the whole journey time for its variance results in a similar model, with an R^2 of 0.92 and coefficients of similar size and direction. The p-values are not statistically significant, which is not surprising considering the small sample size of 8 routes. It makes sense that routes with a lot of data (unique trips), and a tall narrow distribution (high kurtosis and low skew) would have consistent predictions from an ML algorithm.

Let us recall that the Genoa dataset was collected in 2021, when restrictions related to the COVID-19 pandemic were active. This could have an impact on the obtained prediction. Thus, in order to see if the patterns of prediction were related to this reliability, we split the Dublin data in more homogeneous partitions. In particular, we analysed Dublin data from the off-peak hours, determined experimentally by average journey time. The off-peak times for Dublin

Table 4. Linear Regression (OLS) Analysis Results.

Feature	Coefficient	P-value
Kurtosis	−10.98	0.057
Skew	6.24	0.148
Unique_Trips	−5.30	0.253
STD_Whole	−3.59	0.209

Table 5. Dublin Full Results using data before 7:00, from 9:00–16:30 and after 19:00.

Metric	HA	SP	WJP-C	WJP-P
MAE/s	**89.63**	93.05	97.15	93.92
MAPE	**0.129**	0.142	0.139	0.142
RMSE/s	156.33	**146.54**	164.91	146.92

were found to be prior to 7 am, between 9 am and 4:30 pm and after 7 pm. The results of this experiment are shown in Table 5 and Fig. 7 shows a bar chart of the results by route. The magnitude of the results has decreased to values comparable to the Genoa results. We can also see visually, in Fig. 7, that the consistency of the routes has improved, compared to the results in Fig. 4a.

Table 5 shows that the SP is the best performing method, when measured with RMSE. while HA is the best performing method in terms of MAE and MAPE. This is significant and interesting because HA and WJP-C are both very simple prediction methods. So it is reasonable to conclude that, when the chosen metric is MAE or MAPE, on a reliable bus network, the simpler methods perform best. However, that opens another question, why is HA the best performing method in Dublin and WJP-C the best performing method in Genoa? This will be discussed further below.

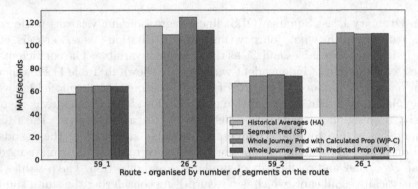

Fig. 7. Average MAE of the four methods versus the standard deviation of the whole journey times for the off-peak data in Dublin

Table 6. Analysis Summary Statistics.

Route ID	Avg Seg Max Max (s)	Last Seg Max Max (s)	C_r (s)	ESE	Hist_minus _WJPC (s)
59_1	241.80	390	35.52	1.61	−0.0019
59_2	196.65	1237	25.92	6.29	−0.0029
26_1	417.81	1728	8.57	4.14	−0.0037
26_2	460.18	872	15.77	1.89	0.0008
044_1	458.56	924	2.46	2.01	0.0015
044_2	424.59	590	2.96	1.40	−0.0005
003_1	527.48	525	2.21	1.00	0.0010
003_2	538.52	257	3.92	0.48	0.0007

4.3   Discussion on the Differences Among Methods

In the full Dublin dataset, the more complex methods, i.e. WJP-P and SP, outperformed the simpler HA and WJP-C. In the Genoa dataset it was a simpler method, WJP-C, that performed best when measured with MAE and MAPE and SP with RMSE. This is possibly due to local factors with the bus network, and are consistent with the findings in the existing literature. Dunne et al.'s results from multiple routes in Dublin showed the other simpler method, HA, performing best on the shorter, most consistent, routes in their dataset. We know the routes in the Genoa dataset are shorter than those in Dublin. The Dublin routes were chosen as they had the closest number of stops to the Genoa dataset, but they still have more stops. Dunne et al. previously reported SP performing better than WJP-P on shorter PTT, of which there are proportionately more on shorter routes. They suggested that there were a number of segments (9) on a partial trip at which the noise in the segment data became greater than any inaccuracy introduced by using the whole journey time prediction. They also reported WJP-P outperforming SP at times of low network reliability and SP slightly outperforming WJP-C at times of high network reliability.

When considering the most homogeneous subset of Dublin, we see a different simple method performing best in each case. All the bus data in this experiment underwent the same outlier removal process. Negative journey times and journey times greater than 12 standard deviations from the mean were removed. We noted a pattern in the Dublin data that the range of the distribution on the last segment of the bus routes tended to be very wide. The last segment journey time distribution had a much longer tail than the intermediate segments and the last segments in the Genoa dataset. Based on local knowledge and observation, we suspected that this might be a result of an accumulation of buses around the last stop, and buses stopping before reaching the terminus bus stop. This results in the AVL not recording the reaching the final stop until the bus is about to embark on its return journey. This is an artificially long time for the last segment and is not representative of the real journey time. We theorised that this End Segment Effect (ESE) would impact the accuracy of the whole journey time predictions, as calculated from departure at the first stop to arrival at the last stop. This can negatively influence the performances of the WJP-C method, as, by definition, it is based on the whole journey time of the route, thus resulting in worse predictions than HA. To investigate this effect, we quantified the ESE as the maximum value in the data distribution of the last segment, as shown in Eq. 6, where JT is the journey times on the last segment (n-1) on a route with n stops. The ESE for the routes can be seen in Table 6.

$$ESE = max(JT_{n-1}) \qquad (6)$$

We also quantified how well the WJP-C method performed compared to the HA method. In particular, for each route r, we defined $Hist\_minus\_WJPC$ as the difference between the MAE of the WJP-C and of the HA, for that route.

Then, to account for differences caused by the length of the routes, we divided
that difference by the mean whole journey time of r (see Eq. 7).

$$Hist\_minus\_WJPC_r = \frac{MAE_{Hist,r} - MAE_{WJP-C,r}}{\overline{WJT_r}} \qquad (7)$$

If the methods perform identically, this value will be 0. On routes where HA
outperforms WJP-C, the value will be negative, while it will be positive on routes
where WJP-C outperforms HA. The resulting values for the $Hist\_minus\_WJPC$
are reported in Table 6.

We examined the data for a correlation between this metric and the ESE.
The plot of the values can be seen in Fig. 8 and the correlation coefficient was
found to be -0.74. This is a strong negative correlation, indicating as the ESE
increases, the Hist_minus_WJPC will decrease. This supports our theory that
this ESE is contributing to the difference in method performance. This is an
important finding, that likely affects other bus networks, apart from Dublin.

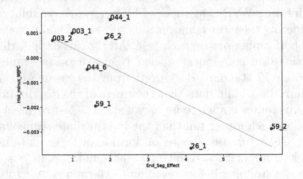

Fig. 8. The End Segment effect vs the Hist_minus_WJP-C

5   Conclusion

This paper on bus journey times includes two disparate bus networks, in different countries. To the best of our knowledge, this is unique in journey time
prediction literature. We have reproduced and validated some recently published
methods and gained insights into bus networks. There is strong evidence that
the accuracy of the predictions is strongly related to the standard deviation of
the whole journey times. This is a useful finding, because it allows us to assess
the likely accuracy of the predictions on unseen routes from simple data analysis.
We discuss and explore the differences in the consistency of the results across
methods and provide a robust explanatory model with an R^2 of 0.93. Identifying
routes that give very similar results with varying methods is useful because for
these routes we can choose to use methods that are fast and computationally
efficient, as there is no benefit from more complex algorithms. We have also identified a previously unreported issue with bus data in Dublin, which we named

the End Segment Effect (ESE) which we attribute to the accumulation of buses at terminus stops. It is very useful to know about a problem, because then we can attempt to solve it. We suggest reducing the threshold for outlier removal to a threshold of 3 standard deviations or providing a limit based on the average maximum on the other segments if this problem is identified in bus data.

Still, due to the significant impact of geospatial context on bus reliability, more routes and more geographical coverage would improve the study. Other planned further work is analysing the impact of specific geospatial features on the data distribution of the bus route.

Acknowledgements. This publication has emanated from research supported in part by a grant from Science Foundation Ireland under Grant number 18/CRT/6183. For the purpose of Open Access, the author has applied a CC BY public copyright licence to any Author Accepted Manuscript version arising from this submission.

References

1. Avenali, A., Catalano, G., Gregori, M., Matteucci, G.: Rail versus bus local public transport services: a social cost comparison methodology. Transp. Res. Interdiscip. Perspect. **7**, 100200 (2020)
2. Cats, O., Loutos, G.: Evaluating the added-value of online bus arrival prediction schemes. Transp. Res. Part A Policy Pract. **86**, 35–55 (2016)
3. Central Statistics Office: Use of Public Transport - CSO - Central Statistics Office (2019). https://www.cso.ie/en/releasesandpublications/ep/p-nts/nationaltravelsurvey2019/useofpublictransport/
4. Cristóbal, T., Padrón, G., Quesada-Arencibia, A., Alayón, F., de Blasio, G., García, C.R.: Bus travel time prediction model based on profile similarity. Sensors **19**(13), 2869 (2019)
5. Currie, G.: Bus transit oriented development - strengths and challenges relative to rail. J. Public Transp. **9**(4), 1–21 (2006)
6. Dastjerdi, A.M., Kaplan, S., de Abreu e Silva, J., Anker Nielsen, O., Camara Pereira, F.: Use intention of mobility-management travel apps: the role of users goals, technophile attitude and community trust. Transp. Res. Part A Policy Pract. **126**, 114–135 (2019)
7. Dunne, L., McArdle, G.: A large scale method for extracting geographical features on bus routes from OpenStreetMap and assessment of their impact on bus speed and reliability. Int. Arch. Photogramm. Remote Sens. Spatial Inf. Sci. **XLVIII-4/W5-2022**, 37–44 (2022)
8. Dunne, L., McArdle, G.: A novel post prediction segmentation technique for urban bus travel time estimation. In: Proceedings Tenth International Workshop on Urban Computing (2021)
9. Dunne, L., McArdle, G.: Bus journey time prediction: a comparison of whole route and segment journey time predictions using machine learning. In: Intelligent Transport Systems (2023, in Press)
10. Gössling, S.: Why cities need to take road space from cars - and how this could be done. J. Urban Des. **25**(4), 443–448 (2020)

11. Jeong, R., Rilett, L.R.: Bus arrival time prediction using artificial neural network model. proceedings. In: The 7th International IEEE Conference on Intelligent Transportation Systems (IEEE Cat. No. 04TH8749), pp. 988–993 (2004)
12. Lacoste, A., Luccioni, A., Schmidt, V., Dandres, T.: Quantifying the Carbon Emissions of Machine Learning (2019). http://arxiv.org/abs/1910.09700
13. Maiti, S., Pal, A., Pal, A., Chattopadhyay, T., Mukherjee, A.: Historical data based real time prediction of vehicle arrival time. In: 17th International IEEE Conference on Intelligent Transportation Systems (ITSC), pp. 1837–1842 (2014)
14. Pałys, L., Ganzha, M., Paprzycki, M.: Machine learning for bus travel prediction. In: Computational Science - ICCS 2022, pp. 703–710 (2022)
15. Serin, F., Alisan, Y., Erturkler, M.: Predicting bus travel time using machine learning methods with three-layer architecture. Measurement **198**, 111403 (2022)
16. Soza-Parra, J., Muñoz, J.C., Raveau, S.: Factors that affect the evolution of headway variability along an urban bus service. Transp. B Transp. Dyn. **9**(1), 479–490 (2021)
17. Treethidtaphat, W., Pattara-Atikom, W., Khaimook, S.: Bus arrival time prediction at any distance of bus route using deep neural network model. In: 2017 IEEE 20th International Conference on Intelligent Transportation Systems (ITSC), pp. 988–992 (2017)
18. United Nations: 2018 Revision of World Urbanization Prospects — Multimedia Library - United Nations Department of Economic and Social Affairs. https://www.un.org/development/desa/publications/2018-revision-of-world-urbanization-prospects.html
19. United Nations: Population. https://www.un.org/en/global-issues/population
20. Xie, Z.Y., He, Y.R., Chen, C.C., Li, Q.Q., Wu, C.C.: Multistep prediction of bus arrival time with the recurrent neural network. Math. Probl. Eng. e6636367 (2021)
21. Zhu, L., Shu, S., Zou, L.: XGBoost-based travel time prediction between bus stations and analysis of influencing factors. Wirel. Commun. Mob. Comput. e3504704 (2022)

A Novel GIS-Based Machine Learning Approach for the Classification of Multi-motorized Transportation Modes

Ali Afghantoloee[1]([✉]), Mir Abolfazl Mostafavi[1], and Bertrand Gélinas[2]

[1] Center for Research in Geospatial Data and Intelligence, Laval University, Quebec, QC, Canada
ali.afghantoloee.1@ulaval.ca,
mir-abolfazl.mostafavi@scg.ulaval.ca
[2] GreenPlay Company, Quebec, QC, Canada
bertrand.gelinas@greenplay.social

Abstract. Transportation sector is the largest contributor to greenhouse gas emissions. Among all means of transportation (road, air, sea), road transportation has the greatest impact in terms of CO_2 emissions in the atmosphere. In order to develop "smart" and sustainable cities and improve the health of the population, it is crucial to re-evaluate our use of various means of transportation for our daily travel to work or leisure and minimize the emissions of pollutants and greenhouse gases. Some smartphone applications currently offer routes to optimize greenhouse gas emissions, but these applications have limitations, particularly due to a lack of environmental data and a lack of multimodality regarding means of transportation (bicycles, walking, running, car, bus, metro, etc.). This paper aims to address these limitations by proposing an intelligent application for detecting the user travel mode based on smart phone sensors information and data from Geospatial Information System (GIS). Specifically, reliable transportation mode detection (TMD) algorithms using the real-time sensors data open new possibilities for travel optimization with minimum greenhouse gas emissions.

Keywords: Transportation mode detection · Machine learning · GIS · Greenhouse gas emissions · Smartphone

1 Introduction

Transportation sector is the largest contributor to greenhouse gas emissions [7, 15]. Among all means of transportation (road, air, sea), road transportation has the greatest impact in terms of CO2 emissions in the atmosphere [4, 10]. A major challenge for future "smart" cities is certainly, particularly in North America, traffic congestion and the resulting pollution emissions [1, 14]. Many studies show the negative effects of urban pollution on health and well-being of the population [5, 14].

At an even finer level of analysis, it is noted that travelling is the potentially large generator of greenhouse gas emissions. Furthermore, it is well documented that the

M. A. Mostafavi and G. Del Mondo (Eds.): W2GIS 2023, LNCS 13912, pp. 121–126, 2023.
https://doi.org/10.1007/978-3-031-34612-5_8

majority of trips between home and work are made by car [13], a mode of transportation that is not sustainable and causes many problems such as traffic congestion, air pollution and road accidents. In general, the transportation sector is the main responsible for greenhouse gas emissions in Canadian cities, and these emissions are mostly due to individuals commuting to their place of work. In light of these findings and given the federal and provincial governments aim at reducing greenhouse gases [6, 11], companies are increasingly being called upon to take a proactive role in sustainable mobility, especially by encouraging a change in their employees' travel habits.

Although some studies have already been done to detect means of transportation [3, 8, 9], they do not correlate the direct effect of GIS information such as locations of transportation infrastructures with the TMD. Other studies, however, propose some solutions on how to correlate GIS data with the TMD in urban areas [2, 12]. In addition, some smartphone applications currently allow to determine routes calculated using data compiled by Google or Apple. Some applications already exist, but they propose routes for common modes (bicycle, walking, running, car) without considering other modes that are more difficult to detect such as bus, train, and metro. While previous studies have focused on implementing transportation mode detection algorithms on servers or cloud computing platforms, this research project aims to develop a machine learning algorithm that can be run directly on smartphones. Therefore, the originality of this paper lies in the integration of GIS information with TMD algorithm for use in smartphones, which can provide more efficient and real-time transportation mode detection and expand the capabilities of existing smartphone applications and provide new insights into transportation patterns and behavior.

The goal of this research project is to propose and implement an algorithm that can automatically identify the mode of transportation of individuals carrying a smart phone. Given the large amount of data from smart phones and the various conditions and exceptions for transportation mode detection, we aim to develop a machine learning algorithm using labeled datasets. The algorithm should be able to distinguish between different modes of transportation including still, walking, running, biking, driving, taking the bus, metro, train. While Google and Apple have already created machine learning algorithms that can classify modes such as still, walking, running, biking, and being in a vehicle, this research aims to propose a new machine learning algorithm that can specifically detect the motorized transportation modes including the car, bus, train, and metro.

2 Methodology

In order to accurately detect the mode of motorized transportation, we opted to train a Multiple Layer Perceptron (MLP) algorithm as a machine learning (ML) model using the TensorFlow framework developed by Google. This allows us to deploy the ML algorithm on the Google Firebase cloud service to predict the transportation mode on smart phones.

The steps to develop the MLP algorithm using smartphones sensors are as follows (Fig. 1):

1. The mode of transportation is detected on the smartphone using the location tracking library in the Flutter framework, considering Google activity and Core ML API for android and iPhone devices.
2. If the mode is detected as in-vehicle, the MLP function is executed on the device based on the inputs (features) to predict the motorized transportation mode.

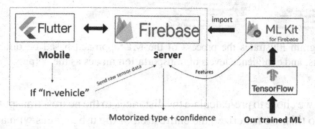

Fig. 1. Process of using the ML approach for transportation mode detection using the Firebase, Flutter, and TensorFlow frameworks.

The MLP algorithm is designed to train the TMD model using the TensorFlow framework. First, we defined the features extracted from the raw sensor data within the smartphone. All the features including used for training the ML models are shown in Fig. 2. These features are classified into non-spatial, and spatial features. The non-spatial features are calculated based on different statistical modes (minimum, maximum, average, and variance) on the raw sensor data including acceleration (for x, y, and z axes), magnitude, accuracy, speed, speed accuracy, heading, heading accuracy within a predefined time window (6 snapshots of 10 s = 6 min). The spatial features include the proximity of user's location and transportation corridors and stops such as bus, train, and subway stations (as the binary variables so that their distance is less than 50 m is 1, otherwise is 0). Additionally, there could be dynamic spatial features such as real-time bus locations within the region provided by bus service companies, however, we have not used these dynamic spatial features in our ML approach due to the high computational time required to request the real-time bus location API and filter the nearest one for each user.

In order to improve the performance of the proposed ML approach, we integrated supplementary spatial information such as proximity to bus stop into the training and prediction processes. However, due to the extremely high computational cost related to the assessment of spatial features such as distance computation to the infrastructures such as bus stops, metro, and train corridors, we could not integrate these features to predict TMD on smartphones. Most research works have used these features on the server side because the volume of the spatial dataset is very high and the computation of distance between the nearest infrastructure to the user location is very time-consuming on mobile devices, which drains the battery life.

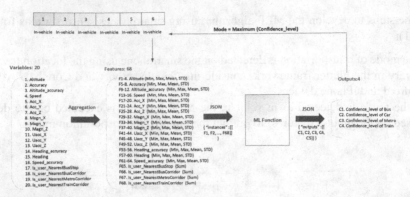

Fig. 2. The diagram illustrates the process of the ML approach based on different variables, features as inputs, and confidence levels of transportation modes as the outputs.

Therefore, we chose to pre-calculate the distances to the nearest transportation infrastructures. To do this, we rasterized the entire area of the urban areas with a resolution of 20 m by 20 m. Afterward, we calculated the distance to the nearest infrastructure like bus stops for each pixel and stored it as the pixel's value. Since the volume of raster data is big and the data covers many pixels that are placed out of the urban region, we converted the raster dataset to a json file (with inputting the i and j ($json[i][j]$) which shows the location of the pixel in the region) and eliminated the items (pixels in the raster dataset) that have a distance more than 50 m to the nearest bus stops to reduce the volume of spatial data.

3 Result

Using the rich sensor data and powerful computational capabilities of modern smartphones, we collected raw sensor data from multiple types of smartphones along with trajectory information (latitude and longitude) in different cities (Quebec, Montreal, and Sherbrooke) at a frequency of 10 s and labeled the transportation mode. We then developed a MLP algorithm that was trained and fitted using the labeled data (Fig. 3a). The algorithm achieved 93% accuracy on test data (which represented 30% of the total data) (Fig. 3b). Our algorithm can accurately identify train, bus, metro, and car as the means of transportation on various smartphone models.

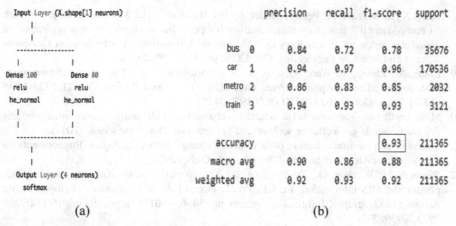

		precision	recall	f1-score	support
bus	0	0.84	0.72	0.78	35676
car	1	0.94	0.97	0.96	170536
metro	2	0.86	0.83	0.85	2032
train	3	0.94	0.93	0.93	3121
accuracy				0.93	211365
macro avg		0.90	0.86	0.88	211365
weighted avg		0.92	0.93	0.92	211365

(a)   (b)

Fig. 3. (a) Configuration of Three-Layer MLP model with the number of neurons in the layer and activation functions, (b) Classification accuracy for each transportation mode including accuracy, precision, recall, and F1-score.

4 Conclusions

Nowadays, mobile applications allow the collection of information about individuals and their surroundings for diverse application thanks to the advances in sensor technologies as well as information and telecommunication technologies. This has also contributed to the advances in TMD using smartphones for monitoring Greenhouse Gas emissions. In this paper, we have proposed a new machine learning method for detecting motorized transportation modes, such as cars, buses, subways, and trains using smartphones.

The proposed approach uses sensor data and GIS information integrated over a one-minute time period into a MLP model. The results indicate that this approach is able to accurately detect different transportation modes with a success rate of 93%, which is 2% higher compared to the case when spatial features are not considered.

References

1. Banister, D.: Cities, mobility and climate change. J. Transp. Geogr. **19**, 1538–1546 (2011)
2. Biljecki, F., Ledoux, H., van Oosterom, P.: Transportation mode-based segmentation and classification of movement trajectories. Int. J. Geogr. Inf. Sci **27**, 385–407 (2013). https://doi.org/10.1080/13658816.2012.692791
3. Du, Z., Zhang, X., Li, W., Zhang, F., Liu, R.: A multi-modal transportation data-driven approach to identify urban functional zones: an exploration based on Hangzhou City. China. Trans. GIS **24**, 123–141 (2020). https://doi.org/10.1111/tgis.12591
4. Environnement et Changement climatique Canada (2020) Indicateurs canadiens de durabilité de l'environnement : Émissions de gaz à effet de serre, Canada statistic, (2020)
5. Gössling, S.: Urban transport justice. J. Transp. Geogr. **54**, 1–9 (2016)
6. Gouvernement du Canada, Progrès vers la cible de réduction des émissions de gaz à effet de serre du Canada, (2020)
7. Hoornweg, D., Sugar, L., TrejosGomez, C.L.: Cities and greenhouse gas emission: moving forward. Environ. Urban. **23**(1), 207–227 (2011)

8. Jiang, X., de Souza, E.N., Pesaranghader, A., Hu, B., Silver, D.L., Matwin, S.: TrajectoryNet: an embedded GPS trajectory representation for point-based classification using recurrent neural networks. In: Proceedings of 27th Annual International Conference on Computer Science and Software Engineering, CASCON, pp. 192–200 (2020)

9. Liang, X., Zhang, Y., Wang, G., Xu, S.: A deep learning model for transportation mode detection based on smartphone sensing data. IEEE Trans. Intell. Transp. Syst. **21**, 5223–5235 (2020). https://doi.org/10.1109/TITS.2019.2951165

10. Ministère de l'environnement et de la lutte aux changements climatiques. Inventaire québécois des émissions de gaz à effet de serre en 2017 et leur évolution depuis 1990 (2019)

11. Ministère de l'environnement et de la lutte aux changements climatiques. Engagements du Québec. Nos cibles de réduction d'émissions de GES, (2020)

12. Stenneth, L., Wolfson, O., Yu, P.S., Xu, B.: Transportation mode detection using mobile phones and GIS information. In: GIS Proceedings of ACM International Symposium on Advance in Geographic Information System, pp. 54–63 (2011). https://doi.org/10.1145/2093973.2093982

13. Transports Québec : Résultats de l'enquête « Origine-destination » de la grande région de Québec (2020)

14. UN-Habitat: Planning and design for sustainable urban mobility. Global report on human settlements. Earthscan, Routledge (2013)

15. United Nations: Cities and Pollution contribute to climate change (2020)

Volunteered Geographic Information (VGI)

CIMEMountainBot: A Telegram Bot to Collect Mountain Images and to Communicate Information with Mountain Guides

Maryam Lotfian[1]([✉]) [iD], Jens Ingensand[1] [iD], Adrien Gressin[1],
and Christophe Claramunt[2] [iD]

[1] Institute INSIT, School of Business and Engineering, University of Applied
Sciences and Arts, 1401 Yverdon-les-Bains, Switzerland
{maryam.lotfian,jens.ingensand,adrien.gressin}@heig-vd.ch
[2] Naval Academy Research Institute, Lanvéoc, France

Abstract. Advancements in technology have led to an increase in the number of Volunteer Geographic Information (VGI) applications, and new smartphone functionalities have made collecting VGI data easier. However, getting volunteers to install and use new VGI applications can be challenging. This article introduces a possible solution by using existing applications, that people use on a daily basis, for VGI data collection. Accordingly, a prototype of a Telegram chatbot is developed to collect mountain images from volunteers, while also providing them with information such as weather conditions and avalanche risk in a given location. The article concludes that using existing platforms like Telegram has benefits, but it is important to consider the specific goals, participants' needs, and interface of a project, and strikes a balance between creating a new application and using existing ones.

Keywords: Volunteered Geographic Information · Telegram bot · Data collection

1 Introduction

For many years, individuals and communities have contributed geospatial content through VGI projects. These types of contributions can be used to supplement existing information or to collect data in hard-to-reach areas. As mentioned by Haklay [1], VGI activities range from leisurely pursuits like geotagging photos of vacations or outdoor activities [2] to other activities such as mapping roads and buildings for disaster management following an earthquake in humanitarian OpenStreetMap project [3,4]. This type of data collection involves volunteers and citizens who contribute and collect data for a variety of purposes, including biodiversity conservation, urban planning, and even health-related issues like using VGI data to assess mobility during the Covid-19 pandemic [5].

M. A. Mostafavi and G. Del Mondo (Eds.): W2GIS 2023, LNCS 13912, pp. 129–138, 2023.
https://doi.org/10.1007/978-3-031-34612-5_9

The advancements in technology, in particular the widespread use of mobile devices with capabilities such as GPS, media recording, and sensors has made it easier to collect VGI data, and has resulted in an increase in the number of VGI mobile applications [6,7]. However, despite the abundance of these VGI mobile applications, it can be difficult to motivate volunteers to contribute to them [8,9]. One reason for this is that people tend to be hesitant to download and install new applications on their mobile devices, and it can be challenging to persuade them to do so [10]. Additionally, there are many VGI applications that serve similar purposes in different domains, and developing new ones from scratch requires a significant investment of both financial and human resources. As a potential solution to these issues, using known applications, that people already use frequently, as a toolkit for data collection could be effective in overcoming these challenges. One of these possible applications can be Telegram[1], one of the most known messaging applications.

Accordingly, in this article we present a toolkit to collect data using Telegram messaging application for our project called CIME. CIME (Choix d'Itinéraire de MontagnE: Choice of Mountain Route) is an European Interreg project[2], which aims at creating decision-making methods and software tools for mountain professionals, to help them in their choice of routes taking into account the avalanche danger zones [11]. This project emphasizes connecting experts, professionals, trainers and researchers in order to create innovative digital tools (virtual reality and augmented reality), which will decrease the daily risk taken by professionals and make it easier for them to make decisions on the field. These tools aim to cover two areas:

- "Mountain Skiing" aspect, focusing on snow-covered terrain and the risk of avalanches;
- "3D Model of Alpine Routes" aspect, focusing on technical terrain (rock, ice, and mixed) that requires precise and often complex route planning.

Therefore, to investigate using existing applications for VGI data collection, real-time communication, information sharing, and data verification, we created a Telegram bot toolkit for collecting mountain images. The aim of data collection for the CIME project is twofold: to construct a 3D model of Alpine routes using mountain images collected by the participants, and to share information with participants as they collect data. While mountain professionals in Switzerland currently use a private WhatsApp group to share information among themselves, the use of a Telegram bot allows for both access to this information as well as the ability to provide real-time information to them, and filter out data that is not relevant to the creation of the 3D model.

The Telegram bot toolkit is currently a prototype for testing the method of collecting mountain data through Telegram. Our goal is for not only mountain professionals but also amateurs to use it while engaging in their leisure activities, while also being able to interact with the toolkit and receive real-time information on weather conditions and avalanche risk zones.

---

[1] https://telegram.org/.
[2] https://interreg.eu/.

The article is structured as follows: The next step introduces the different approaches for VGI data collection. This is followed by presenting our toolkit and the different functionalities developed within this toolkit. Finally, we discuss the limitations of this toolkit for mountain data collection, summarize the findings and draw a few directions for extending the prototype functionalities.

2 VGI Data Collection

There are many different applications that can be used to collect VGI data for a variety of purposes. These applications are tailored to the specific needs and objectives of each project, but they mostly serve a similar purpose: data collection. To facilitate this process, it is beneficial to use a tool that can be used across multiple projects, rather than one that is specific to a single project. An example of an open source toolkit for data collection is Open Data Kit (ODK). ODK[3] is a well-known and widely used tool for creating forms, collecting data, and managing data in the field. It can be used for a wide range of applications, from research data collection to humanitarian aid purposes. Furthermore, it is free and open source, which means it may be modified and adapted to meet the particular needs of a project.

Despite the availability of open-source toolkits for data collection, these tools must be customized for each project. One challenge that can arise is that the user interface may not be user-friendly, which may cause participants to become frustrated and potentially disengage from the project. Additionally, the tool must be installed on participants' devices, which can present a number of challenges, such as potential issues with compatibility between the tool and the operating systems or versions. Furthermore, convincing participants to install an additional application on their devices can be difficult, as research has shown that individuals typically stick to a limited number of applications on their phone [12]. This is because many people already have a large number of applications on their devices, and therefore may not be willing to install another one unless there is a motivating reason to do so. Additionally, there may be instances where participants are unable to install the tool due to limited memory on their devices. Thus, data collection using an application that people use on a daily basis may be a way to address the aforementioned issues.

Telegram with more than 700 million users is one of the most used messaging applications. One of the reasons for Telegram's success is the possibility to create chat-bots using the Telegram bot API. As a result, Telegram is quickly becoming a popular platform for data collection projects. One example is the collection of species data, where researchers can use Telegram bots to gather information from participants in real-time. An advantage of using Telegram for data collection is the ability to exchange messages between the bot and the participants. This allows for real-time feedback and can sustain the participants' motivation to continue their contribution. Additionally, Telegram's group chat feature allows for exchange among the participants and can be another motivating factor. Participants can share their experiences and discoveries with each

---

[3] https://opendatakit.org.

other, discuss the project, and even collaborate on data collection. This can foster a sense of community and belonging among the participants, which can in turn increase their motivation and engagement.

The Telegram bot works as follows: When a user sends a message to the Telegram bot, it is first sent to the Telegram server. The Telegram server then acts as an intermediary, forwarding the message to the bot server for processing. The bot server is where the message is analyzed and a response is generated. The response is then sent back to the Telegram server, which then forwards it back to the user. This entire process is illustrated in Fig. 1. The next section presents our prototype development based on the Telegram bot API and applied to the CIME project, and whose objective is to collect mountain images.

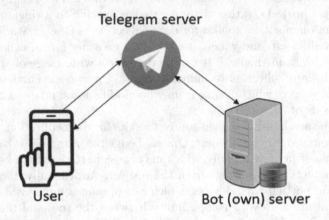

Fig. 1. Communication between user and Telegram chatbot

3   CIMEMountainBot

As mentioned earlier the objective of CIME project is to guide mountain professionals with their choice of mountain routes especially in risky situations such as avalanches. We have analyzed the needs of mountain guides in terms of communication. In order to meet the needs we analyzed several existing platforms that allow both communication between different people, but also to add additional features. Currently, mountain guides communicate mainly with WhatsApp groups where different types of information are communicated such as weather conditions, and terrain conditions, e.g. snow, risks, etc. However, due to some limitations of WhatsApp at the time of developing the prototype, we used Telegram messaging application for data collection. Some of the WhatsApp's limitations include restrictions on data size that can be shared, limited user interface customization options, and end-to-end encryption, which makes obtaining user data for various data collection purposes difficult. Telegram bots, on the other hand, provide more possibilities for data access while protecting user privacy and security. We have thus used Telegram bot, which allows us to create bots to communicate with the members of a group, to transmit and process photos and to include external resources.

Accordingly, the main objectives of using Telegram bot for CIME project are the followings:

- To collect mountain images that can be used to generate a 3D model of Alpine areas
- To exchange information with mountain guides such as real-time information on weather conditions and avalanche risk in a given location
- To filter out mountain images from other images

The Telegram bot was implemented in Python within the Flask framework, and using the Telegram Bot API[4]. There were four main commands defined in this bot including /start, /help, /UploadPhoto, and /GetMeteo. The /start and /help command were for giving general information to the user explaining how to communicate with this chat bot (Fig. 2a).

The other two commands (/UploadPhoto and /GetMeteo) are for collection of images and communicating with the participant about avalanche risk and weather conditions while collecting data. Therefore, four main functionalities were developed in the CIMEMountainBot:

Guiding Participant on Uploading Mountain Images: Participants are instructed to take four photos of a mountain area, each from a slightly different location (about 20 m away from the previous one). A message will appear after each photo is uploaded, indicating how many more photos are required and reminding the participant to move their location before taking the next photo. Additionally, the bot will extract metadata from the images and provide the participant with information on the avalanche risk and weather conditions at the location where the photo was taken. If there is no metadata in the image, or if there is no GPS info in the EXIF file, a message is sent to the participant. The Fig. 2b shows the messages exchanged between the participant and the bot after uploading a photo.

Verify if an Image is a Mountain Image or Not: To sort mountain images from other types of images that mountain guides share with each other, we used an API called Clarifai. Clarifai[5] is a computer vision company that offers access to their trained algorithms through their API, which is free up to 1000 API calls per month. Clarifai's general model has been used widely in scientific research, and that is why we have utilized it in this study [13,14]. They also allow for custom algorithms to be trained using your own dataset. We employed their general model to filter out images that are not mountains. Each time an image is sent to the Clarifai API, the model generates a set of tags for the elements present in the image along with their probabilities. We used these predicted tags

---

[4] https://github.com/python-telegram-bot/python-telegram-bot.
[5] https://www.clarifai.com/.

to determine if an uploaded image is a mountain image or not (Fig. 2c), which simplifies the verification process later on [15].

Return Weather Condition in a Given Location: To obtain the weather condition at a specific location, participants can either share their location via Telegram or provide the coordinates (latitude and longitude). We utilized a free API[6] that returns the weather for the given coordinates. While the weather information provided by this API may not be highly accurate, it was suitable for testing this prototype (Fig. 2d). For actual usage, a more accurate source of weather information should be provided to participants.

Return Avalanche Risk in a Given Location: To communicate avalanche risk, we utilized data from the Swiss Federal Institute for Snow and Avalanche Research (SLF) regarding maps of zones classified by level of risk[7]. We obtained the map through WMS and converted it to a Tiff file, which was then used to determine the pixel value for a given location. The pixel values included an RGB color code, which we then converted to readable colors. Based on the color, we extracted the risk of an avalanche for the location, using the legend defined by SLF (Fig. 2d). It is worth noting that, while this information from SLF was sufficient for the purposes of implementing this prototype and conducting a pilot test, for future improvements, more accurate information on avalanche risk should be used. There is a risk of misinterpretation from color to risk level, and it is better to use standard color codes already in use by mountain guides, as well as information that is closer to real-time, rather than a raster file based on data from the previous year, for example.

4   Limitations and Future Improvements

The CIMEMountainBot project is currently in its prototype phase and has yet to be field-tested by mountain guides. However, the prototype has been presented and discussed with mountain guides, who have shown interest in using the tool as an alternative to their traditional WhatsApp group. Despite this interest, mountain guides have suggested several improvements that need to be made before the tool can be used effectively.

One key area for improvement is the accuracy of the data used for communication. This includes using more accurate information for communicating avalanche risk in a given location, as well as using standard colors for risk communication that are commonly used among mountain professionals. Additionally, using a more accurate source for weather information is also suggested.

Another important aspect discussed by mountain guides is the issue of data sharing. They sometimes may not be willing to share all the exchanged information with other users or third party sources, such as weather APIs or the Clarifai API. Therefore, it is important to establish clear guidelines and agreements on data sharing before implementation.

---

[6] https://api.weatherapi.com.
[7] https://www.slf.ch/en/projects/avalanche-terrain-maps.html.

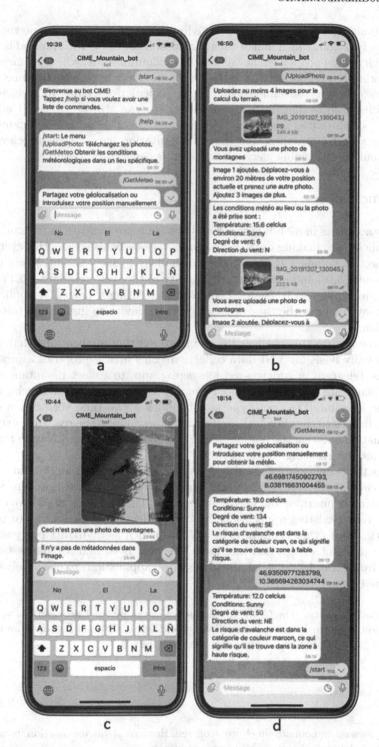

Fig. 2. Different fonctionalities in the CIMEMountainBot, a) start and help commands, b) upload photo, c) verify photo, and d) get weather conditions and avalanche risk

Additionally, Telegram bots have the limitation of requiring an internet connection to function, which makes them unsuitable for areas with limited internet connectivity. This poses a challenge for CIMEMountainBot, which requires real-time information exchange that relies on mobile data networks. In some areas, network access may be limited, making it difficult for guides to receive real-time feedback on avalanche risk. However, data can still be collected in these areas and synchronized with the project's database once an internet connection is established. It is worth noting that this limitation may not be as relevant in Switzerland, as the mobile network coverage is generally widespread[8].

5   Conclusions

The advancements in mobile technology have led to an increase in the number of VGI applications, making data collection in various fields easier. However, VGI data collection comes with its own set of challenges, such as motivating people to contribute [8,9], and evaluating the quality of the collected data [16,17]. One of the main challenges is getting people to start using a new VGI application, as they may not have the time or space on their device to install and use a new application.

One solution to this challenge is to utilize existing applications that people use on a daily basis for VGI data collection. This article proposes a prototype that uses Telegram, a widely used messaging app, to collect mountain images and communicate information about weather conditions and avalanche risk in a specific location. The prototype also includes a real-time verification of the collected images to simplify data verification later on, and the real-time exchange of information between the bot and participants can serve as motivation for them to continue contributing to the project.

While the benefits of using existing applications like Telegram for data collection are clear, there may still be cases where a new VGI application is needed to meet particular interface and user requirements. The idea presented here emphasizes the use of existing applications for data collection of media files or textual information, but other types of data collection such as digitizing polygons may require a different design and interface. The goal is to find a balance between starting from scratch and using already existing applications to effectively collect the desired data.

Acknowledgements. The CIME project is supported by the European cross- border cooperation program Interreg France-Switzerland 2014-2020 and has been awarded a European grant (European Regional Development Fund).

---

[8] https://www.comcom.admin.ch/comcom/en/Homepage/documentation/facts-and-figures/mobile-telephony/mobile-coverage.html.

References

1. Haklay, M.: Citizen science and volunteered geographic information: overview and typology of participation. In: Sui, D., Elwood, S., Goodchild, M. (eds.) Crowdsourcing Geographic Knowledge, pp. 105–122. Springer, Dordrecht (2012). https://doi.org/10.1007/978-94-007-4587-2_7

2. Sun, Y., Fan, H., Helbich, M., Zipf, A.: Analyzing human activities through volunteered geographic information: using flickr to analyze spatial and temporal pattern of tourist accommodation. Prog. Location-Based Serv. 57–69 (2013)

3. Moradi, M.: Evaluating the quality of OSM roads and buildings in the Québec Province. Université Laval, Québec (2020)

4. Bonafilia, D., Gill, J., Basu, S., Yang, D.: Building high resolution maps for humanitarian aid and development with weakly-and semi-supervised learning. In: Proceedings of the IEEE/CVF Conference on Computer Vision and Pattern Recognition Workshops, pp. 1–9 (2019)

5. Vannoni, M., McKee, M., Semenza, J., Bonell, C., Stuckler, D.: Using volunteered geographic information to assess mobility in the early phases of the COVID-19 pandemic: a cross-city time series analysis of 41 cities in 22 countries from March 2nd to 26th 2020. Globalization Health **16** (2020)

6. Neis, P., Zielstra, D.: Recent developments and future trends in volunteered geographic information research: the case of OpenStreetMap. Future Internet **6**, 76–106 (2014). https://doi.org/10.3390/fi6010076

7. Antoniou, V., et al. The future of VGI. In: Mapping and the Citizen Sensor, pp. 377–390 (2017). https://doi.org/10.5334/bbf.p

8. Fritz, S., See, L., Brovelli, M.: Motivating and sustaining participation in VGI. In: Mapping and the Citizen Sensor, pp. 93–117 (2017)

9. Lotfian, M., Ingensand, J., Brovelli, M.: A framework for classifying participant motivation that considers the typology of citizen science projects. ISPRS Int. J. Geo Inf. **9**, 704 (2020)

10. Oxoli, D., Pessina, E., Brovelli, M.: Geo collector bot: a telegram-based open toolkit to support field data collection. Int. Arch. Photogramm. Remote Sens. Spatial Inf. Sci. **XLVIII-4/W1-2022**, 351–356 (2022). https://doi.org/10.5194/isprs-archives-xlviii-4-w1-2022-351-2022

11. Pagnier, F., Pourraz, F., Coquin, D., Verjus, H., Mauris, G.: A multilevel clustering method for risky areas in the context of avalanche danger management. In: Information Processing and Management of Uncertainty in Knowledge-Based Systems, pp. 54–68 (2022)

12. Böhmer, M., Hecht, B., Schöning, J., Krüger, A., Bauer, G.: Falling asleep with angry birds, Facebook and kindle. In: Proceedings of the 13th International Conference on Human Computer Interaction With Mobile Devices and Services (2011). https://doi.org/10.1145/2037373.2037383

13. Nanne, A., Antheunis, M., Van Der Lee, C., Postma, E., Wubben, S., Van Noort, G.: The use of computer vision to analyze brand-related user generated image content. J. Interact. Mark. **50**, 156–167 (2020)

14. Iadanza, E., Benincasa, G., Ventisette, I., Gherardelli, M.: Automatic classification of hospital settings through artificial intelligence. Electronics **11**, 1697 (2022)

15. Lotfian, M., Ingensand, J., Brovelli, M.: The partnership of citizen science and machine learning: benefits, risks, and future challenges for engagement, data collection, and data quality. Sustainability **13**, 8087 (2021). https://doi.org/10.3390/su13148087

16. Xie, X., Zhou, Y., Xu, Y., Hu, Y., Wu, C.: OpenStreetMap data quality assessment via deep learning and remote sensing imagery. IEEE Access **7**, 176884–176895 (2019)
17. Moradi, M., Roche, S., Mostafavi, M.: Exploring five indicators for the quality of OpenStreetMap road networks: a case study of Québec, Canada. Geomatica **75**, 178–208 (2021). https://doi.org/10.1139/geomat-2021-0012

A Novel Feature Matching Method for Matching OpenStreetMap Buildings with Those of Reference Dataset

Milad Moradi[✉], Stéphane Roche, and Mir Abolfazl Mostafavi

Center for Research in Geospatial Data and Intelligence, Université Laval, Quebec, QC G1V 0A6, Canada
`milad.moradi.1@ulaval.ca`

Abstract. Numerous studies have attempted to assess the quality of Open-StreetMap's building data by comparing it to reference datasets. Map matching (feature matching) is a critical step in this method of quality assessment, involving the matching of polygons in the two datasets. Researchers commonly use two main polygon matching algorithms: 1) the buffer intersection method and 2) the centroid comparison method. While these methods are effective for the majority of OSM building footprints, they may not achieve high accuracy in complex situations. One possible reason is that both methods only consider the position of the OSM polygon compared to that of the reference polygon. To improve these matching algorithms and propose a more robust solution, this study proposes an algorithm that considers shape similarity (using average distance method) in addition to position similarity to better identify corresponding polygons in the two datasets. The experiment results for five cities in the Province of Quebec indicate that the proposed algorithm can reduce the matching error of previous map matching algorithms from approximately 8% to approximately 3%. Furthermore, the study found that the proposed polygon matching algorithm performs more accurately than previous methods when buildings consist of multiple polygons.

Keywords: OpenStreetMap · Feature Matching · Map Matching · OSM Polygon Matching · OSM Buildings Footprint Quality · Volunteered Geographic Information · Spatial Data Quality

1 Introduction

Over the past two decades, several researchers have attempted to assess the usefulness and quality of Volunteered Geographic Information (VGI) in different geomatics applications [1–13]. OpenStreetMap (OSM) has garnered significant attention due to its provision of a free, editable, and readily available map of the world, which is collaboratively created by thousands of contributors [14]. OSM is emerged after Web 2.0 technology that allows the users (OSM contributors) to create content (such as text, image or video) and send it towards the server to be shared with other users [2, 15–18]. Since any contributor with no required level of knowledge in geomatics can modify OSM data, the quality of OSM

M. A. Mostafavi and G. Del Mondo (Eds.): W2GIS 2023, LNCS 13912, pp. 139–152, 2023.
https://doi.org/10.1007/978-3-031-34612-5_10

data is not guaranteed [19–21]. Thus, many researchers tried to evaluate the quality of OSM data (road network or building footprint) [11, 17, 18, 22–25]. Comparing the OSM data to an authoritative dataset is one of the methods that is widely used to evaluate the quality of OSM database [7, 17, 26–29].

In order to compare the OSM data to authoritative data, we have to match features in OSM dataset with corresponding features in the reference dataset [30]. Therefore, developing a reliable feature matching algorithm is an important part of the OSM quality assessment [18]. Currently, there are two methods that are widely used for matching OSM buildings to the reference datasets; buffer intersection and centroid comparison methods [18]. Since both methods find corresponding features only based on the comparison of the position of the two features in the two datasets (OSM and reference), these methods have high error rates when the buildings are complex. In other words, when multiple buildings in OSM are corresponding to only one big polygon in the reference dataset, and those OSM polygons are displaced by ± 5 m, there is a high probability that some of the OSM buildings are not recognized as corresponding polygons of the reference dataset. This research does feature matching not only based on the similarity of the position of the two features, but also based on the similarity of their shapes. Furthermore, the proposed matching algorithm can indicate correspondence type with a much higher accuracy than the previous matching methods.

The remainder of this article is structured as follows: Sect. 2 discusses the concept of feature matching and feature matching algorithms in OSM, Sect. 3 explains the proposed feature matching algorithm, Sect. 4 discusses the results of the implementation of the proposed method in five cities in the province of Quebec, and Sect. 5 concludes the findings of this research.

2   Feature Matching

Feature matching is a process that aims to find corresponding features between multiple databases [7, 31]. Typically, a tolerance level is considered, and the similarity and dissimilarity of two features are assessed based on this tolerance level. The two features are then identified as corresponding or independent. As a geographic feature can be characterized by both a geometry and a set of attributes, similarity measures can be based on lexical information, feature position, shape, or even the attributes describing the feature. Feature matching is considered a crucial stage in data integration, data updates, change detection, and data versioning [32].

Matching features in OpenStreetMap (OSM) presents a greater challenge than matching features in authoritative databases due to the heterogeneous nature of OSM data. In some neighborhoods, there may be a high density of data, while in others, the density may be low. Moreover, OSM features do not consistently contain the same level of detail [33]. It is because OSM does not force the contributors to use a unique way of data creation [34]. For example, a contributor can select any tag that she wants for describing the feature. Another example is that a contributor may digitize a very complex building footprint with only 4 points. Generally, the building footprints in OSM are less detailed (more generalized) than the actual footprints [30]. As a result of polygon generalization, it cannot be expected that the same level of detail in building footprints will be present in OSM as in authoritative databases. While buildings in authoritative databases may adhere to consistent levels of detail, this is not necessarily the case for OSM. Overall, a comparison of attributes (tags) or geometry between an OSM feature and a reference feature is far more complicated than comparing two authoritative databases.

A number of researchers proposed models of feature matching for OpenStreetMap. A method was suggested by [35] to match the OSM road network with a reference road network, which involves a seven-step comparison algorithm that can automatically identify corresponding roads [35]. The method computes geometrical and topological aspects of a line such as distance and direction as well as attributes of the line such as the name of the street [35]. This method seems to be computationally complex since it computes many measures. However, in [32] the author holds the view that the efficiency of this method is limited due to the presence of topological inconsistencies in the OSM database. Consequently, another feature matching method is proposed by the author [32]. The proposed method employs a tolerance level, which creates a buffer around the geometry and then evaluates the location of the second geometry in relation to this buffer. The second geometry may be within, partly within, or entirely outside of the buffer. The length of the buffer determines the maximum allowable difference between the two geometries. Additionally, the method compares the lexical information of the two features to measure their similarity. This step involves comparing the strings in which the lexical information is usually stored [32]. Although this algorithm produced satisfactory results in certain regions, it appears to be computationally burdensome. Furthermore, the majority of buildings in OSM do not have a name, which reduces the effectiveness of comparing them by name or other tags. Unlike road network matching, the name comparison approach is not as efficient in the case of buildings.

Prior research on OSM building quality has predominantly utilized two methods to match OSM building footprints with a reference database. The more commonly used approach is the area overlapping method, which was introduced by [7]. The area overlapping method is founded on the assumption that the polygon displacement between OSM and the reference database is negligible [7]. Hence, the overlapping area between the two polygons can be utilized as a criterion for identifying corresponding features [7]. The tolerance for feature matching is considered 30% of the area [7]. In cases where the overlap area between the OSM and reference features is less than 30%, the two features will not be considered corresponding. This is because it is assumed that the overlap is caused by the spatial displacement of neighboring polygons. However, if the overlap area between any two features in the OSM and reference data is greater than 30%, they will be regarded as corresponding features [7]. The following equation is proposed by [7] for finding corresponding building footprints:

$$\frac{Area_{overlap}}{Min(Area(Foot_{osm_i}), Area(foot_{ref\_j}))} > 30\% \qquad (1)$$

Majority of researchers who evaluated the quality of OSM building footprint data used this method [36–39]. The tolerance of 30% is not a fixed value and some of the other researchers considered other values as tolerance. For example, [36] used a tolerance of 50% for feature matching.

An additional method for feature matching was proposed by [30], which calculates completeness by utilizing the centroids of OSM polygons and comparing them to the reference database. Correspondence is established if the centroid of an OSM building footprint falls within a building footprint of the reference database [30]. The aforementioned method was employed by [30] to assess the object-based completeness of OSM building footprints. Additionally, several researchers have utilized the centroid method for feature matching [36, 38, 40, 41].

The second method of feature matching is proposed by [22]. The centroid method for feature matching calculates the distance between the centroids of the two datasets, and considers the nearest polygons as matching. A tolerance of 20m is utilized, with only OSM polygons that have a nearest reference polygon within 20m being considered corresponding pairs [22]. This method is considered the simplest among the proposed methods. However, there is no available research that compares the quality of all these feature matching methods, so a comparison of their quality cannot be made.

2.1 Correspondence Types

The correlation between OSM features and reference features can be complex, especially in the case of building footprints due to potential errors during data creation. For instance, a group of five buildings may be depicted as a single building in OSM since it can be challenging to identify the precise boundary between rooftops in aerial imagery. Additionally, OSM polygons typically represent rooftops rather than footprints, which can result in some displacement due to the oblique angle of the sensor capturing the image [42]. Hence, the OSM building footprints are susceptible to various sources of errors, such as a combination of reference buildings, a generalized depiction of reference buildings, positional displacements, or a combination of these factors. These discrepancies may arise from difficulties in identifying precise boundaries between roofs and footprints in the areal imagery, resulting in a generalized representation. Furthermore, the OSM polygons may only capture the roofs of the buildings, which can cause positional inaccuracies due to the sensor's oblique view. [7] argued that the relationship between OSM footprints and the footprints in the reference databases can be one of the following cases: (OSM: reference).

a. **1: 1** – This refers to a 1:1 relationship between an OSM building and a reference building, where each building is matched to only one corresponding building in the other dataset. This is considered the ideal scenario from a data quality perspective, as both datasets are fully matched with no missing or redundant features.
b. **1: 0** – this scenario arises when an OSM building is not associated with any corresponding polygon in the reference database. According to the ISO standard, this is known as "data commission" [43].
c. **1: n** – this case occurs when one OSM building is associated with multiple buildings in the reference database. It is a common occurrence in OSM because the boundaries between adjacent building rooftops are not always clear in aerial imagery, and sometimes a group of buildings is represented by a single polygon in OSM [32, 43].
d. **0: 1** – this case occurs when a building exists in the reference database but there is no corresponding polygon in the OSM database. According to the ISO standard, this situation is referred to as "data omission" [43].
e. **n: 1** – this case indicates that multiple buildings in the OSM database are matched with a single building in the reference database [43]. It is also common in OSM

because variations in the elevation of different parts of a building may lead digitizers to interpret them as separate buildings.

f. **n: m** – this case pertains to the matching of multiple buildings in OpenStreetMap to multiple buildings in a reference database [43]. This study indicates that this is more common in large structures, like commercial or industrial buildings, compared to small residential ones.

Figure 1 illustrates some issues regarding OSM feature matching. In this figure, all polygons are moved towards northeast in comparison to the reference polygons. Polygon 1 is generalized in comparison to the reference corresponding polygon. In addition, the centroid of the OSM polygon is outside of the reference polygon and it is within another reference polygon. The centroid of polygon 2 of OSM, is outside of the corresponding reference one. However, it does not fall inside any other polygon. In case of polygon 3, it has a considerable overlap with a wrong reference polygon. Polygons 4 and 5 are moved towards northeast and they are generalized in comparison to the corresponding reference polygon. Generally, OSM polygons may have their centroids withing a wrong reference polygon or they may have a considerable overlap with a wrong reference polygon.

To overcome the previously mentioned problems in feature matching and have a more reliable one, we propose to add a shape comparison to the previous methods. In addition, the comparison and feature matching should be done for all the possible subsets of the set of candidate polygons. In the next section, the algorithm developed for this purpose is discussed.

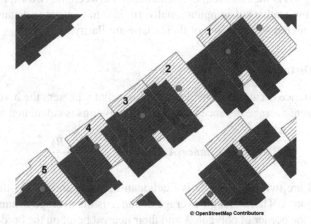

Fig. 1. Issues related to OSM buildings footprints (OSM: green, reference: red) (Color Figure Online)

2.2 Shape Similarity

The buildings of OSM are usually digitized by the contributors from the areal imageries. [1, 7] mentioned that the buildings of the OSM are in fact, a simplified representation of the buildings of the reference database. Therefore, from one hand, the shapes of the polygons are not digitized with the same level of details as the reference database [7, 41]. On the other hand, sometimes there are some errors in the digitization process due to the lack of geographic knowledge of the contributors or even vandalism activities. Thus, a shape dissimilarity can happen based on different reasons. It is necessary to evaluate how similar are the shapes of the buildings in OSM to the shapes of the buildings in the reference database.

[7] defined the shape accuracy as the similarity between the footprints in the two databases. [7] proposed the use of a turning function to measure the similarity of the polygons. This method was used by a number of other researchers [7, 22, 38]. This method represents each polygon with a set of tangents of the edges and the length of each edge [7]. The length of each edge should be normalized by the perimeter of the polygon so that different polygons can be compared [7]. The dissimilarity of two polygons can then be calculated by comparing these two functions.

[25] proposed using a discrete Fourier Transform for calculating the shape similarity between the two databases. This method first finds the polygons with 1:1 relationship. Then, each polygon will be considered as a signal and Fourier transformation is used to express that signal in terms of a complex exponential [25]. The measure of the similarity of the two polygons is then defined, by the distance between the two exponentials [25]. This method is innovative but computationally. In this study average distance of the two polygon is considered as a measure of their shape similarity.

2.3 Average Distance

The average distance is calculated between the lines that represent the border of the two polygons. Discrete average distance between two polygons is calculated as [44]:

$$AverageDistance(A, B) = \frac{\sum_{i=1}^{n} d(p_i^A, B)}{n} \tag{2}$$

where A and B are two polygons. D is Euclidean distance and p_i^A is i-th point on the border of polygon A. Therefore, the average distance is the average distance between a set of points on the border of polygon A and their nearest point on the border of polygon B.

In this method, firstly, the two polygons will become concentric. Then, a set of points will be generated on the border of the first polygon. Finally, the distance of each point to the border of the second polygon will be calculated. If the average distance between the two polygons is 0, it means that the two shapes are exactly similar. If the average distance is high, it means that the corresponding points of the two polygons are far from each other, which means that the two shapes are not similar.

3   Proposed Matching Method

As mentioned in the previous section, there are several issues regarding feature matching for OSM buildings. Due to the displacement, the centroid may not necessarily fall within the correct reference polygon. The positional accuracy of OSM polygons is relatively acceptable and for most of the cases, the centroid falls within the correct object. However, there are still few cases where the centroid is not within the corresponding polygon due to the poor spatial accuracy (displacement of the polygons). Moreover, this displacement can cause an overlay between the target OSM polygons and several incorrect reference features. To tackle this issue, we proposed a method that matches the features based on the comparison of both position and shape of the polygons (shape similarity is calculated using Eq. 2). Therefore, the results will be more reliable than comparing only the position of the polygons.

In addition, the other problem is that sometimes the difference in the elevation of different parts of a roof may cause errors in digitizing the roof in the areal images. [32] found that a few OSM buildings are in fact a block of buildings in reality but the border between them is not clearly visible in the areal images and they are digitized as one polygon. Therefore, it is possible that a group of polygons in OSM is corresponding to a polygon in the reference database or vice versa. To tackle this issue, we proposed an algorithm that first finds the candidate polygons and then check if any group of these candidates can be corresponding to a polygon in the reference database.

The flowchart of the algorithm is explained in Fig. 2. This algorithm has two inputs: the OSM polygons and the reference polygons. Then, for each polygon in OSM, all the candidate reference polygons are identified using a polygon overlay method (calculating the intersection between the OSM polygon and all reference polygons). The candidate polygons are those ones that have more than int_tol% intersection with the OSM polygon. The set of the candidate reference polygons is called T. Then, based on the cardinality of the set, 3 possible feature matching cases can happen. If $|T| = 0$, then there are no candidate polygons in the reference database, and it means that the OSM polygon has no match in the reference database, and it is a commission. If $|T| = 1$, then it means that the feature has only one matching polygon in the reference database which indicates a good quality. If $|T| > 1$, then there is more than one candidate for the OSM polygon. In this case, further investigation is required to find out the correct matching polygons. Therefore, a shape similarity evaluation using average distance method is done between the OSM polygon and all possible subsets of T. Since it is not possible to compare the shape of one polygon with two separate polygons, a concave hull is calculated for each subset of T. Then, the shape of the OSM polygon is compared to the shape of the concave hull. If the concave hull of any subset of T has an average distance (shape similarity) to the OSM polygon greater than shp_tol%, then, the members of that subset of T will be considered as the corresponding polygons of the OSM polygon and the relation will be 1: n.

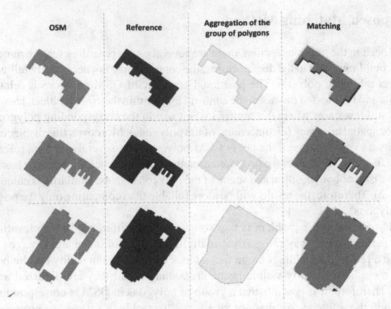

Fig. 2. The polygon aggregation for feature matching [18]

Figure 2 illustrates several examples when the aggregation of a group of polygons is matched with one single polygon. The aggregated polygon may no t be exactly like the reference polygon but if the similarity is greater than shp_tol %, they will be considered as matching features.

The main steps of the proposed algorithm are:

Firstly, find all candidates by comparing their location to the location of the OSM polygon. Secondly, find which group of candidates has a shape that better fits the OSM polygon.

When the relationship between OSM and reference database is evaluated, then, the relation between reference database and OSM should be evaluated using the same algorithm and just by flipping the inputs. This reverse relation evaluation facilitates the discovery of the other types of relations that are not in the flowchart of Fig. 3.

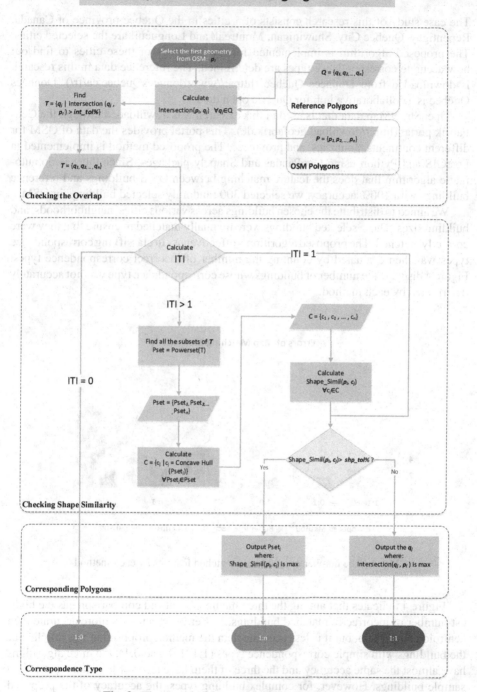

Fig. 3. The proposed feature matching algorithm [18]

4 Results and Discussion

The case study of this research consists of 5 cities in the Quebec province of Canada. Repentigny, Quebec City, Shawinigan, Montreal, and Longueuil are the selected cities. The proposed algorithm is implemented for the buildings of these cities to find out how accurate correspondence types are determined. The reference data in this research is downloaded from Données Québec (https://www.donneesQuebec.ca/fr/). Données Québec is a collaborative hub for Québec open data.

OpenStreetMap data that is used in this research was downloaded through the Geo-Fabrik portal (http://download.geofabrik.de). This portal provides the data of OSM for different continents, countries, and provinces. The proposed method is implemented in PostGIS and Python using GeoPandas and Shapely packages. Since there is no automatic algorithm that does the feature matching between OSM buildings and reference buildings with 100% accuracy, we selected 300 randomly selected buildings in OSM.

We aimed to distribute the chosen buildings across various cities, neighborhoods, and building sizes. These selected buildings were manually matched to ensure that they were correctly matched. The proposed algorithm's effectiveness in classifying correspondence types was then evaluated by counting the number of incorrect correspondence types. Figure 4 displays the number of buildings whose correspondence type was not accurately determined by each method.

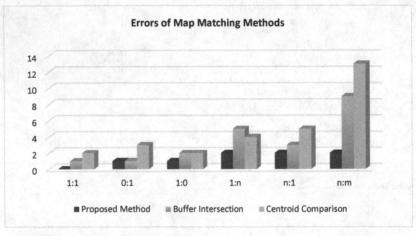

Fig. 4. The number of incorrectly matched features by each method

Figure 4 indicates that among the three methods, centroid comparison has the highest number of incorrectly matched buildings. Buffer intersection is more accurate than centroid comparison, but it is less accurate than the method proposed in this article. For the buildings with simple correspondence types (1:1, 1:0, and 0:1), the three algorithms have almost the same accuracy and the three of them have an error less that 3 out of 300 sample buildings. However, for complex building types, the accuracy of the proposed method is much higher than the two other methods. In case of n:m correspondence type, the proposed method has classified only 2 buildings incorrectly, while buffer intersection and centroid comparison have classified 9 and 13 buildings incorrectly, respectively.

It is illustrated in Fig. 4 that among the three map matching methods, the proposed method has the highest overall accuracy especially in the case of complex buildings where shape similarity is necessary to identify the corresponding buildings correctly. Montreal has more complex buildings that smaller cities of the Province of Quebec. As a result, the proposed method performed more accurately in Montreal than centroid comparison and buffer intersection. The proposed method neglects the attributes of the two polygons when it finds the corresponding buildings, but we believe that adding attribute similarity to the proposed method may increase its accuracy.

5 Conclusion

This article proposes a new algorithm for matching OpenStreetMap building polygons with those of reference dataset. The proposed algorithm improves previous feature matching methods by adding shape similarity check (using average distance method) to the algorithm. Since in the case of complex buildings, sometimes m polygons in OSM are corresponding to n polygons in reference dataset, centroid comparison and buffer intersection methods fail to find all corresponding features correctly. In other worlds, the accuracy of OSM polygon matching by buffer intersection and centroid comparison methods is relatively low when the building consists of multiple polygons. We realized that the two mentioned methods sometimes miss few polygons when multiple polygons in OSM are corresponding to single or multiple polygons in reference dataset. The proposed method, on the other hand, has a reliable accuracy in case of complex buildings because it finds the corresponding polygons not only based on the similarity of the position of polygons in two datasets, but it also measures the similarity of their shapes to make sure that the corresponding polygons are detected correctly. However, the implementation showed that the proposed method is computationally heavier than the two previous methods. Future works may improve the algorithm by adding attribute similarity to the proposed algorithm.

References

1. Törnros, T., Dorn, H., Hahmann, S., Zipf, A.: Uncertainties of completeness measures in OpenStreetMap – a case study for buildings in a medium-sized German city. ISPRS Ann. Photogramm. Remote Sens. Spatial Inf. Sci. **II-3/W5**, 353–357 (2015). https://doi.org/10.5194/isprsannals-II-3-W5-353-2015
2. Neis, P., Goetz, M., Zipf, A.: Towards automatic vandalism detection in OpenStreetMap. ISPRS Int. J. Geo-Inf. **1**, 315–332 (2012). https://doi.org/10.3390/ijgi1030315
3. Lotfian, M., Ingensand, J., Brovelli, M.A.: The partnership of citizen science and machine learning: benefits, risks, and future challenges for engagement, data collection, and data quality. Sustainability **13**(14), 8087 (2021). https://doi.org/10.3390/su13148087
4. Lotfian, M., Ingensand, J., Brovelli, M.A.: A framework for classifying participant motivation that considers the typology of citizen science projects. ISPRS Int. J. Geo-Inf. **9**(12), 704 (2020). https://doi.org/10.3390/ijgi9120704

5. Lotfian, M., Ingensand, J., Brovelli, M.A.: an Approach for Real-Time Validation of the Location of Biodiversity Observations Contributed in a Citizen Science Project. The International Archives of the Photogrammetry, Remote Sensing and Spatial Information Sciences **XLVIII-4/W1-2022**, 271–278 (2022). https://doi.org/10.5194/isprs-archives-XLVIII-4-W1-2022-271-2022

6. Camboim, S., Bravo, J., Sluter, C.: An investigation into the completeness of, and the updates to, OpenStreetMap data in a heterogeneous area in Brazil. ISPRS Int. J. Geo-Inf. **4**, 1366–1388 (2015). https://doi.org/10.3390/ijgi4031366

7. Fan, H., Zipf, A., Fu, Q., Neis, P.: Quality assessment for building footprints data on OpenStreetMap. Int. J. Geogr. Inf. Sci. **28**, 700–719 (2014). https://doi.org/10.1080/13658816.2013.867495

8. Hacar, M., Kılıç, B., Şahbaz, K.: Analyzing OpenStreetMap road data and characterizing the behavior of contributors in Ankara. Turkey. ISPRS Int. J. Geo-Inf. **7**, 400 (2018). https://doi.org/10.3390/ijgi7100400

9. Fonte, C.C., et al.: Assessing VGI data quality. In: Mapping and the Citizen Sensor, pp. 137–163 (2017)

10. Sui, D., Elwood, S., Goodchild, M. (eds.): Crowdsourcing Geographic Knowledge: Volunteered Geographic Information (VGI) in Theory and Practice. Springer Netherlands, Dordrecht (2013). https://doi.org/10.1007/978-94-007-4587-2

11. Haklay, M.(Muki), Basiouka, S., Antoniou, V., Ather, A.: How many volunteers does it take to map an area well? The validity of Linus' law to volunteered geographic information. Cartogr. J. **47**, 315–322 (2010). https://doi.org/10.1179/000870410X12911304958827

12. Moradi, M., Delavar, M.R., Moshiri, B.: A GIS-based multi-criteria decision-making approach for seismic vulnerability assessment using quantifier-guided OWA operator: a case study of Tehran. Iran. Ann. GIS. **21**, 209–222 (2015). https://doi.org/10.1080/19475683.2014.966858

13. Moradi, M., Delavar, M.R., Moshiri, B.: A GIS-based multi-criteria analysis model for earthquake vulnerability assessment using Choquet integral and game theory. Nat. Hazards **87**(3), 1377–1398 (2017). https://doi.org/10.1007/s11069-017-2822-6

14. Bertolotto, M., Mc-Ardle, G., Schoen-Phelan, B.: Volunteered and crowdsourced geographic information: The openstreetmap project. J. Spat. Inf. Sci. **20**, 65–70 (2020). https://doi.org/10.5311/JOSIS.2020.20.659

15. Antoniou, V., Morley, J., Haklay, M.: Web 2.0 geotagged photos: assessing the spatial dimensions of the phenomenon. Geomatica. **64**, 99–110 (2010)

16. Goodchild, M.F.: Citizens as sensors: the world of volunteered geography. GeoJournal **69**, 211–221 (2007). https://doi.org/10.1007/s10708-007-9111-y

17. Moradi, M., Roche, S., Mostafavi, M.A.: Exploring five indicators for the quality of OpenStreetMap road networks: a case study of Québec Canada. Geomatica. **31**, 1–31 (2022). https://doi.org/10.1139/geomat-2021-0012

18. Moradi, M.: Evaluating the quality of OSM roads and buildings in Quebec Province (2020)

19. Fan, H., Yang, B., Zipf, A., Rousell, A.: A polygon-based approach for matching OpenStreetMap road networks with regional transit authority data. Int. J. Geogr. Inf. Sci. **30**, 748–764 (2016). https://doi.org/10.1080/13658816.2015.1100732

20. Funke, S., Schirrmeister, R., Storandt, S.: Automatic extrapolation of missing road network data in OpenStreetMap. CEUR Workshop Proc. **1392**, 27–35 (2015)

21. Funke, S., Storandt, S.: Automatic tag enrichment for points-of-interest in open street map. In: Brosset, D., Claramunt, C., Li, X., Wang, T. (eds.) Web and Wireless Geographical Information Systems. LNCS, vol. 10181, pp. 3–18. Springer, Cham (2017). https://doi.org/10.1007/978-3-319-55998-8_1

22. Müller, F., Iosifescu, I., Hurni, L.: Assessment and visualization of OSM building footprint quality. In: Proceedings of the 27th International Cartographic Conference, Rio de Janeiro (2015)
23. Wang, M., Li, Q., Hu, Q., Zhou, M.: Quality analysis of open street map data. Int. Arch. Photogramm. Remote Sens. Spatial Inf. Sci. **XL-2/W1**, 155–158 (2013). https://doi.org/10.5194/isprsarchives-XL-2-W1-155-2013
24. Zhou, Q., Tian, Y.: The use of geometric indicators to estimate the quantitative completeness of street blocks in OpenStreetMap. Trans. GIS. **1**, 1550–1572 (2018). https://doi.org/10.1111/tgis.12486
25. Xu, Y., Chen, Z., Xie, Z., Wu, L.: Quality assessment of building footprint data using a deep autoencoder network. Int. J. Geogr. Inf. Sci. **31**, 1929–1951 (2017). https://doi.org/10.1080/13658816.2017.1341632
26. Antoniou, V., Skopeliti, A.: Measures and indicators of VGI quality: an overview. ISPRS Ann. Photogramm. Remote Sens. Spatial Inf. Sci. **II-3/W5**, 345–351 (2015). https://doi.org/10.5194/isprsannals-II-3-W5-345-2015
27. Tveite, H., Langaas, S.: An accuracy assessment method for geographical line data sets based on buffering. Int. J. Geogr. Inf. Sci. **13**, 27–47 (1999). https://doi.org/10.1080/136588199241445
28. Touya, G., Antoniou, V., OlteanuRaimond, A.-M., Van Damme, M.-D.: Assessing crowd-sourced POI quality: combining methods based on reference data, history, and spatial relations. ISPRS Int. J. Geo-Inf. **6**, 80 (2017). https://doi.org/10.3390/ijgi6030080
29. Hochmair, H.H., Zielstra, D., Neis, P.: Assessing the completeness of bicycle trail and lane features in OpenStreetMap for the United States. Trans. GIS. **19**, 63–81 (2015). https://doi.org/10.1111/tgis.12081
30. Hecht, R., Kunze, C., Hahmann, S.: Measuring completeness of building footprints in Open-StreetMap over space and time. ISPRS Int. J. Geo-Inf. **2**, 1066–1091 (2013). https://doi.org/10.3390/ijgi2041066
31. Jin, M., Claramunt, C., Wang, T.: A map-matching approach for travel behavior analysis. In: 2017 4th International Conference on System Informatics, ICSAI 2017. 2018-January, pp. 1405–1410 (2017). https://doi.org/10.1109/ICSAI.2017.8248506
32. Du, H., Alechina, N., Jackson, M., Hart, G.: A method for matching crowd-sourced and authoritative geospatial data. Trans. GIS. **21**, 406–427 (2017). https://doi.org/10.1111/tgis.12210
33. Senaratne, H., Mobasheri, A., Ali, A.L., Capineri, C., Haklay, M. (Muki): A review of volunteered geographic information quality assessment methods. Int. J. Geogr. Inf. Sci. **31**, 139–167 (2017). https://doi.org/10.1080/13658816.2016.1189556
34. Mooney, P., Corcoran, P.: The annotation process in OpenStreetMap. Trans. GIS. **16**, 561–579 (2012). https://doi.org/10.1111/j.1467-9671.2012.01306.x
35. Koukoletsos, T.: A Framework for Quality Evaluation of VGI linear datasets (2012)
36. Jacobs, K.T.: Quality Assessment of Volunteered Geographic Information : An Investigation into the Ottawa-Gatineau OpenStreetMap Database, (2018)
37. Zhou, X., Chen, Z., Zhang, X., Ai, T.: Change detection for building footprints with different levels of detail using combined shape and pattern analysis. ISPRS Int. J. Geo-Inf. **7**(10), 406 (2018). https://doi.org/10.3390/ijgi7100406
38. Hung, K.-C., Kalantari, M., Rajabifard, A.: Assessing the quality of building footprints on OpenStreetMap: a case study in Taiwan. In: Smart World, p. 237 (2016)
39. Huerta, J., Schade, S., Granell, C. (eds.): Connecting a Digital Europe Through Location and Place. LNGC, Springer, Cham (2014). https://doi.org/10.1007/978-3-319-03611-3
40. Copes, N.: A Planning based Evaluation of Spatial Data Quality of OpenStreetMap Building Footprints in Canada (2019)

41. Siebritz, L.-A.: Assessing the accuracy of openstreetmap data in south africa for the purpose of integrating it with authoritative data (2014). https://open.uct.ac.za/handle/11427/9148
42. Zhuo, X., Fraundorfer, F., Kurz, F., Reinartz, P.: Optimization of OpenStreetMap building footprints based on semantic information of oblique UAV images. Remote Sens. **10**(4), 624 (2018). https://doi.org/10.3390/rs10040624
43. ISO: ISO 19157: Geographic information-data quality (2013)
44. Gil de la Vega, P., Ariza-López, F.J., Mozas-Calvache, A.T.: Models for positional accuracy assessment of linear features: 2D and 3D cases. Surv. Rev. **48**(350), 347–360 (2016). https://doi.org/10.1080/00396265.2015.1113027

Network Analysis and Geovisualization

Geovisualisation Generation from Semantic Models: A State of the Art

Matthieu Viry[1] and Marlène Villanova[2]([✉])

[1] Université de Paris, UAR RIATE, CNRS, 75013 Paris, France
matthieu.viry@cnrs.fr
[2] Univ. Grenoble Alpes, CNRS, Grenoble INP (Institute of Engineering Univ.
Grenoble Alpes), LIG, Grenoble, France
marlene.villanova@univ-grenoble-alpes.fr

Abstract. Geovisualisation is a first-choice approach when it comes to support a user's reasoning process to explore geographical information or solve a spatial problem. More and more data relevant for geovisual analysis is published in the Web, sometimes even directly described using the RDF formalism and made available through SPARQL endpoints. Beyond exploiting Semantic Web data, we claim that Semantic Web-based Geovisualisation is a field that also offers an opportunity to make methods, techniques and tools of geovisualisation evolve so they fully exploit the possibilities offered by the Semantic Web technologies stack. In this paper we review some works of the literature that have addressed the issues of cartography and geovisualisation of data formalised or published using Semantic Web technologies, ranging from domain knowledge representation only to frameworks supporting knowledge-based process for geovisualisation generation. As a contribution to this field, and based on lessons learned from the state of the art, we introduce the CoViKoa framework we have designed and implemented. Then, taking stock of our experience, we introduce some challenges we still envision in the field of Semantic Web-based Geovisualisation. We present some of them as open questions, but also draw some guidelines, for future works in the field.

Keywords: Geovisualisation · Semantic Web · generation process · state of the art

1 Introduction

Geovisualisation is a first-choice approach when it comes to support a user's reasoning process to explore geographical information or solve a spatial problem. More and more data relevant for geovisual analysis is published in the Web, sometimes even directly described using the RDF formalism and made available through SPARQL endpoints. León *et al.* [12] identified the need for a tool to explore and visualize RDF geospatial datasets. They proposed a geospatial browser, named Map4RDF, that facilitates the publishing of geospatial data stored in a triplestore. It displays GeoSPARQL data grouped under different

M. A. Mostafavi and G. Del Mondo (Eds.): W2GIS 2023, LNCS 13912, pp. 155–165, 2023.
https://doi.org/10.1007/978-3-031-34612-5_11

categories and allows users to interact with them (accessing detailed information, sharing the resource on Twitter, editing of the resource, etc.). Trillos Ujueta *et al.* [19] propose a JavaScript library, RDF2Map to display RDF individuals on a Leaflet map. RDF2Map offers an interesting level of abstraction since it allows to retrieve RDF individuals from a turtle file loaded beforehand or from DBpedia, and to deliver them as JavaScript objects directly usable by Leaflet. However, the filtering options are limited to the geometric type of the data. No filter option according to an RDFS/OWL class or other more complex conditions (value of a property, etc.) is provided, thus not exploiting the potentially rich semantics of the RDF data to be depicted.

Indeed, beyond the structuration and description of Web data, RDF offers a powerful framework for knowledge management that remains underexploited in the Geographical Information Science field. Methods, techniques, and tools of geovisualisation for using natively these GIS data expressed in the languages of the Semantic Web are still needed, open the path to a Semantic Web-based Geovisualisation (Fig. 1). In this paper, we explore approaches that can be used to automate the geovisualisation of data described by Semantic Web models.

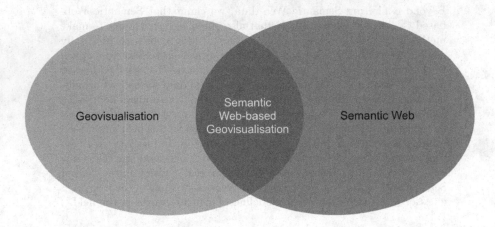

Fig. 1. Semantic Web-based Geovisualisation.

Numerous studies aim at evaluating the contribution of Semantic Web technologies to encode and to exploit knowledge with a geospatial component. Among them, research focuses on:

- formalisation of such a geospatial knowledge (for example by [1,11,17,25]),
- its querying (this issue is covered extensively in [26]),
- its integration (on which [13,15,26] offer interesting findings for example)

Nevertheless, the use of Semantic Web technologies for the specific purpose of concretely building geovisualisation is rarely addressed when geospatial semantics issues are tackled (e.g. by [6,11]).

Regarding more specifically issues dealing with visualization, challenges were identified rather early as stated for instance by Fabrikant [4]: "an ontological approach to visualization seems particularly adequate for formalizing semantic and semiotic transformation components of web-enabled geovisualisation". In [21], Villanova-Oliver draws the contours of an approach based on ontologies for organising at a semantic level the concepts exploited in a automatised process of an geovisualisation creation. She proposes the GVR Matching ontologie that establishes the correspondence between concepts from an application ontology (that contains the data) and the geovisual portrayal concepts that can be associated with them. Geovisual portrayal concepts descriptions are given in the GEOVIS ontology. This proposal does not result in the formalisation of ontologies that can be directly exploited by a machine but is explained on paper with the help of diagrams and Description Logics.

In the next sections, we first present a bibliographical review of works that have addressed the issues of cartography and geovisualisation of data formalised or published using Semantic Web technologies, ranging from domain knowledge representation only to frameworks supporting knowledge-based process for geovisualisation generation. Then, we introduce some challenges we still envision in the field of Semantic Web-based Geovisualisation before we conclude.

2 Where Geovisualisation Meets Semantic Web Data or Models

2.1 Ontologies for Appropriate Cartographic Portrayal

Iosifescu-Enescu and Hurni [10] identify the lack of mechanisms for formalising cartographic rules as one of the elements that can impact on the cartographic quality of the maps produced. They propose two OWL ontologies: the Cartographic Domain Ontology which describes the vocabulary needed to describe maps, and the Cartographic Task Ontology which describes the cartographic rules to be implemented (these rules are only presented in natural language in the article). They also describe a generic architecture of a cartographic library that can be used for a symbolisation process based on these ontologies. This offers the possibility of formalising mapping rules independently of any specific mapping software. Software based on these ontologies would not need to write additional code when adding new representation functionalities but would simply exploit an updated version of the ontologies. Moreover, separate vocabularies related to mapping from the rules that use them makes it possible to reuse them in another context, and to have different sets of cartographic rules depending on the purposes. A significant limitation to this work is that it seems their ontologies have not been published on the Web and the generic architecture of the cartographic library not implemented.

Smith [18] proposes ontologies for the construction and the successful execution of an expert system dedicated to thematic cartography. The ontologies are described in detail on the paper and reuse parts of those proposed in [10].

The result is a Map Ontology, formalized in OWL, that organizes the following concepts: Attribute, Graphic, Layout Element, Map, Map Projection, Production Medium, Spatial Phenomenon and Visual Variable. The relations necessary to create a well-formed map (sometimes in the form of "has exactly one" restrictions for example) are encoded in the ontology. The independence on specific software is also emphasized in this proposal. This work however does not provide an example of a map description using this vocabulary neither a software implementation based on it.

Brus *et al.* [2] address the design of an intelligent system for cartography that could assist users in creating correct maps. The authors consider that map making, initially the apanage of cartographers who know the rules, has become more democratic and that the production of right maps must also be a goal for non-cartographers. To this end, the authors first propose a cartographic ontology based on knowledge acquired from expert cartographers. An interesting aspect of the approach lies in the double hierarchy: that of data types (with the three subtypes AttributeDate, DataTypeDomain and GraphicData) on the one hand, and that of possible representation types (CartographyMethod) on the other. Then they imagine a system of rules specific to cartography that could be implemented in the Business Rules Management Systems Drools[1] using terms from their ontologies (such as "when there exists PointFeature then insert PointSymbol"). Nevertheless, elements are missing to concretely describe the different cartographic methods and no real implementation based on the ontology and derived from Drools rules is shown. If they surprisingly choose to encode the rules in a dedicated formalism that does not belong to the Semantic Web ecosystem, their approach foreshadows a trend that will develop as shown in the next section.

An OGC report [5] addresses the specification of semantic information models and REST APIs for Semantic Registry, Semantic Mediation and Semantic Portrayal Services, aiming at federating and unifying the information produced by different OGC catalog services. It has given rise to the formalisation of various semantic information models allowing the description of style information as well as the composition of graphic symbolizers. To this end, Fellah [5] proposes:

- a Style Ontology, that defines the concept of Style and Portrayal Rules,
- a Symbol Ontology that defines the concepts of SymbolSet and Symbol,
- a Symbolizer Ontology that defines the concept of Symbolizer (and its subclasses PointSymbolizer, LineSymbolizer, PolygonSymbolizer, TextSymbolizer, RasterSymbolizer and CompositeSymbolizer),
- a Graphic Ontology that defines the different graphical elements that allow to create symbolizers.

Based on the study of different specifications (such as the Scalable Vector Graphics format, MapCSS, CartoCSS and SLD/SE to mention only the best known), the vocabulary and the conceptual organization of this proposal is very close to the SLD/SE specifications. The essential differences are in the formalism

---

[1] https://www.drools.org/.

used in [5], that of the Semantic Web, unlike SLD/SE which uses the hierarchical XML format. Fellah [5] also introduces the concept of Symbol, absent from SLD/SE vocabularies, for facilitating the reuse of the same symbols with different styles and grouping symbols into sets to which applying a same style for instance. The ontologies described in this OGC Testbed are however not available directly with the report in a computer-readable form.

2.2 Towards the Automatisation Based on Rules

Carral *et al.* [3] propose an ontology design pattern for map scaling using OWL. The extension of the OWL RL profile they define can be used to describe scaling applications, to reason over scale levels and geometric representations, notably thanks to formal constraints they express for concepts. This makes it possible to check automatically whether data representations from scaling applications are compatible with respect to their scale levels, and thus, can be meaningfully displayed in a single map.

In their paper [9], Huang *et al.* also tackle a problem encountered during the realization of cartographic mash-ups, when the geometrical representations between the base-map and overlaying thematic data do not fully match. They propose a relative positioning approach to synchronize geometric representations for map mashups. They formalize knowledge about relative positioning and implement it using ontologies based on the GeoSPARQL vocabulary and linked data. They both demonstrate the power of GeoSPARQL ontologies to solve complex tasks and provide a technical answer to a problem that can be encountered when creating geovisualisations.

Ruzicka *et al.* [16] and Penaz *et al.* [14] formalize declarative knowledge related to cartography in order to integrate it into an intelligent application based on a rules system. Both proposals use OWL as well as the Drools rule engine. In [14], precise insights are given on modelling cartographic knowledge by adapting the main OWL functionalities (property restrictions, inverse properties, functional properties) to a case study on thematic cartography. The authors' goal is to express as much information as possible about the maps to be created and especially good cartographic practices in their ontological model (such as "the map page contains at least one element of map composition which is title and subtitle"). They also organize in a hierarchy portrayals methods adapted to the type of data (for instance they identify a set of QuantitativeThematicMapMethod).

2.3 Exploiting More the Semantics of the Data or the Model

Varanka and Usery [20] make a particularly interesting proposal from a conceptual point of view. They propose to design and implement what they call the map as a knowledge base so that both humans and machines can interpret it. The authors discuss the technical and architectural challenges facing this approach. The proofs of concept they implement show that advances in Semantic Web technologies and linked data make them viable for mapping, allowing for a map product in which RDF triples are accessible behind the visual vocabulary shown to the user. The authors show two ways of using the map as a knowledge base. The first uses SPARQL queries to fetch the objects of interest to be mapped according to some constraints. They for instance exploit a graph from the U.S. Geological Survey to ask for, in SPARQL: "EPA pollution sites within 5 km of the Pittsburg, Missouri Volunteer Fire Station". The second is using what they call the "browsable graph approach" where new data is retrieved by selecting a resource from data already present on the map. While this approach not directly aims exploiting the semantics of an existing data model, it can contribute to the creation of an intelligent geovisualisation infrastructure. The main limitation however is the lack of discussion about vocabularies to describe the graphical representation of objects shown on the map which is however indispensable to fully concretize the concept of map as a knowledge base.

In [24], Wagner et al. describe the implementation of a system for exploring linked data that semantically integrate geospatial data from various sources. This provides more detailed information on the implementation of the system described by [20], with a strong emphasis on how integrating data into their system. Some interesting points are raised regarding methods of symbolization at cartographic user interface design level that supports linked data (in particular the grouped display of objects in clusters depending on the zoom level).

Huang et al. [7] propose a system that allows formal representation of geo-visual knowledge in a machine-readable way. They propose several ontologies covering the cartographic scale, the data portrayal and the geometry source. The vocabulary proposed for the scale is particularly interesting. Based on the works [3] and [9] (section previous sub-section), it differs from them by allowing the implementation of a conditional portrayal in which the symbolization depends on the visualisation scale and attribute/geometric data associated with the feature. The vocabularies proposed for data portrayals are notably based on the work of the OGC Testbed for Semantic Portrayal [5] also presented previously. In the approach of [7], the definition of the graphical elements is therefore carried out in RDF and the semantic rules that allow to link individuals and these graphical elements are written using SPIN. To demonstrate the potential of the approach, the authors show how SPIN rules[2] (called geometry source rules) are used to choose the geometry of the entities to be represented according to both a zoom level and the availability or not of geometries in the datasets. Conditional portrayal possibilities can be handled through these rules (i.e. filter the entities to which they apply). Nevertheless, rules must be written for each geovisualisation to be created (i.e. adding new graphical elements does not only require to code them in RDF but also to define new SPIN rules so they can be used). Therefore, one of the main limitations is the lack of genericity of the approach as well as the quantity of SPIN rules to be written to obtain a choropleth portrayal for which there are well-defined codes (such as the mapping of continuous values to classes represented by a colour). We note, however, that their ontologies and rules are readily available online, which facilitates rapid iteration

---

[2] Twelve portrayals rules and two geometry source rules specific to their use-case about geovisualisation of heritage building in central Stockholm.

on this work, although the data is not published (for licensing reasons) nor the source code of the implementation.

In the case study presented in [8], Huang *et al.* use the portrayal vocabularies proposed by [7] with a specific focus on the geovisualisation of urban bicycling suitability. In this work, the approach is still based on the SPIN inference mechanism, but SHACL constraints are also added to validate the integration of the data to be exploited by the geovisualisation. They try to remedy the lack of genericity of [7] by using new concepts formalising high-level cartographic knowledge and reusing part of the work of [2]. In particular, the authors formalize the types of data that can be mapped (using the AttributeData and GraphicData concepts and their hierarchies unchanged from [2]) and link these types to continuous colour progressions (they propose vocabulary elements for this in their ontology). Depending on the number of classes required by the data encountered by their system, a rule interpolates the colour progression into the correct number of colours. Despite this, a lack of genericity remains the main limitation: as with previous approach, it requires writing SPIN rules specific to the data to be exploited in order to link individuals and their symbolizers. The ontologies used are available online, together with the source code of the implementation.

In [22,23], we present the CoViKoa Framework. Our proposal first consists in including the concepts of the geovisualisation field into the Semantic Web through new vocabularies to ensure their interoperability with the existing bricks. We propose a stack of compatible ontologies for geovisualisation ([22], Chapter 5): a geovisualisation ontology, a context ontology, an interaction ontology, a colour palette ontology and an ontology of cartographic solutions. We also modify the symbol, symbolizer and scale ontologies and reuse the graphic ontology from [7]. Together these ontologies form a vocabularies ecosystem enabling the description of the main components of a geovisualisation. This constitutes a first contribution in terms of knowledge representation for the field of Semantic Web-based Geovisualisation. As a step further, in [22] Chapter 6, we propose a model of RDF specification document allowing describing the geovisualisation to be created a priori, meaning before any implementation, and declaratively, thanks to the previous vocabularies we define. The description of the geovisualisation is done through a specification document, the Derivation Model, which describes in RDF, using the aforementioned ecosystem of ontologies, how the data should be represented in the geovisualisation components. In this sense, we extend and improve the approach described in [7,8] by making our approach purely declarative. A framework is described that allows transforming this specification into a well-shaped RDF graph ready to be exploited by a geovisualisation interface. A generic geovisualisation interface is also available as a ready-to-use functional template.

The proposals presented in this last section bring considerable progress regarding both the technical challenge of exploiting Semantic Web data for geovisualisation and the challenge of finely leveraging the semantics of the data. However, the architecture proposed by these solutions remains cumbersome and non-standard and does not fully bridge the gap between Semantic Web geospatial data and their geovisual exploitation. Indeed, the proposals of [7, 22] place themselves, like a map server (like GeoServer and MapServer) as an additional infrastructure element to be deployed for knowledge engineers moving towards such a solution, without however disseminating their data by exploiting the well-known OGC specifications that are the WMS and WFS for example. The evolution of the state of the question since the 2000s s and the strengths but also the weaknesses of the latest proposals in the field allow us to identify the remaining challenges and to draw guidelines for what could be a true knowledge-based geovisualisation.

3   Some Challenges for Future Work

First, we identify two main categories of tasks dealing with geovisualisations issues that could benefit from an approach based on the exploitation of data semantics:

- Task 1: the construction of geovisualisation applications (we adopt here the point of view of the application developer, who must make choices concerning the data to be presented to the user and their representation),
- Task 2: visualisation for exploratory purposes of Semantic Web data (we adopt here the point of view of the user or data analyst who wants to discover information through data). In both cases, improvements can be envisioned for three main areas that refer to the Web infrastructure (client, server, etc.), as the support of the Semantic Web, and that tends to be the prime choice for hosting geovisualisations.

3.1   Server Side

In [22], based on [5], we propose geospatial feature selection rules, close to those proposed in SLD/SE but adapted to semantic Web data (selection according to subsumption relation, selection according to the value read after traversing a property path, etc.). However, one of its limitations is that it proposes a non-standard infrastructure but require an additional specific component in the whole web architecture. An interesting approach from an engineering point of view could be to integrate into existing map servers (GeoServer or MapServer for example) a functionality allowing 1) to connect to triplestores and 2) to define the representation rules, not with SLD/SE but with rules dedicated to Semantic Web data, like those of [22]. This could take the form of *adhoc* plugins offering editorial facilities to declare rules as introduced in [22] (Chapter 9). Such a proposal would take advantage of data semantics upstream of visualisation, since the data to be geovisualised would still be published through standard OGC protocols (such as WMS and WFS). This maintains interoperability with well-known practices and is therefore particularly suitable for improving the achievement of Task 1.

3.2   Client Side

Unlike data stored in traditional DBMSs, a significant amount of Semantic Web data is exposed directly on the Web. This invites thinking about how this data can be consumed directly (i.e. without going through a map server or even other infrastructure elements) from a Web client such as a browser. This is thus linked to Task 2, that could be tackled by the creation of a data exploration and visualisation platform (like Tableau) allowing to load data from the Semantic Web. Such a platform should be able to exploit all the particularities of RDF data when querying. In such an approach, the application could be able, thanks to the exploitation of the semantics of the data to be explored and thanks to the exploitation of the various knowledge bases dedicated to cartography (that can notably be found in [2,8,10,22]) to propose adapted representations (allowing a correct and near-automatic representation). This could be made possible if, to some extent as in the proposals of [7,22], the geovisualisation presented to the user was internally fully described in the form of an RDF graph linking the visualised data to elements, themselves RDF, describing the geovisual aspects (symbols, zoom level, etc.). Moreover, such a tool could also perform (machine) learning operations on the basis of the representations chosen by the user in order to improve its representation suggestion system and parallely, in a subjacent way, make general knowledge about the geovisualisation field evolve.

3.3   In Terms of Knowledge Bases

As stated in Sect. 2, several knowledge bases on cartographic representations are proposed by various authors. They could be completed and/or made operational in order to encode more general knowledge on what a geospatial data visualisation is, and on the possible and appropriate representations methods for data. This could allow to intervene on both Task 1 and Task 2. Especially, the selection mechanisms we proposed in [22] could be extended and completed, making it possible to describe more rules for selecting individuals both for integration in a cartographic server (Task 1, server side) and in the context of a Semantic Web data exploration and visualisation application (Task 2, client side). For example, considering the existing knowledge bases, little work is needed to, given a rule for selecting geospatial RDF individuals, identify the type (in the cartographic sense) of a property qualifying them (qualitative, quantitative variable, etc.) and propose a set of representation rules (necessity to discretise or not the values, formulas for the construction of proportional symbols if necessary, etc.) and appropriate colour palette (already described and classified according to whether the values correspond to a sequential, divergent or categorical scheme in the dicopal ontology we proposed in [22]).

4   Conclusion

Beyond exploiting Semantic Web data, we claim that Semantic Web-based Geo-visualisation is a field that also offers an opportunity to make methods, techniques and tools of geovisualisation evolve so they fully exploit the possibilities offered by the Semantic Web technologies stack. This motivated an approach we have developed [22], based on the state of the art of the last 15 years we have introduced in this paper, whether works be architectural, conceptual or concrete, (namely [2,5,7,8,10,18,20,21]). Based on lessons learned from the state of the art, and on our own work when we have designed, implemented and applied to various case studies our proposal (the framework CoViKoa), we have taken stock of our experience, and introduced some challenges that still have to be faced to improve methods, techniques, and tools for building geovisualisation using geospatial data of the Semantic Web in a more fluid way. We have presented some of them as open questions, but also draw some guidelines, for future works in the field.

Acknowledgements. This work was supported by the French National Research Agency (ANR) as part of the Program ANR-16-CE23-0018 - CHOUCAS.

References

1. Abadie, N., Mechouche, A., Mustière, S.: OWL-based formalisation of geographic databases specifications. In: 17th International Conference on Knowledge Engineering and Knowledge Management (EKAW 2010), Lisbon (Portugal) (2010)
2. Brus, J., Zdena, D., Kanok, J., Pechanec, V.: Design of intelligent system in cartography. In: 9th RoEduNet IEEE International Conference, pp. 112–117 (2010)
3. Carral, D., Scheider, S., Janowicz, K., Vardeman, C., Krisnadhi, A.A., Hitzler, P.: An ontology design pattern for cartographic map scaling. In: Cimiano, P., Corcho, O., Presutti, V., Hollink, L., Rudolph, S. (eds.) ESWC 2013. LNCS, vol. 7882, pp. 76–93. Springer, Heidelberg (2013). https://doi.org/10.1007/978-3-642-38288-8_6
4. Fabrikant, S.: Building task-ontologies for geovisualization. In: Pre-Conference Workshop on Geovisualization on the Web (2001)
5. Fellah, S.: OGC Testbed-12 Semantic Portrayal, Registry and Mediation. Open Geospatial Consortium (2017). http://www.opengis.net/doc/PER/t12-A066
6. Hu, Y.: Geospatial semantics. In: Comprehensive Geographic Information Systems, pp. 80–94. Elsevier (2018)
7. Huang, W., Harrie, L.: Towards knowledge-based geovisualisation using semantic web technologies: a knowledge representation approach coupling ontologies and rules. Int. J. Digit. Earth **13**, 976–997 (2020). https://doi.org/10.1080/17538947.2019.1604835
8. Huang, W., Kazemzadeh, K., Mansourian, A., Harrie, L.: Towards knowledge-based geospatial data integration and visualization: a case of visualizing urban bicycling suitability. IEEE Access **8**, 85473–85489 (2020). https://doi.org/10.1109/ACCESS.2020.2992023
9. Huang, W., Mansourian, A., Abdolmajidi, E., Xu, H., Harrie, L.: Synchronising geometric representations for map mashups using relative positioning and Linked Data. Int. J. Geogr. Inf. Sci. **32**, 1117–1137 (2018). https://doi.org/10.1080/13658816.2018.1441416
10. Iosifescu-Enescu, I., Hurni, L.: Towards cartographic ontologies or "how computers learn cartography". In: Proceedings 23rd International Cartographic Conference, pp. 4–10 (2007)

11. Janowicz, K., Scheider, S., Adams, B.: A geo-semantics flyby. In: Rudolph, S., Gottlob, G., Horrocks, I., van Harmelen, F. (eds.) Reasoning Web 2013. LNCS, vol. 8067, pp. 230–250. Springer, Heidelberg (2013). https://doi.org/10.1007/978-3-642-39784-4_6

12. León, A.D., Wisniewki, F., Villazón-Terrazas, B., Corcho, O.: Map4rdf - faceted browser for geospatial datasets. In: Proceedings of the First Workshop on USING OPEN DATA, W3C (2012)

13. Maué, P., Schade, S.: Data integration in the geospatial semantic web. J. Cases Inf. Technol. 11, 100–122 (2009). https://doi.org/10.4018/jcit.2009072105

14. Penaz, T., Dostal, R., Yilmaz, I., Marschalko, M.: Design and construction of knowledge ontology for thematic cartography domain. Episodes 37, 48–58 (2014). https://doi.org/10.18814/epiiugs/2014/v37i1/006

15. Prudhomme, C., Homburg, T., Ponciano, J.-J., Boochs, F., Cruz, C., Roxin, A.-M.: Interpretation and automatic integration of geospatial data into the Semantic Web. Computing 102(2), 365–391 (2019). https://doi.org/10.1007/s00607-019-00701-y

16. Ruzicka, J., Ruzickova, K., Dostal, R.: Expert system for cartography based on ontology. In: 2013 Fourth Global Congress on Intelligent Systems, pp. 159–163. IEEE (2013)

17. Scheider, S., Ballatore, A., Lemmens, R.: Finding and sharing GIS methods based on the questions they answer. Int. J. Digit. Earth 12, 594–613 (2019). https://doi.org/10.1080/17538947.2018.1470688

18. Smith, R.: Designing a cartographic ontology for use with expert systems. In: Proceedings of the ASPRS/CaGIS 2010 Specialty Conference (2010)

19. Trillos Ujueta, J.M., Trillos Ujueta, A.C., Fernandes Rotger, L.D.: Transforming RDF data into maps: Rdf2map library, pp. 1–10 (2018)

20. Varanka, D.E., Usery, E.L.: The map as knowledge base. Int. J. Cartogr. 4, 201–223 (2018). https://doi.org/10.1080/23729333.2017.1421004

21. Villanova-Oliver, M.: Représentations de connaissances spatiales évolutives: des ontologies aux géovisualisations, Habilitation à Diriger des Recherches, Communauté Université Grenoble Alpes (2018). https://hal.archives-ouvertes.fr/tel-01935490. (in French)

22. Viry, M.: A declarative approach based on Semantic Web technologies to specify and generate adaptive geovisualisations (2021)

23. Viry, M., Villanova-Oliver, M.: How to derive a geovisualization from an application data model: an approach based on Semantic Web technologies. Int. J. Digit. Earth 14, 874–898 (2021). https://doi.org/10.1080/17538947.2021.1900937

24. Wagner, M., Varanka, D.E., Usery, E.L.: A system design for implementing advanced feature descriptions for a map knowledge base. Reston, VA (2020)

25. Zhang, C., Zhao, T., Li, W.: Geospatial Semantic Web (2015)

26. Zhang, C., Zhao, T., Li, W., Osleeb, J.P.: Towards logic-based geospatial feature discovery and integration using web feature service and geospatial semantic web. Int. J. Geogr. Inf. Sci. 24, 903–923 (2010). https://doi.org/10.1080/13658810903240687

A Heterogeneous Information Attentive Network for the Identification of Tourist Attraction Competitors

Jialiang Gao[1,2], Peng Peng[1,2(✉)], Christophe Claramunt[1,3],
and Feng Lu[1,2]

[1] State Key Laboratory of Resources and Environmental Information System,
Institute of Geographic Sciences and Natural Resources Research, Chinese Academy
of Sciences, Beijing 100101, China
pengp@lreis.ac.cn
[2] University of Chinese Academy of Sciences, Beijing 100049, China
[3] Naval Academy Research Institute, 29240 Lanvéoc, France

Abstract. Tourist attraction competition amongst tourist destinations
is a crucial com-ponent of a sustainable growth of tourism destinations,
and it still deserves appropriate studies to identify them as well as appropriate management solu-tions. Existing studies usually focus on mining
tourism locations correla-tions using available statistical data or inference mechanisms applied to tex-tual and cartographical reports. However, a few works apply a combination of qualitative and quantitative
approaches, based on multiple contextual characteristics, to infer tourism
attraction patterns and competition patterns. Over the past few years,
the emergence of social media and Location-Based Services (LBS) in the
tourism sector such as geo-tagged reviews, photos, consuming behaviors, and itineraries, provides a new paradigm for extracting and understanding competition among attractions. This research introduces a Het-
erogenous Information Network (HIN) and Graph Neural Network-based
model to capture the complex contextual features for and identifica-tion
of attraction competitions. Specifically, three categories of LBS data
are processed, extracted, and integrated into a unified HIN, including
tourists' journeys, online text, and spatial attributes. This supports the
exploration of significant regularities of attraction competing contexts.
The GNN-based model, so-called Competitor-GAT, extract spatial distribution properties and semantic correlations. The experiments applied
on a real-world dataset demonstrate the effectiveness of our method.

Keywords: Competitor Identification · Graph Neural Network ·
Heterogeneous Information Network · Spatial Dependency · Semantic
Context · Location-based Service

This research was supported by the National Key Research and Development Program
(2022YFB3904200).

M. A. Mostafavi and G. Del Mondo (Eds.): W2GIS 2023, LNCS 13912, pp. 166–178, 2023.
https://doi.org/10.1007/978-3-031-34612-5_12

1   Introduction

An effective understanding of the competitive environment of the tourism sector has long been a focus of tourism management and business marketing research. This competitive environment is typically volatile, uncertain, complex, and ambiguous (VUCA) [1], implying that customer behaviors must be constantly adapted. Owing to a relatively lower market entry threshold, and changeable tourist demands, tour-ism businesses are confronted with a high risk of losing market share or attractive image collapse. Furthermore, information overload induced by the big data era makes it difficult for tourism businesses to discover new competitors and develop targeted competitive strategies, especially for potential threats with weak signals in peripheral vision. Therefore, competitor identification, as the first step of competi-tive environment screening, has become particularly important.

Most existing studies on detecting competitive relationships are based on entities co-existing in text, and reference relations via websites or social medias. However, these methods are rarely applicable to the tourism sector. The main reasons are two-fold: 1) tourism is not a technology-oriented industry, with quite low data references available 2) Co-existence and co-reference patterns are relatively sparse then mak-ing their identification and non-straightforward task.

Competitor identification in the tourism field can be categorized at two different scales. At the micro-scale, price competition behaviors, for instance among accom-modations or catering, can be identified. For instance, observed daily Best Available Rates along the booking were analyzed via Granger Causality to find the emergence of leader-follower or independent/collusive patterns [2]. At the macro level, a quan-titative analyses of destinations' revenue relationships has been developed (e.g., spatial spillover or shielding effect by Geographically Weighted Regression [3]), or studied using qualitative discussions on tourist destinations' policies. Whereas tour-ist attractions - as the core element of tourism competitiveness - are seldomly inves-tigated, and these above methods are mostly unsuitable for competing attraction detection, partly due to the huge volumes of data generated.

Nowadays, Location-based Service (LBS) data offers new opportunities for min-ing competitive relationships among tourism attractions [4]. Tourism-oriented LBS data is multimodal and multisource, including online reviews, images, travel notes, journeys, and map services, and which provides a comprehensive perspective for attraction competing contexts. However, the integration of large LBS data resources associated to tourism, geo-tagged and temporal data is a non-straightforward task that required the development of appropriate modelling mechanisms. This study introduces a modelling framework for attraction competitor identification based on heterogeneous information networks (HIN) and graph neural networks (GNN). HIN integrates three modes of LBS data as three corresponding subgraphs of a unified schema, including tourists' journeys, online text, and spatial attributes. Contextual characteristics of attraction competitions are studied, particularly, spatial regulari-ties, flows, and semantic relationships. A contextual-based GNN-based model is designed, so-called Competitor-GAT, and that integrates three components: feature generation fused with the spatial distribution and semantic context; feature propagation via a distance-dependency Graph Attentive Network (GAT) [5]; feature output for accurate detecting competitors for attractions.

2   Overview

2.1   Preliminaries

This section introduces the background principles of our network-based models and a few notations.

Theorem 1. *Tourist flow network. A tourist flow network $\{N,E\}$ is defined by a set of journeys associated to a destination city, where nodes N are attractions and edges E valued by tourist flow weights. Edge weights are valued per journey and are aggregated towards a complete graph that denotes all possible relationships between destinations. A complete network model specification is given in [6].*

Theorem 2. *Competitive Relationship. The intuitive understanding of competitive relationship is that attractions i and j frequently emerge in two highly-coincident tourist journeys, e.g. $\{n_1, n_2, \ldots, n_{10}, i\}$ and $\{n_1, n_2, \ldots, n_{10}, j\}$, however, i and j seldomly co-visited in the same journey. In other words, there is a strong fungibility between two attractions. The specific definition is referred to [7] as follow.*

$$w_{ij}/(\frac{(\sum_{(k\in CN(i,j))} w_{ik} + \sum_{(k\in CN(i,j))} w_{jk})}{(2|CN(i,j)|)}) < 0.2 \qquad (1)$$

where $CN(i,j)$ is the common neighbors of i and j, and w_{ij} is the edge weight between i and j. In this study, we consider the competitive relation to have direction, namely, to be asymmetrical. If the tourist volume of current attraction i lower than j, the j is the potential competitor of i, i.e. $y_{(i \leftarrow j)} = 1$.

Theorem 3. *Competitor identification task. The objective of our competitor identification task is to associate each pairs of attraction ij with label $y_{(i \leftarrow j)} \in \{0,1\}$. The proposed Competitor-GAT is to output the possibility of each pairs of attraction in a destination based on HIN G, i.e. $func : (i \times j|G) \rightarrow Y$.*

2.2   Research Framework

The overview of the research framework is illustrated in Fig. 1, which can be divided into three modules: HIN construction, competition context analysis, and

Com-petitor-GAT model. For a comprehensive understanding of the competition phenom-enon among attractions, three modes of data sources are adopted, including tourists' journey data, tourism textual data, and spatial attribute data. First, multimodal data are fused into a unified HIN, where three sources are transformed into three sub-graphs of HIN: spatial distribution, tourist flow network, and Knowledge Graph (de-tails are given in Sect. 3.4). Second, based on HIN, we conduct multiple analyses on the contextual factors of the competition of attractions. The contextual rules of the competition are revealed, respectively corresponding to three aspects: spatial, movement, and semantic. Third, we proposed a new GNN-based deep model to cap-ture the above contextual rules via specific architectures, including spatial-oriented distribution, KGE, and distance dependency. Finally, through this framework, the complete competitive status within a destination can be reflected.

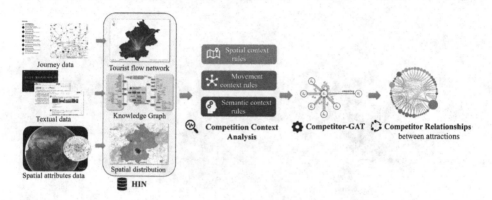

Fig. 1. The overview of the research framework.

2.3   Competition Context Analysis

Spatial Context. Naturally, travel activity is a type of geographical phenomenon with significant spatial context characteristics, such as distance friction and location advantage. It is deemed that these spatial context characteristics will also impact the market competitions among attractions. In this section, the spatial context rules of attraction competing are investigated in three sub-aspects: distance-dependency, spatial distribution, and orientation differentiation. The data used for the analyses come from the famous online travel agency (OTA) platform, MaFengWo.com.

Distance-Dependency. The frequencies of competing relations between two attraction within the same destination city on spatial distance are illustrated in Fig. 2 It demonstrates an approximate Poisson distribution characteristic.

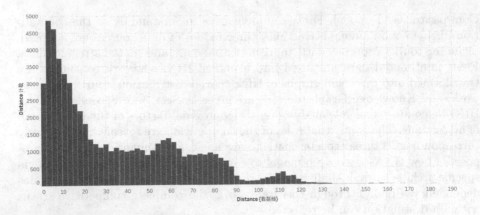

Fig. 2. The frequencies of competing relations on a certain spatial distance interval.

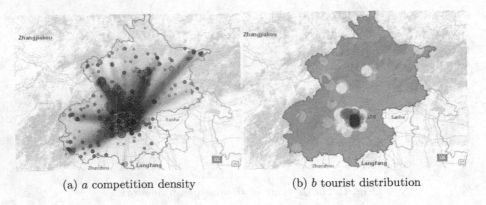

(a) *a* competition density   (b) *b* tourist distribution

Fig. 3. The spatial distribution of competition relationships and tourist volume.

Spatial Distribution. The line density of attraction competitions within the same destination city and tourist volume density are respectively demonstrated in Fig. 3 (a) and (b). A significant correlation between competition and tourist distribution can be observed in space, which means the emergence of competitors has related to their locations.

Orientation Differentiation. The distributed orientation characteristic of competitors can be reflected by Standard Deviational Ellipse (SDE) [8]. We randomly sample three attractions and calculate the SDEs for their competitors, respectively. It demonstrated a distinct orientation differentiation of competitors (Fig. 4).

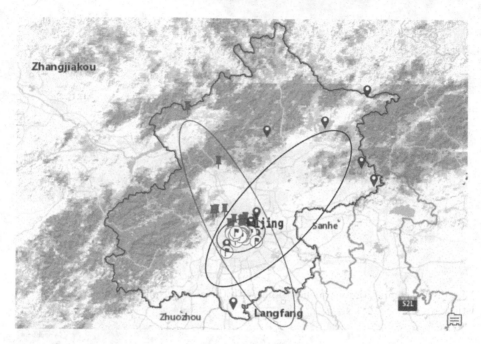

Fig. 4. Standard Deviational Ellipse of competitor-orientated distribution.

Movement Context. The tourist movement context has a decisive influence on competition among attractions. We observe the correlation between the core-periphery structural characteristics of the tourist flow network and the competition frequency. The core-periphery structure represents the modularity characteristics of tourist flow network, which means the close-connected core part, the spare-connected periphery part, and well-connected links between core and periphery. As Fig. 5 illustrated, the overwhelming majority of competition emerges in periphery ← core, namely, the peripheral attractions tend to be under competitive threat by core attractions.

Semantic Context. There is an intuitive phenomenon that the experience, service, activity, or cognition that two attractions provide are more similar, they are more likely to compete. This intuition can be testified by a tourism KG with rich semantic profile information about attraction, whether two attractions with more common semantic aspects within KG (e.g. resource types, activity information, cognitive features and so on) are more frequently competing. The result in Fig. 6 demonstrates that the competing attractions have more common semantic aspects.

2.4 HIN Construction

We integrate three modes of tourism data into a unified HIN schema, where three data sources can be processed, extracted, and transformed into the correspond-

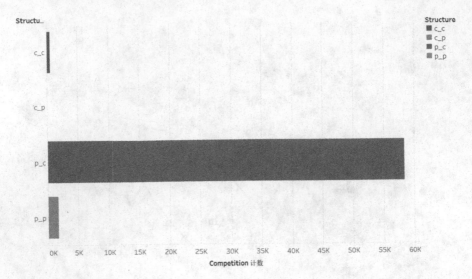

Fig. 5. The competition frequency along with the core-periphery structural characteristics.

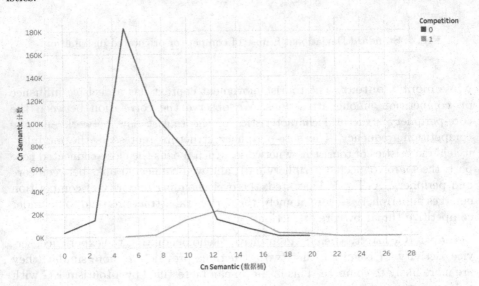

Fig. 6. The similarity between attractions reflected by tourism KG can reflect competition.

ing subgraphs of HIN: spatial density distribution, tourist flow network, and knowledge graph. First, to depict the spatial context of competition, we conduct kernel density estimation for tourist volume with the destination space and add density value as an attraction attribute. Second, tourist flows link attractions to form the movement topological structure. Third, multi-source tourism online text is extracted by a pre-trained language model for the construction of tourism KG, including reviews, publicity profiles, and encyclopedias. The detailed construction procedure and results of tourism KG are referred to [9].

3 Competitor-GAT

The principles of the Competitor-GAT architecture are illustrated in Fig. 7. Competitor-GAT is made of three components: feature generation, propagation, and output. First, feature generation captures the spatial distribution of the attraction in terms of location and orientation, and associates them to their semantic using a KG. Next, feature propagation aggregates the attraction features according to the structure of the tourist flow network to capture movement patterns, and utilize distance to mediate the attention calculation in the GAT model. Third, we transform the three kinds of attraction features to output the existence possibility of competitive relation $i \leftarrow j$.

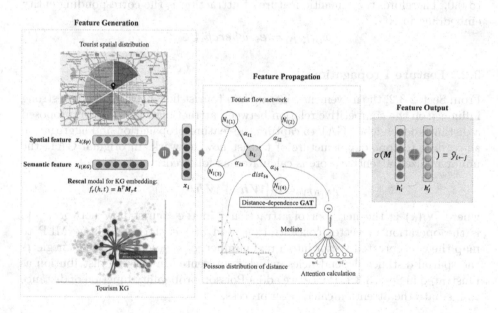

Fig. 7. The Framework of Competitor-GAT architecture.

3.1 Feature Generation

Spatial Feature Generation. From Sect. 2.3.1, the competition relations are highly correlated to the spatial distribution of tourists and biased on different orientations. To capture this spatial context feature, we build the circle buffer area for every attraction, with the radius L regarded as a hyper-parameter.

The buffer is further divided into several oriented sectors (e.g. 6). The tourist density of each oriented sector is set as the dimension of spatial feature vector $x_{(i(Sp))}$. For the convenience of aggregation to the semantic feature, we align the dimension by linear transformation and set element as 0 when the dimension exceeds the number of orientations.

$$x_{(i(Sp))} = W_{align} x_{(i(Sp))}^6 \tag{2}$$

Semantic Feature Generation. From Sect. 2.3.3, the pair of attractions with similar semantic context are more likely to compete. We obtain the semantic feature of attraction from the tourist KG in virtue of KGE model, RESCAL [10]. The score function $f_r(h, t)$ of a triple (h, r, t) in KG is defined as followed,

$$f_r(h, t) = h^T M_r t \tag{3}$$

where the M_r is the matrix of relation r, h and t are the embedding of head h and tail t entity. If the triple exists in KG, the $f_r(h, t)$ should gain on 1.0; reversely to 0.0. Therefore, the semantic feature of attraction is the corresponding entity embedding in KG.

$$x_{(i(KG))} = e_i, where h, t \in e \tag{4}$$

3.2   Feature Propagation

From Sect. 2.3.2, the movement context from tourist flow network exerts a strong influence on the competitive relation between attractions. This section proposed a distance-dependency GAT to capture the feature propagation and aggregation ac-cording to topology structure of tourist flow network. In original GAT, the unnor-malized attentive score is calculated as followed:

$$e_{i,N_{(i(k))}} = a([W h_i \| W h_{(N_i(k))}]) \tag{5}$$

where $N_i(k)$ is the neighbor of attraction i in the tourist flow network, $[\cdot\|\cdot]$ is the operation of vector concentration, and $a(\cdot)$ is the single large MLP to map the concentrated vector into a real number, $e_{i,N_{(i(k))}}$. This process neglects the spatial distance dependencies, which is presented in Poisson distribution as illustrated in Sect. 3.3.1. Hence, we add a Poisson probability function of distance to mediate the attention calculation process.

$$e_{i,N_i(k)}' = P(dist) \cdot e_{i,N_i(k)} = \frac{\lambda^{dist}}{dist!} \exp{-\lambda} \cdot e_{i,N_i(k)}, dist = 0, 1, \cdots \tag{6}$$

where $dist$ is the discretization internal index of distances between attraction with the interval length (e.g. 2 km), namely, $dist = 0, when 0 \le distance_{i,N_{(i(k))}} < 2km$.

Then, $e_{i,N_{i(k)}}'$ is normalized by $Softmax(\cdot)$ and $LeakyReLU(\cdot)$.

$$\alpha_{i,N_i(k)} = \frac{exp(LeakyReLU(e_{i,N_{i(k)}}'))}{\sum_{k \in N_i} exp(LeakyReLU(e_{i,N_i(k)}'))} \tag{7}$$

$$LeakyReLU(x) = \max{(0, x)} + leak \times min(0, x), e.g.leak = 0.02 \qquad (8)$$

Next, we utilize $\alpha_{i,N_{i(k)}}$ to aggregate the neighbors' message $h_{N_i(k)}$ to update h_i.

$$h'_i = \sigma(sum_{k \in N_i} alpha_{i,N_{i(k)}} W_{\alpha} h_{N_i(k)}) \qquad (9)$$

Attention $alpha_{i,N_{i(k)}}$ can be a multi-head attentive mechanism, and the final h'_i is calculated as follow,

$$h'_i(H) = \prod_{h=1}^{H} \sigma(sum_{k \in N_i} \alpha_{i,N_{i(k)}} W_{\alpha}^h h_{N_i(k)}) \qquad (10)$$

where H is the number of ensemble channels.

3.3 Feature Output

The existence possibility of competing relation $i \leftarrow j$ is predicted by a fully-connected layer with joint h'_i and bmh'_j.

$$\hat{y}_{i \leftarrow j} = sigmoid(W_o \cdot (h'_i \bigoplus h'_j)) \qquad (11)$$

The Cross-Entropy loss function is adopted to train Competitor-GAT over all labeled pairs of attractions i←j.

$$\mathcal{L} = \sum_{i \leftarrow j \in Pairs} y(i \leftarrow j) log \hat{y}_{i \leftarrow j} + (1 - y_{i \leftarrow j}) log(1 - \hat{y}_{i \leftarrow j}) + \| \theta \|_2^F \qquad (12)$$

where the second term is $F2$ regularization for all parameters in Competitor-GAT.

3.4 Learning Process

The training process of Competitor-GAT is as follows.

4 Experiment

4.1 Settings

Dataset. We testify the performance of Competitor-GAT on two real-world datasets in Beijing and Shanghai, which contains 832 attractions. The ground truth of com-petitive relations is constructed by the tourism data from January 2013 to April 2019, which amounts to 60,597. **Baselines.** Two types of base-lines are compared, i.e. GCN and KGE models. Specifi-cally, GraphSAGE [11] on behalf of GCN is conducted on a competitive network among attractions con-structed from competition relations. TransH [12] -a repre-sentative KGE model- is adopted to link-prediction on an enhanced KG, which in-cludes competitive relation as a triplet. **Evaluation Metrics.** Area Under Curve (AUC) is selected as the evaluation metric for the performance of competitor identification.

Algorithm 1   *Competitor-GAT* training process

Input: three contextual features: $\{\mathcal{G}_{geo}, \mathcal{G}_{semantic}, \mathcal{G}_{behaviour}\}$

   competition relationship set: $\{y_{i \leftarrow j} | Y\}$

Output: competition prediction function: $func: (i \times j | G) \rightarrow Y$

1. Spatial feature calculation: [Calculation of tourist density in buffer zone]

$$x_{i(Sp)} = W_{align} x^6_{i(Sp)}$$

2. Semantic feature generation: [KGE by RESCAL model]

$$x_{i(KG)} = e_i, where\ h, t \in \mathcal{G}_{semantic}$$

3. while $\triangle|\Theta|$ do:
4.   for *Head* do:
5.   for Hop do:
6.   The aggregation attention of adjacent attractions is calculated according to

   equations (5, 6, 7): $e'_{i,N_{i(k)}}, \ a_{i,N_{i(k)}}$

7.   Information aggregation of adjacent attractions as equation (9):

$$x'_i = \sigma(\textstyle\sum_{k \in N_i} a_{i,N_{i(k)}} W_a x_{N_{i(k)}})$$

8.   end
9.   Concatenate the features of the head attention according to Equation (10):

$$x'_i(Head) = x'_i(Head - 1) || x'_i$$

10.   end
11.   Calculate the loss function according to Equation (11):

$$\mathcal{L} = \textstyle\sum_{i \leftarrow j \in Pairs} y_{i \leftarrow j} log \hat{y}_{i \leftarrow j} + (1 - y_{i \leftarrow j}) log(1 - \hat{y}_{i \leftarrow j}) + ||\Theta||^F_2$$

12.   Gradient descent updates the model parameters:

$$\partial \mathcal{L} / W_a, \ \partial \mathcal{L} / W_{align}$$

13. end
14. return $\hat{y}_{i \leftarrow j} = func(x'_i, x'_j)$

4.2   Results

Compared with state-of-the-art baselines in competitor identification, our Competi-tor-GAT achieves 10.1 19.5% performance improvement. This result certifies the effectiveness of modeling multiple contextual rules in GNN to realize precise pre-diction (Table 1).

5   Conclusion

This study addresses the competitor identification problem for tourist attractions, which is conducive to the tourism management domain. Three modes of tourism data about attractions are integrated into a unified HIN, and the comprehensive ex-ploration of the regularities of multiple contextual characteristics

Table 1. Performance of competitor identification

Model	Beijing AUC	Shanghai AUC
GraphSAGE	0.750	0.682
TransH	0.691	0.656
Competitor-GAT	0.826	0.781

is conducted. Based on the HIN, we design the Competitor-GAT model aiming at capturing the special rules of attraction competition and overcoming the limitations of GNN's feature generation and message-passing. The experimental results on real-world datasets testify to the effectiveness of Competitor-GAT over baselines on attraction competitor mining.

Acknowledgements. This research was supported by the National Key Research and Development Program (2022YFB3904200) and the National Natural Science Foundation of China (42001391). The authors also appreciate Chinese Academy of Sciences President's International Fellowship Initiative (2021VTA0002) and the Yongth Project of Innovation LREIS (YPI002).

References

1. Werle, M., Laumer, S.: Competitor identification: a review of use cases, data sources, and algorithms. Int. J. Inf. Manag. **65**, 102507 (2022)
2. Guizzardi, A., Pons, F.M.E., Ranieri, E.: Competition patterns, spatial and advance booking effects in the accommodation market online. Tour. Manage. **71**, 476–489 (2019)
3. Yang, Y., Fik, T.: Spatial effects in regional tourism growth. Ann. Tour. Res. **46**, 144–162 (2014)
4. Li, S., et al.: Competitive analysis for points of interest. In: Proceedings of the 26th ACM SIGKDD International Conference on Knowledge Discovery & Data Mining 2020, Virtual Event, USA, vol. 1050, p. 20 (2020)
5. Velickovic, P., et al.: Graph attention networks. Stat **1050**, 20 (2017)
6. Xu, Y., et al.: Impact of COVID-19 on tourists' travel intentions and behaviors: the case study of Hong Kong, China. In: Karimipour, F., Storandt, S. (eds.) Web and Wireless Geographical Information Systems. Springer, Cham (2022). https://doi.org/10.1007/978-3-031-06245-2_2
7. Gao, J., et al.: A multi-scale comparison of tourism attraction networks across China. Tour. Manage. **90**, 104489 (2022)
8. Gong, J.: Clarifying the standard deviational ellipse. Geogr. Anal. **34**(2), 155–167 (2002)
9. Jialiang, G., et al.: Construction of tourism attraction knowledge graph based on web text and transfer learning. Geomat. Inf. Sci. Wuhan Univ. **47**(8), 1191–1200 (2022)
10. Nickel, M., Tresp, V., Kriegel, H.-P.: A three-way model for collective learning on multi-relational data. In: Proceedings of the 28th International Conference on International Conference on Machine Learning 2011, Bellevue, Washington, USA, pp. 809–816 (2011)

178   J. Gao et al.

11. Hamilton, W., Ying, Z., Leskovec, J.: Inductive representation learning on large graphs. In: Proceedings of the 31st International Conference on Neural Information Processing Systems 2017, Red Hook, NY, USA, vol. 30, pp. 1025–1035 (2017)
12. Wang, Z., et al.: Knowledge graph embedding by translating on hyperplanes. In: Proceedings of the AAAI Conference on Artificial Intelligence, Canada, pp. 1112–1119 (2014)

Poly-GAN: Regularizing Polygons with Generative Adversarial Networks

Lasith Niroshan(✉) and James D. Carswell(✉)

Technological University Dublin, Dublin, Ireland
d19126805@mytudublin.ie, james.carswell@TUDublin.ie

Abstract. Regularizing polygons involves simplifying irregular and noisy shapes of built environment objects (e.g. buildings) to ensure that they are accurately represented using a minimum number of vertices. It is a vital processing step when creating/transmitting online digital maps so that they occupy minimal storage space and bandwidth. This paper presents a data-driven and Deep Learning (DL) based approach for regularizing OpenStreetMap building polygon edges. The study introduces a building footprint regularization technique (*Poly*-GAN) that utilises a Generative Adversarial Network model trained on irregular building footprints and OSM vector data. The proposed method is particularly relevant for map features predicted by Machine Learning (ML) algorithms in the GIScience domain, where information overload remains a significant problem in many cartographic/LBS applications. It addresses the limitations of traditional cartographic regularization/generalization algorithms, which can struggle with producing both accurate and minimal representations of multisided built environment objects. Furthermore, future work proposes a way to test the method on even more complex object shapes to address this limitation.

Keywords: Geographic Information System · Polygon
Regularization · Generative Adversarial Networks · OpenStreetMap

1 Introduction

Polygon *regularization*, also known as simplification/generalization, is a vital image processing step when digitising object shapes predicted from aerial/satellite imagery using Machine Learning (ML)/Deep Learning (DL) change detection algorithms. Overcoming the formation of built environment objects (e.g. buildings) with stair-like edges or otherwise irregular shapes (Fig. 1a) remains a challenging topic much discussed in the computer vision and GIScience/Digital Earth domain [9].

Many related studies propose statistical or ML/DL based solutions for polygon detection/regularization. For example, in our previous work, an ML-based spatial change detection mechanism (called *OSM-GAN*) was proposed using satellite images and OpenStreetMap (OSM) vector data [12,13]. The output

M. A. Mostafavi and G. Del Mondo (Eds.): W2GIS 2023, LNCS 13912, pp. 179–193, 2023.
https://doi.org/10.1007/978-3-031-34612-5_13

of this approach is an outline of any changed building object(s) in raster format, which then needs to be vectorised prior to uploading into online mapping platforms like OSM [14]. However, the outlined object first needs to be simplified (regularized) to represent the same map feature using a minimum number of vertices before the vectorisation process begins (Fig. 1b). This new research extends previous work by appending to the DeepMapper [10] automated map update workflow an additional ML-based regularization process (called *Poly*-GAN) designed to produce fully vectorized map features having a minimum number of nodes.

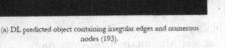

(a) DL predicted object containing irregular edges and numerous nodes (193).

(b) A simplified (regularized) version of the object containing a minimum number of nodes (6).

Fig. 1. Non-regularized (a) and regularized (b) building footprints.

In other words, this investigation mimics the ML-based OSM-GAN change detection mechanism already used by *DeepMapper* to now include *Poly*-GAN, another Generative Adversarial Network (GAN) model - this time specifically trained to the purpose of polygon regularization.

This paper is structured into five sections, including this Introduction. Section 2 follows by providing more background on the topic of polygon regularization and the challenges it presents for image analysis. Section 3 provides a detailed explanation of the *Poly*-GAN modelling mechanism, highlighting its advantages and innovations. It describes the complete polygon regularization methodology including data preparation, pre- and post-processing, and refining polygon edges with GANs. Section 4 presents some experimental results and a discussion of their implications. Finally, Sect. 5 concludes the paper and discusses potential future research directions.

2 Background

Traditional cartographic regularization approaches have issues with producing both accurate and minimal representations of complex built environment structures. These algorithms depend on pre-defined threshold values that need to be discovered empirically or consist of deterministic rules (IF-THEN-ELSE) instead of rules derived from the data - as in Machine Learning approaches. Consequently, traditional methods to address these issues can adversely affect polygon regularization accuracy, while ML/DL-based methods can produce more consistently reliable results.

Briefly, traditional regularization algorithms commonly include the *Lang simplification algorithm* [6], the *Ramer-Douglas-Peucker* (RDP) algorithm [16], the *Zhao-Saalfed algorithm* [27], *Opheim simplification* algorithm [15] and the *Reumann-Witkam* algorithm [17]. Figure 2 illustrates the behaviour of each algorithm applied to a sample non-regularized building footprint. In addition to these algorithms, *perpendicular distance simplification*[1] was also implemented and tested in this study.

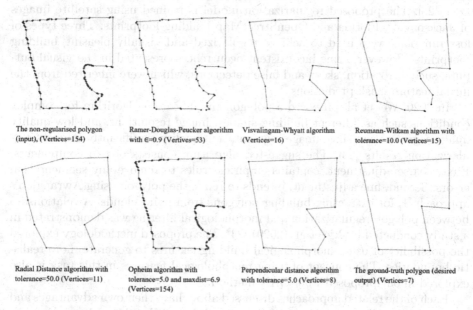

The non-regularised polygon (input), (Vertices=154)   Ramer-Douglas-Peucker algorithm with ∈=0.9 (Vertives=53)   Visvalingam-Whyatt algorithm (Vertices=16)   Reumann-Witkam algorithm with tolerance=10.0 (Vertices=15)

Radial Distance algorithm with tolerance=50.0 (Vertices=11)   Opheim algorithm with tolerance=5.0 and maxdist=6.9 (Vertices=154)   Perpendicular distance algorithm with tolerance=5.0 (Vertices=8)   The ground-truth polygon (desired output) (Vertices=7)

Fig. 2. A comparison of traditional regularization algorithms on a noisy polygon in terms of node reduction, shape simplification, and edge smoothness. The total number of nodes (vertices) produced in each case is also given.

In 2012, Sohn et al. proposed a regularization method for building rooftop models using LiDAR data [20]. The proposed method is based on Minimum

---

[1] https://psimpl.sourceforge.net/perpendicular-distance.html.

Description Length (MDL) theory and comprises two stages: 1) Hypothesis generation and 2) Global Optimisation. Lu et al. (2018) used a richer convolutional feature (RCF) network to create an edge probability map (i.e. a map of building footprints) and an edge refinement process according to morphological analysis of the topographic surface [8]. These approaches primarily tried to improve the edge refinement process by addressing issues such as stair-like noise, isolated points, and outliers using a non-maximal suppression (NMS) algorithm. Their methods outperform the NMS algorithm in terms of accuracy.

A study by Zhao et al. investigated a data-driven approach for boundary regularization along with a machine-learning approach to building extraction from satellite images [26]. This approach includes three steps: 1) Initial modelling, 2) Hypothesis generation, and 3) Minimum Description Length (MDL) optimisation. At the initial modelling, the Ramer-Douglas-Peucker algorithm was applied to simplify the initial polygon. In the next phase, local hypothetical models were generated using a set of temporal points and lines. Finally, MDL optimisation was performed to assert the optimal hypothesis among local hypotheses.

Zorzi and Fraundorfer (2019) proposed an approach inspired by style transfer techniques that utilise adversarial losses to generate accurate building boundaries [28]. The proposed regularization model is trained using satellite images of Jacksonville, Florida and OpenStreetMap building footprints. Three types of loss functions were used to achieve regularized and visually pleasing building footprints. However, some inconsistent occurrences presented in the visual outputs, such as rotation, skew, and false detections, which were inherited from the initial feature mask predictions.

In 2020, Wei et al. proposed a polygon simplification algorithm for complex conditions such as different building shapes, image resolutions, and low-quality image segmentation since image segmentation quality significantly impacts regularization results [23]. The suggested algorithm consists of two components. First, coarse adjustment, contains empirical rules to remove any segmentation errors. Second, fine adjustment, intends to refine the polygon using Awrangjeb's approach [1] for extracting building polygons from point clouds. A relationship between polygon regularization and morphological filtering was demonstrated in a study conducted by Xie et al. (2020) [24]. The proposed methodology explored the possibility of using morphological building features to generate more realistic boundaries. The concept of using morphological features in this task is also explored in our proposed *Poly*-GAN method.

Each of the related approaches discussed above have their own advantages and disadvantages. When working with geospatial data, it has been shown that the method used must be specifically adapted to the characteristics of the area being mapped. In other words, classification performance depends on the morphological features and other local spatial data attributes. Such uncertainty encouraged this study to utilise state-of-the-art Deep Learning techniques and crowdsourced geo-data to propose a more reliable regularization mechanism. As such, this paper introduces *Poly*-GAN, a novel solution inspired by image-to-image translation for addressing the polygon regularization problem that uses large volumes of crowd-sourced geo-data to train data-hungry real-world ML models.

3   Methodology

The following Sections describe in more detail the proposed GAN-based polygon regularization algorithm (*Poly*-GAN), including pre- and post-processing procedures.

3.1   Data Preparation

Data preparation is a necessary part of ML-based research, particularly for Deep Learning models [7]. To develop an effective DL model for polygon simplification, both noisy and corresponding ground truth data are essential for training. This study uses OSM-GAN predicted building polygons for noisy data, while OSM building footprints were used as the ground truth component for training polygon simplification models.

After the OSM-GAN model generates the feature-map for a given satellite image, the noisy predicted building polygons are separated using an *instance segmentation* process. Following the creation of these predicted footprint segments, a lookup process is launched to retrieve the corresponding OSM building footprint in a local vector map database. A filtering mechanism removes anomalous data (i.e. incorrect OSM-GAN polygons) from the dataset when both components are present. Finally, the filtered data is combined into a 600×300 pixel image for input into the DL model training process. The building footprints were not zoomed to the size of the input images to maintain consistency of prediction results. Figure 3 (left half) illustrates some of the different building objects predicted by the OSM-GAN model together with their "ground truth" counterparts.

3.2   *Poly*-GAN Modelling

The Generative Adversarial Network (GAN) modelling architecture consists of two main components (each a Neural Network): the *Generator* and the *Discriminator*. The Generator component of the GAN is responsible for producing new

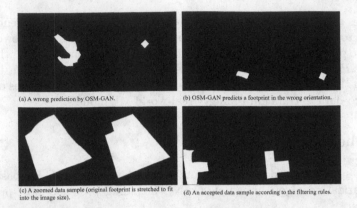

(a) A wrong prediction by OSM-GAN.

(b) OSM-GAN predicts a footprint in the wrong orientation.

(c) A zoomed data sample (original footprint is stretched to fit into the image size).

(d) An accepted data sample according to the filtering rules.

Fig. 3. Different forms of data samples used in this study. All left side objects were predicted by OSM-GAN model; right side objects are "ground truth" building footprints taken from OSM. First two samples (a and b) were not accepted and filtered out of the *Poly*-GAN training dataset.

(but fake), regularized polygons by learning from a dataset of previously regularized polygons (ground truth data). The Discriminator component then attempts to determine whether the generated polygons are real or fake to improve the Generator's ability to produce realistic polygons. The two components work together in a competition, with the Generator trying to produce more realistic polygons and the Discriminator trying to become better at identifying fake polygons.

The main idea behind image-to-image translation in a ML context is that a given input image (e.g. sketch/outline of an object) translates or transforms into another higher-level representation (e.g. photo-realistic image) of the set of input information. Isola et al. [4] presented several generalized uses of Conditional GAN based image-to-image translation, such as labels-to-street scenes, black&white images-to-colour images, sketches-to-photos, and especially aerial images-to-maps, which is important for this study. Pix2Pix is their implementation of image-to-image translation, which is freely available for use on GitHub[2].

This study uses an updated version of Pix2Pix in its polygon regularization modelling experiments. Once data samples were prepared and split into *train* and validation categories, they were then uploaded to Kay[3], Ireland's national supercomputer, to train the proposed *Poly*-GAN regularization model. Kay cuts model training times from a few days on a typical "gamer-spec" laptop to a few hours - allowing to train and test multiple models relatively quickly with different hyperparameters and datasets [11]. The following hyperparameters (Table 1) were applied to train the *Poly*-GAN model.

---

[2] https://github.com/junyanz/pytorch-CycleGAN-and-pix2pix.
[3] https://www.ichec.ie/about/infrastructure/kay.

Table 1. Values for key hyperparameters used in the *Poly*-GAN model training process.

Name	Value	Description
batch_size	1	Number of images in a batch
gan_mode	vanilla	The type of GAN objective. (i.e. vanilla, lsgan, wgangp)
init_gain	0.02	Scaling factor for the network
init_type	normal	Network initialisation method
input_nc	1	Number of input image channels
output_nc	1	Number of output image channels
lr	0.0002	Initial learning rate for adam optimisation
lr_policy	linear	Learning rate policy
n_epochs	100	Number of epochs with the initial learning rate
ndf	64	Number of discriminative filters in the first conv layer
ngf	64	Number of generative filters in the first conv layer
netD	basic	The type of the discriminator architecture
netG	unet_256	The type of the generator architecture
pre-process	resize_and_crop	Scaling and cropping of images at load time

3.3 A Combined Regularization Method

Poly-GAN aims to improve the accuracy and efficiency of polygon regularization by combining data-driven and DL-based regularization methods into a single solution. Using a Generative Adversarial Network in this approach allows for a supervised learning technique, where the network can learn from a dataset of previously regularized polygons. Once an irregular building footprint is obtained (predicted) from the OSM-GAN change detection process, a pre-processing step stores its geo-referenced coordinates. Simultaneously, the Ramer-Douglas-Peucker (RDP) algorithm processes the building's shape to reduce the number of redundant polygon nodes and simplify it for input to the GAN-based regularization modelling procedure.

The refined/simplified polygon is then further processed to generate an input data sample for training the *Poly*-GAN model. An overview of the process is shown in Fig. 4 and consists of two phases: the training phase and the prediction phase. The training phase involves the use of a dataset of ground-truth building footprints to train the *Poly*-GAN model. The prediction phase involves the use of the now trained *Poly*-GAN model to regularize the predicted building footprints obtained from the OSM-GAN change detection process.

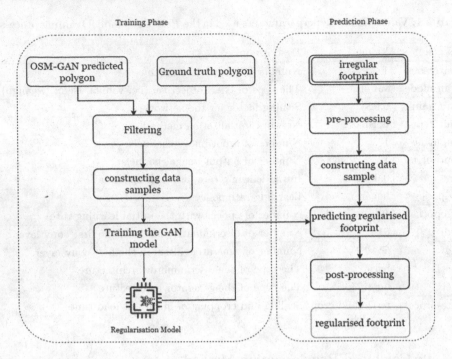

Fig. 4. Schematic diagram of the polygon regularization process linking the *Poly*-GAN model training phase to the (predicted) building regularization phase.

Pre-processing. As mentioned, the pre-processing step for the proposed building regularization procedure begins by storing the geo-referenced coordinates of the predicted building footprint generated by the OSM-GAN change detection algorithm. However, analysis of the OSM-GAN results show that the generated footprints can contain a considerable number of redundant nodes, which can affect the accuracy of polygon regularization. In this case, the RDP algorithm is applied to perform node reduction while preserving the overall shape of the predicted building footprint.

The RDP algorithm is a popular algorithm for polygon simplification that aims to reduce the number of vertices in a polygon while preserving the shape of the polygon as much as possible. The simplification is performed by identifying and removing redundant vertices that are not essential to the overall shape of the polygon. The algorithm works by iteratively removing vertices that are within a specified distance tolerance, called *epsilon*, from a straight line connecting the start and end vertices of the polygon. The RDP algorithm is simple, fast, and efficient, making it a popular choice for polygon regularization in GIScience, cartography, and computer vision domains [21]. Additionally, this algorithm is easy to implement and does not require complex parameter tuning, making it useful for various dataset types. In Fig. 5, the footprints generated by the

OSM-GAN change detection algorithm are compared with the simplified foot-prints produced by RDP.

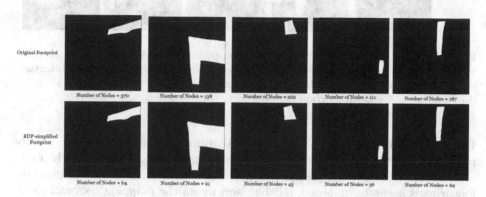

Fig. 5. Comparison of original input footprints returned from OSM-GAN algorithm (top row) and RDP-simplified footprints (bottom row). The captions show the number of nodes in each.

After applying the RDP algorithm, the pre-processed footprint is saved into a 300×300 pixel black&white image; this is used as the inference data sample in the next step. This pre-processing procedure ensures that the input data to the GAN-based regularization algorithm is a cleaned, pre-processed version of the initially predicted (noisy) footprint. This helps to produce a more accurate and reliable regularization of the building's footprint in the next step.

Refining Polygon Edges with Generative Adversarial Networks. The above pre-processed building footprint is then combined with an empty mask, resulting in an image that is 300×600 pixels in size. The empty mask, which is 300×300 pixels, serves as a placeholder for the generator to fill in with the regularized polygon. By providing the generator with a clear distinction between the building footprint and the area to be regularized, the GAN can focus on making changes to the specific area of the image that needs to be regularized. This process continues until the Generator produces polygons (i.e. buildings) that are indistinguishable from real ones. The final *Poly*-GAN regularization model developed in this work also reshapes irregular building footprints in order to make them more "regular". The result of this combined approach is dependent on the quality of the dataset used for training the GAN, as well as the specific architecture and hyperparameters chosen for the GAN. Finally, the predicted footprint is passed through a post-processing procedure to assess its quality and create an OSM-acceptable changeset. Figure 6 illustrates the prediction results from the GAN-based regularization model.

188   L. Niroshan and J. D. Carswell

Fig. 6. Regularized building footprints after applying the GAN-based regularization method to map objects shown in bottom row of Fig. 5. The *Poly*-GAN architecture learns to reshape the irregular building footprints while preserving the overall shape of the building and other important features such as corners.

Post-processing. Once *Poly*-GAN regularization simplifies the building footprint, the result is passed through a post-processing procedure to refine the footprint further. Overall, the post-processing steps aim to ensure that the building footprint is accurate, minimal, reliable, and meets the mapping conventions of OSM. The output of this step is a high-quality regularized building footprint that can be uploaded to the online OSM dataset.

The first step in the post-processing phase is to extract the GAN-regularized footprint from the 300 × 600 pixel image and re-apply the coordinates that were recorded in the pre-processing phase. Then a *perpendicular distance algorithm* (PD) is applied to the extracted footprint since experiments show this to be a reliable and accurate method for producing building footprints with minimal nodes while preserving the overall shape of the building (See Fig. 2).

This algorithm works by measuring the perpendicular distance between a point and a line and removing the point if it falls within a specified threshold distance from the line (Fig. 7). The algorithm does not require complex parameter tuning, which makes it useful for various dataset types, and it is relatively fast and efficient, which makes it suitable for use in real-time applications.

After the PD algorithm is applied, the *Poly*-GAN generated footprints are re-georeferenced using the geo-data stored during the pre-processing step. Re-georeferencing the footprints using the pre-processing stored geo-data assumes that the original geo-data is accurate and that the GAN-generated footprints are aligned with the original raster image.

Finally, an OSM-acceptable changeset is built, containing any modifications made to the *Poly*-GAN simplified footprint that passed the post-processing procedure. The post-processing procedure aims to ensure that the resulting footprint is of high quality and meets the requirements of OSM mapping conventions. This may include editing the positions of building vertices, merging or splitting polygons, and adding/removing attributes for polygons. The output from this step is a reliable, accurate, and regularized building footprint which can be uploaded to the online OSM dataset.

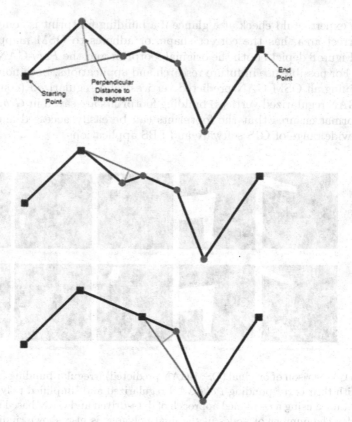

Fig. 7. The perpendicular distance algorithm for polygon simplification. Initially, the first and third nodes are used to define a line segment, and the perpendicular distance to the second node is calculated and compared against a given threshold. After that, the algorithm is moved to the next node pairs which are the second and fourth. If the calculated distance is lower than the threshold the node gets removed from the polygon, and so on.

4   Results and Discussion

In the ML domain of generative models, such as GANs, it is suggested that qualitative analysis is often more informative and effective than quantitative analysis, as it provides a more comprehensive understanding of the generated samples [5,22]. Quantitative analysis metrics, for instance, *Fréchet Inception Distance* [3] or *Inception Score* [18], can provide a good indication of the quality of the generated data samples, but these metrics only provide a limited view of generated samples.

When working with GANs, qualitative analysis can help to understand the biases that the model has learned from the training data, which can be important for avoiding unwanted consequences. In relation to *Poly*-GAN, qualitative analysis was used in the experiments, which has several advantages. For example, a human expert could check at a glance if a building footprint is complete, covers the correct area, has the correct shape, or adheres to OSM mapping conventions. Figure 8 depicts both the original footprint and the *Poly*-GAN regularized result. For possible use in future research and applications, both non-regularized (containing all OSM-GAN predicted vertices) and regularized (containing only *Poly*-GAN regularized vertices) building footprints are saved in *GeoJson* format. This format ensures that the footprints can be easily accessed and integrated into a wide range of GIS software and LBS applications.

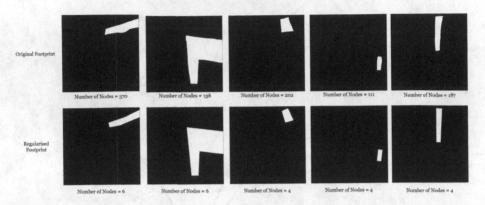

Fig. 8. Comparison of original (OSM-GAN predicted) irregular building footprints (top row) with their corresponding *Poly*-GAN regularized and simplified polygons (bottom row) obtained using a combined approach of data-driven and GAN-based regularization methods. The number of nodes in the final polygons is also shown, indicating object complexity reduction while preserving the building's overall shape.

Polygon regularization is important in the context of digital maps, such as OpenStreetMap, because it helps to improve the accuracy and uniformity/consistency of online map data [2,19]. The regularization process can correct errors and inconsistencies in the map data and make it more consistent with the real world. In the case of OSM, map data is often contributed by many volunteers, which can lead to inconsistencies in the data. For example, building footprints can be irregular and inconsistent in shape, size, and orientation. Regularization can correct these inconsistencies and make the building footprints more uniform with surrounding real-world buildings. Polygon regularization can also improve the quality of map data used for further analysis in other mapping applications - like 3D modelling, solar exposure/energy consumption analysis, and emergency planning. Additionally, regularization can reduce the overall complexity of map data, which can make it easier to work with and improve the performance of LBS applications by helping to reduce information overload [25].

It is important to note that the quality of the *reshaping* produced by *Poly*-GAN is dependent on several factors. The dataset used for training the GAN should be of high quality, containing a diverse set of building footprints that are representative of the real-world buildings that the GAN will be used to regularize. Additionally, the architecture and hyperparameters of the GAN should be carefully chosen to ensure that it can effectively reshape the footprints while preserving the overall shape of the building and important building features such as corners.

One limitation of the method presented is that it has not yet been tested on circular objects or other complex building shapes, such as buildings with empty areas (holes) inside. These types of shapes can present unique challenges for regularization and simplification, as they may require different threshold values or algorithms compared to more uniform, orthogonal building shapes. This limitation highlights the need for further research and experimentation to develop methods to effectively handle these types of shapes. In this regard, the effectiveness of the approach should be trained and tested on larger geographic datasets to optimise the architecture and hyperparameters of the GAN model and further improve the reshaping performance to suit the built environment where it is used.

5   Conclusions

The experiments carried out in this study show promising results in terms of extracting the key building vertices needed to preserve the overall shape of a building, and the final regularized polygon being acceptable for updating online mapping platforms such as OSM.

This combined polygon regularization approach integrates data-driven and Deep Learning-based methods. It was applied to irregular building footprints obtained from OSM-GAN change detection, where a pre-processing step involved storing geo-referenced coordinate data and applying the RDP algorithm (*epsilon* = 0.9) to reduce redundant polygon nodes. The reduced polygon was then used as input for the *Poly*-GAN algorithm, which aimed to regularize building footprints while preserving their overall shape. As a post-processing step, the regularized polygons were further refined using the Perpendicular Distance algorithm to extract key building vertices (e.g. corners) while continuing to maintain the overall shape of the building.

The work presented in this paper is a part of a comprehensive online map updating solution (called *DeepMapper*) that endeavours to provide an end-to-end automated workflow for populating OSM [10]. The complete solution is in final stages of development and includes several important components: geo-data (raster/vector) crawling and indexing, GAN-based change detection, GAN-based regularization, quality analysis, and OSM changeset creation and map updating. This fully integrated prototype aims to improve the accuracy, consistency, and efficiency of the online map-updating process by automating many of the manual tasks that VGI mappers typically carry out. This research is a step forward in improving the consistency and quality of crowdsourced maps and is expected to lead to further developments (e.g. regularizing complex objects and other map feature types) in the future.

Acknowledgements. The authors wish to thank all VGI contributors involved with the OpenStreetMap project. This research is funded by Technological University Dublin College of Arts and Tourism, SEED FUNDING INITIATIVE 2019-2020. The authors wish to acknowledge the Irish Centre for High-End Computing (ICHEC) for the provision of supercomputing facilities. We also gratefully acknowledge Ordinance Survey Ireland (OSi) for providing both raster and vector ground truth data used to verify accuracy experiments.

References

1. Awrangjeb, M.: Using point cloud data to identify, trace, and regularize the outlines of buildings. Int. J. Remote Sens. **37**(3), 551–579 (2016)
2. Grinberger, A.Y., Minghini, M., Juhász, L., Yeboah, G., Mooney, P.: OSM science-the academic study of the openstreetmap project, data, contributors, community, and applications (2022)
3. Heusel, M., Ramsauer, H., Unterthiner, T., Nessler, B., Hochreiter, S.: GANs trained by a two time-scale update rule converge to a local nash equilibrium. In: Advances in Neural Information Processing Systems, vol. 30 (2017)
4. Isola, P., Zhu, J.Y., Zhou, T., Efros, A.A.: Image-to-image translation with conditional adversarial networks. In: Proceedings of the IEEE Conference on Computer Vision and Pattern Recognition, pp. 1125–1134 (2017)
5. Karras, T., Laine, S., Aila, T.: A style-based generator architecture for generative adversarial networks. In: Proceedings of the IEEE/CVF Conference on Computer Vision and Pattern Recognition, pp. 4401–4410 (2019)
6. Lang, T.: Rules for the robot draughtsmen. Geogr. Mag. **42**(1), 50–51 (1969)
7. LeCun, Y., Bengio, Y., Hinton, G.: Deep learning. Nature **521**(7553), 436–444 (2015)
8. Lu, T., Ming, D., Lin, X., Hong, Z., Bai, X., Fang, J.: Detecting building edges from high spatial resolution remote sensing imagery using richer convolution features network. Remote Sens. **10**(9), 1496 (2018)
9. Mooney, P., Corcoran, P.: Has openstreetmap a role in digital earth applications? Int. J. Digit. Earth **7**(7), 534–553 (2014)
10. Niroshan, L., Carswell, J.: Deepmapper: automatic updating crowdsourced maps. Poster, Technological University Dublin, College of Arts and Tourism (2020). https://arrow.tudublin.ie/gradcamoth/3
11. Niroshan, L., Carswell, J.D.: Machine learning with kay. AGILE: GIScience Ser. **3**, 11 (2022)
12. Niroshan, L., Carswell, J.D.: OSM-GAN: using generative adversarial networks for detecting change in high-resolution spatial images. In: Bourennane, S., Kubicek, P. (eds.) ICGDA 2022, pp. 95–105. Springer, Cham (2022). https://doi.org/10.1007/978-3-031-08017-3_9
13. Niroshan, L., Carswell, J.D.: Post-analysis of OSM-GAN spatial change detection. In: Karimipour, F., Storandt, S. (eds.) W2GIS 2022, pp. 28–42. Springer, Cham (2022). https://doi.org/10.1007/978-3-031-06245-2_3
14. OpenStreetMap: Openstreetmap (2004). https://www.openstreetmap.org. Accessed 04 Mar 2023
15. Opheim, H.: Fast data reduction of a digitized curve (1982)

16. Ramer, U.: An iterative procedure for the polygonal approximation of plane curves. Comput. Graph. Image Process. **1**(3), 244–256 (1972). https://doi.org/10.1016/S0146-664X(72)80017-0. https://www.sciencedirect.com/science/article/pii/S0146664X72800170
17. Reumann, K.: Optimizing curve segmantation in computer graphics. In: International Computing Symposium 1973, Amsterdam, pp. 467–472 (1974)
18. Salimans, T., Goodfellow, I., Zaremba, W., Cheung, V., Radford, A., Chen, X.: Improved techniques for training GANs. In: Advances in Neural Information Processing Systems, vol. 29 (2016)
19. See, L., et al.: Crowdsourcing, citizen science or volunteered geographic information? the current state of crowdsourced geographic information. ISPRS Int. J. Geo Inf. **5**(5), 55 (2016)
20. Sohn, G., Jwa, Y., Jung, J., Kim, H.: An implicit regularization for 3D building rooftop modeling using airborne lidar data. ISPRS Ann. Photogramm. Remote Sens. Spatial Inf. Sci. **1**(3), 305–310 (2012)
21. Szeliski, R.: Computer Vision: Algorithms and Applications. Springer, Cham (2022)
22. Theis, L., Oord, A.V.D., Bethge, M.: A note on the evaluation of generative models. arXiv preprint arXiv:1511.01844 (2015)
23. Wei, S., Ji, S., Lu, M.: Toward automatic building footprint delineation from aerial images using CNN and regularization. IEEE Trans. Geosci. Remote Sens. **58**(3), 2178–2189 (2019)
24. Xie, Y., et al.: Refined extraction of building outlines from high-resolution remote sensing imagery based on a multifeature convolutional neural network and morphological filtering. IEEE J. Sel. Top. Appl. Earth Obs. Remote Sens. **13**, 1842–1855 (2020)
25. Yin, J., Carswell, J.D.: Spatial search techniques for mobile 3D queries in sensor web environments. ISPRS Int. J. Geo Inf. **2**(1), 135–154 (2013)
26. Zhao, K., Kang, J., Jung, J., Sohn, G.: Building extraction from satellite images using mask R-CNN with building boundary regularization. In: Proceedings of the IEEE Conference on Computer Vision and Pattern Recognition Workshops, pp. 247–251 (2018)
27. Zhao, Z., Saalfeld, A.: Linear-time sleeve-fitting polyline simplification algorithms. In: Proceedings of AutoCarto, vol. 13, pp. 214–223 (1997)
28. Zorzi, S., Fraundorfer, F.: Regularization of building boundaries in satellite images using adversarial and regularized losses. In: IGARSS 2019–2019 IEEE International Geoscience and Remote Sensing Symposium, pp. 5140–5143. IEEE (2019)

Author Index

M. A. Mostafavi and G. Del Mondo (Eds.): W2GIS 2023, LNCS 13912, p. 195, 2023.
https://doi.org/10.1007/978-3-031-34612-5